TWENTIETH CENTURY VIEWS

The aim of this series is to present the best in contemporary critical opinion on major authors, providing a twentieth century perspective on their changing status in an era of profound revaluation.

Maynard Mack, *Series Editor*
Yale University

WORDSWORTH

WORDSWORTH

A COLLECTION OF CRITICAL ESSAYS

Edited by

M. H. Abrams

Prentice-Hall, Inc.   *Englewood Cliffs, N.J.*

Library of Congress Cataloging in Publication Data

ABRAMS, MEYER HOWARD, comp.
   Wordsworth: a collection of critical essays.

   (Twentieth century views)   (A Spectrum Book)
   Bibliography: p.
   1. Wordsworth, William, 1770–1850.   I. Title.
PR5888.A27   821'.7   72–4888
ISBN   0–13–965079–7
ISBN   0–13–965061–X (pbk.)

Quotations from *Coleridge on Imagination*, by I. A. Richards, W. W. Norton & Company, Inc., New York, N.Y., 1950, are reprinted with the permission of the publisher.

10   9   8   7   6   5   4   3   2   1

PRENTICE-HALL INTERNATIONAL, INC. (*London*)
PRENTICE-HALL OF AUSTRALIA PTY. LTD. (*Sydney*)
PRENTICE-HALL OF CANADA, LTD. (*Toronto*)
PRENTICE-HALL OF INDIA PRIVATE LIMITED (*New Delhi*)
PRENTICE-HALL OF JAPAN, INC. (*Tokyo*)

To Harold Bloom

Contents

Introduction:
Two Roads to Wordsworth

by M. H. Abrams

The first critic of Wordsworth's poetry was Wordsworth himself, and in his criticism, as in his poetry, he speaks with two distinct voices. The first voice is that of the "Preface" to *Lyrical Ballads,* in which Wordsworth powerfully applies to his poetry some humanistic values of the European Enlightenment. In his "Preface" the controlling and inter-related norms are the essential, the elementary, the simple, the universal, and the permanent. The great subjects of his poetry, Wordsworth says, are "the essential passions of the heart," "elementary feelings," "the great and simple affections," "the great and universal passions of men," and "characters of which the elements are simple . . . such as exist now, and will probably always exist," as these human qualities interact with "the beautiful and permanent forms of nature." His aim is a poetry written in a "naked and simple" style that is "well adapted to interest mankind permanently." And the poet himself, as "a man speaking to men," both affirms and effects the primal human values: the joy of life, the dignity of life and of its elemental moving force, the pleasure principle, and the primacy of the universal connective, love. The poet "rejoices more than other men in the spirit of life" both within him and without, pays homage "to the grand elementary principle of pleasure, by which he knows, and feels, and lives, and moves," and is "the rock of defense of human nature, carrying everywhere with him relationship and love."

Wordsworth's second critical voice has been far less heeded by his readers. It speaks out in the "Essay, Supplementary to the Preface" of his *Poems* of 1815, and reiterates in sober prose the claims he had made, years before, in the verse "Prospectus" to *The Recluse* (reprinted in his "Preface" to *The Excursion*) and in the opening and closing passages of *The Prelude*: claims that it is his task to confront and find consolation in human suffering—whether the "solitary agonies" of rural life or the "fierce confederate storm / Of sorrow" barricadoed within the walls of cities—since he is a poet who has been singled out "for holy services" in a secular work of man's "redemption." In his "Essay" of 1815, Wordsworth addresses himself to explain and justify those aspects of novelty and strangeness in his poetry that have evoked from critics "unremitting hostility, . . . slight . . . , aversion, . . . contempt." He does so by asserting that he, like every "truly original poet," has qualities that are "peculiarly his own," and in specifying his innovations, he does not now take his operative concepts from eighteenth-century humanism, but imports them from theology; that is, he deliberately adapts to poetry the idiom hitherto used by Christian apologists to justify the radical novelty, absurdities, and paradoxes of the Christian mysteries. For Wordsworth claims in this essay that there are "affinities between religion and poetry," "a community of nature," so that poetry shares the distinctive quality of Christianity, which is to confound "the calculating understanding" by its contradictions:

> For when Christianity, the religion of humility, is founded upon the proudest quality of our nature [the imagination], what can be expected but contradictions?

In the "Essay" of 1815, accordingly, Wordsworth does not represent poetry as elemental and simple, but stresses instead its "contradictions" —that is, its radical paradoxicality, its union of antitheses, its fusion of the sensuous and the transcendant, its violation of the customary, and its reversal of status between the highest and lowest. Poetry, for example, imitates the supreme contradiction of the Incarnation itself: it is "etherial and transcendant, yet incapable to sustain her existence without sensuous incarnation." The higher poetry unites the "wisdom of the heart and the grandeur of imagination" and so achieves a "simplicity" that is "Magnificence herself." Wordsworth's own poems manifest "emotions of the pathetic" that are "complex and revolutionary." As for "the sublime"— he is specifically a poet "charged with a new mission to extend its kingdom, and to augment and spread its enjoyments." For as one of the poets who combine the "heroic passions" of pagan antiquity with Christian wisdom he has produced a new synthesis—an "accord of sublimated humanity." And his chief enterprise as a poet is expressed in a Christian paradox—he must cast his readers down in order to raise them up: their spirits "are to be humbled and humanized, in order that they may be purified and exalted."

Wordsworth as primarily the simple, affirmative poet of elementary feelings, essential humanity, and vital joy, and Wordsworth as primarily the complex poet of strangeness, paradox, equivocality, and dark sublimities—these diverse views, adumbrated by Wordsworth himself, were established as persistent alternative ways to the poet by Matthew Arnold and by A. C. Bradley. The cause of Wordsworth's greatness, Arnold said, taking his cue from Wordsworth's "Preface" to *Lyrical Ballads,* "is simple, and may be told quite simply. Wordsworth's poetry is great because of the extraordinary power" with which he feels and renders and makes us share "the joy offered to us in nature, the joy offered to us in the simple, primary affections and duties." And from the naturalness of his subject and the sincerity of his feeling, his characteristic and matchless style is that of "the most plain, first-hand, almost austere naturalness." [1] Wordsworth's great boon to us in "this iron time," Arnold says in his verses, is that he has restored our lost capacity for spontaneous and uncomplicated responsiveness, "the freshness of the early world." He adds, however, that Wordsworth achieved his "sweet calm" only by the expedient of averting his ken "From half of human fate." [2]

Although Bradley did not publish his great essay on Wordsworth (here reprinted in part) until 1909, thirty years later than Arnold's, he set out explicitly to supplement what he regarded as Arnold's valid but incomplete view of the poet by specifying other qualities without which "Wordsworth is not Wordsworth." His challenge to Arnold's way to Wordsworth is direct and uncompromising: "the road into Wordsworth's mind must be through his strangeness and his paradoxes, and not round them." In pursuing this road Bradley follows the lead, not of Wordsworth's "Preface," but of his vatic poetic pronouncements, which Arnold had noted only to derogate as the style "more properly . . . of eloquent prose." As Bradley's other essays make evident, his critical concepts, and his sensitiveness to negative and paradoxical elements in literature, also owe a great deal to the philosophy of Hegel. As Hegel himself had noted, however, his categories of negation, contradiction, and synthesis are (like Wordsworth's concept of the "contradictions" in the products of the modern poetic imagination) the conceptual equivalents of the paradoxes and the *coincidentia oppositorum* of the Christian mysteries. In the Hegelian cast of his critical concepts, then, Bradley is in broad accord with the spirit of Wordsworth's own "Essay, Supplementary to the Preface" of 1815.

In Bradley's view, that which is most distinctive in Wordsworth's poetry is "peculiar," "audacious," "strange," and Wordsworth's characteristic attitudes are a complex of contraries or contradictions. Although Wordsworth sang of joy and love, "he did not avert his eyes" from anguish or evil, but often represents "a dark world"; and though he undertook to show that suffering and misery can in fact be the conditions of happiness, strength, and glory, he did not pretend that this possibility solved "the riddle of the painful earth"—"the world was to him in the end 'this unintelligible world.' " Wordsworth is "preeminently the poet of solitude," yet "no poet is more emphatically the poet of community."

---

[1] "Wordsworth" (1879), in *Essays in Criticism: Second Series* (London, 1891), pp. 153, 159.
[2] "Memorial Verses" (1850), lines 43, 57; "Stanzas in Memory of the Author of 'Obermann' " (1859), lines 54, 79.

His native bent was not to simplicity, but to "sublimity"; and in this "mystic" or "visionary" strain "there is always traceable a certain hostility to 'sense,' " an intimation of something illimitable, eternal, infinite that is "in some way a denial" of the limited sensible world, "contradicting or abolishing the fixed limits of our habitual view." As Bradley describes the paradoxical qualities of a Wordsworthian spot of time, using a portentous term, "Everything here is natural, but everything is apocalyptic." [3]

Twentieth-century critics of Wordsworth have tended to follow either Arnold's or Bradley's road to the poet, and the diverse approaches have yielded two Wordsworths. One Wordsworth is simple, elemental, forthright, the other is complex, paradoxical, problematic; one is an affirmative poet of life, love, and joy, the other is an equivocal or self-divided poet whose affirmations are implicitly qualified (if not annulled) by a pervasive sense of mortality and an ever-incipient despair of life; one is the great poet of natural man and the world of all of us, the other is a visionary or "mystic" who is ultimately hostile to temporal man and the world of sense and whose profoundest inclinations are toward another world that transcends biological and temporal limitations; one is the Wordsworth of light, the other the Wordsworth of chiaroscuro, or even darkness. Criticism since mid-century continues to manifest, and often to sharpen, this division, although the commentators who take either the one or the other of the old roads to Wordsworth have introduced new critical concepts that make their work seem, in the 1970s, distinctively "modern." I shall try to identify a few of the more conspicuous innovations within both of the traditional perspectives.

I. The Simple Wordsworth

In *The Poet Wordsworth* (1950) Helen Darbishire is an unqualified Arnoldian: Wordsworth is a poet whose motive power was "the depth and force of his feeling for humanity," who vindicated "sense-experience as the foundation of knowledge" and represented "simple men and women who are moved by the great emotions." [4] John F. Danby's poet, in a book published a decade later, is also, as his title asserts, *The Simple Wordsworth*; the innovative element is Danby's view that Wordsworth was an inventive craftsman whose simplicity was an "achieved" simplicity by "an alert and conscious artist," who controls the reader's responses by his management of the narrative personae, "tones of voice," and "masks."

---

[3] "Wordsworth," in *Oxford Lectures on Poetry* (London, 1909), pp. 133, 130–31 (see also footnote, pp. 140–41), 134. (*Note:* in this and the following footnotes, references are given only to passages not included in the essays reprinted in this volume.)
[4] *The Poet Wordsworth* (Oxford, 1950), pp. 26, 161, 172.

Danby's critique of "The Idiot Boy," reprinted here, is a belated recognition that Wordsworth is an accomplished comic poet. Its focus is on the interplay of the narrative voice, the voices of the characters, and the poet's own voice in sustaining the fine balance of humor and human warmth in the evolving story.

Danby expressly opposed his treatment of Wordsworth as intentional artificer to the New Critical approach to a poem as a free-standing and autonomous structure of meanings, to be judged without recourse to the artist or his intention. Cleanth Brooks's essay on Wordsworth's "Intimations Ode" (1947), also included in this volume, demonstrates what can be achieved by such a close reading of the poem "as an independent poetic structure," interrogated for what it "manages to say" entirely "in its own right" as a primarily ironic and paradoxical deployment of thematic imagery. Having assimilated the insights made possible by this strict limitation of perspective in the New Criticism, many critics in the last decade or two have undertaken, like Danby, to rehumanize poetry by viewing the poet, in Wordsworth's phrase in the "Preface," as "a man speaking to men," and by exploiting concepts such as "voice," "persona," "tone," and "point of view," which emphasize the poet's own involvement, as well as his management of the reader's participation, in the fictional process.

Such a revitalized rhetoric of poetry is prominent in many recent writings about Wordsworth. In the third chapter of *The Music of Humanity*, for example, Jonathan Wordsworth demonstrates the essential role, in *The Ruined Cottage*, of the interplay between Wordsworth's two "poetic selves," the Pedlar and the Poet, in effecting the reader's imaginative consent to the author's own attitudes toward the tragic story. In an essay reprinted in this volume that has been much debated, Stephen Parrish reads "The Thorn" not as a quasi-supernatural story, but as an artful dramatic monologue, in which the controlling principle is the revelation of the mental workings of its credulous narrator, the old sea captain. Neil Hertz's essay "Wordsworth and the Tears of Adam"—with a shift of emphasis from Wordsworth's rhetorical artistry to the characteristic disjunction of consciousness in his poetry—discriminates "the transformation of the voice" in a short verse passage, and details the interaction among three "aspects of Wordsworth's self" and a fourth subjectivity, that of the responding reader.

II. The Problematic Wordsworth

In the 1960s there appeared a new mode of criticism in America whose appeal to younger critics presages its growing importance in studies of romantic literature. The primary terms of this criticism are "conscious-

ness" (or "self-consciousness") and the "dialectic" of its dealings with
what is not-consciousness, and its characteristic procedure is to find something "problematic" in the surface meaning of single passages and to
regard this as a clue to a deep structure manifesting an unspoken preoccupation of the poet. The proximate source of this critical procedure
are the diverse movements in European thought loosely classified as
"phenomenology," "existentialism," and "structuralism," but its central
idiom and concerns derive ultimately from Hegel; so that, when applied
to Wordsworth, it can be regarded as a revived form of Bradley's neo-
Hegelian approach to that poet. The focus, however, is much sharper
than Bradley's, and the chief operative concepts much more restricted.
For as Hegel in his *Phenomenology of the Spirit* translated the manifold
particularities of human and individual history into diverse moments of
the transactions between consciousness and its alienated other, so these
critics view the manifold surface particularities of romantic poems as
generated primarily by a single submerged plot: the sustained struggle
of the poet's consciousness (operating in the mode often called "imagination") to achieve "autonomy," or absolute independence from that adversary which is not itself—namely "nature," the world of sensible objects.

In his influential essay, "Intentional Structure of the Romantic Image,"
first published in 1960, Paul de Man sets out from the observation that
there is a "dialectic" that is "paradoxical"—a "fundamental ambiguity"
or "tension" that "never ceases to be problematic"—in romantic attempts
to link the polarities of consciousness, or imagination, and nature. De
Man's paradigmatic instance is Mallarmé, who is represented as a revealing point of reference because he is a late romantic who took over
what had hitherto been an implicit tension of polar attitudes, "the alternating feeling of attraction and repulsion that the romantic poet experiences toward nature," and made it explicit as a "conscious dialectic of
a reflective poetic consciousness." Mallarmé, unlike earlier romantic
poets, "always remained convinced of the essential priority of the natural
object," so that his writings as an extreme "anti-natural poet" are a
defiantly hopeless struggle by consciousness (or by the language in which
consciousness manifests itself) to annihilate, by reducing to its own self,
a nature that Mallarmé knows to be ultimately indefeasible. Wordsworth's
poetry, on the other hand, with its "radical contradictions" in the representation of landscape (de Man's example is the passage on crossing the
Alps in *The Prelude,* Book 6), puts into question "the ontological priority
of the sensory object," by recourse to the faculty he calls "imagination,"
which "marks . . . a possibility for consciousness to exist entirely by and
for itself, independently of all relationship with the outside world."

Geoffrey Hartman also finds that Wordsworth's treatment of nature is "problematic," and that a number of passages in *The Prelude* which "overtly celebrate nature" in fact "share a motif opposed to the overt line of argument." Hartman's repeated reference, however, is not to Mallarmé but to Blake, the extreme representative of a deliberate commitment to a visionary and anti-natural imagination. "Wordsworth," Hartman imagines Blake as saying, "is of his party without knowing it." The difference is that Wordsworth, when he comes face to face with his "autonomous imagination," fears it, shies from it, or veils it. In consequence, his poetry constitutes "a series of evaded recognitions" of imagination and "an avoidance of apocalypse"—where imagination is defined by Hartman as "consciousness of self raised to apocalyptic pitch" and apocalypse signifies "any strong desire to cast out nature and to achieve an unmediated contact with the principle of things," hence as "involving a *death* of nature." It is this "unresolved opposition between Imagination and Nature"—through Wordsworth's "fear of the death of nature"—that "prevents him from becoming a visionary poet." [5]

Two essays in this volume represent another approach to Wordsworth that emphasizes the duplicity and the strain between contradictions in his writings; its major operative concept, however, is not a revived Hegelian opposition between consciousness and an alien other, but the post-Freudian distinction between manifest and latent, conscious and unconscious content. The basic claim is that Wordsworth's overt or surface meaning often overlies a covert countermeaning that expresses what the poet profoundly felt and believed, as against what he rationalized himself into believing.

David Perkins's *Quest for Permanence* undertakes to "go beneath the surface" of Wordsworth's poetry in order to explore the "negative implications" that are sometimes "contrary to his overt intentions and obiter dicta"; for any interpretation that concentrates on Wordsworth's obiter dicta "is not touching what is deepest in him." Under Wordsworth's overt claims that certitude and peace attend upon "the union of mind with nature," Perkins finds a contrary sense that there is a "gulf between human nature . . . and the rest of nature," and that man is doomed to be an isolated being, estranged both from nature and other men. There are symptoms also of "a kind of schizoid retreat" from situations that threaten the poet's composure, which in its extreme form manifests itself in Wordsworth as an attraction to the ultimate security of the grave. [6]

In *The Limits of Mortality,* published in the same year as Perkins's *Quest for Permanence* (1959), David Ferry's aim is to discover in Words-

---

[5] *Wordsworth's Poetry, 1787–1814* (New Haven, 1964), pp. x, 17–18, 39, 61, 63, 101, 124, 184, 211, 226–27, 233, 338.
[6] *The Quest for Permanence* (Cambridge, Mass., 1959), pp. 24, 30, 40, 45, 47, 48, 50, 55, 89–90.

worth "ideas and feelings which can in some way be related to our own
deepest feelings and ideas." Ferry penetrates to this modern element, as
he says, by "a special way of reading his poems." This way to Wordsworth is to strike a sharp dichotomy between the " 'surface' of his poems"
and the "deeper" and "hidden" meanings which are in "tension" or
"conflict" with the surface meanings, and to assert the prepotency of the
hidden and antithetic meanings as constituting the "ultimate subject
matter" of a poem. As Ferry formulates this semantic peripety:

> [The] apparent subject matter is a kind of cipher or hieroglyph for mean-
> ings which reject or devaluate the very experiences which express them.
> . . . The symbolic meanings of [Wordsworth's] poems tend to reject their
> sensuous, dramatic surfaces.

Like A. C. Bradley a half-century earlier, Ferry sets out, as he says, to
correct Arnold's "tendency to take Wordsworth's vocabulary of feeling
at face value," hence to evaluate him as "the poet of the primary affections and simple feelings." By Ferry's interpretative strategy, however,
the paradoxical Wordsworth works free from Bradley's careful qualifica-
tions to become the polar opposite of Arnold's Wordsworth. The sophisticated modern reader is now enabled to look right through Wordsworth's
surface assertions of reverence for a "sacramental" nature, love for elemental man, and esteem for the simple affections and ordinary experience, in order to discern a countermeaning of which the poet himself remained unaware—that is, a "mystical" yearning for an eternal and
unchanging realm of being to which nature and man and even the
articulations of poetry itself (since all are alike trapped in the conditions
of time, space, and vicissitude) are an intolerable obstruction, an offense
against the purity of eternity. Hence to the knowing reader Wordsworth's
"sacramentalist" poems, far from being simple and natural in style, often
turn out to be "contradictions of themselves" and to express a yearning
"for their own destruction," and Wordsworth's "mystical imagination"
is recognized to be "a hater of temporal nature" and "the enemy of
poetry as of all distinctively human experience." Ferry's closing summa-
tion of the Wordsworth of the great decade is that "his genius was his
enmity to man, which he mistook for love, and his mistake led him into
confusions which he could not bear. But when he banished his confusions, he banished his distinctive greatness as well." [7]

Even the confirmed Arnoldian must admit the plausibility of some of
the insights achieved by the recent critics who premise their reading of
Wordsworth on the paradoxical strains and equivocal attitudes in his
poetry. And it is a measure of the range and magnitude of Wordsworth's

[7] *The Limits of Mortality* (Middletown, Conn., 1959), pp. ix, 32–33, 51–53, 160, 173.

achievement that he continues to speak to us and our interests when interpreted by neo-Hegelian concepts, or when viewed as a proto-Mallarmé, or as a Blake manqué, or as, under the brave surface, really one of us in our age of alienation, anguish, and existential absurdity. An inveterate under-reading of the textual surface, however, turns readily into an habitual over-reading. The problem is, to what extent do these recent critical perspectives on Wordsworth simply bring into visibility what was always, although obscurely, there, and to what extent do they project upon his poems the form of their own prepossessions?

This is not the place to argue out the difficult issue. Instead, I shall cite some contemporary critics represented in this volume who, like A. C. Bradley, believe that Arnold described what is really there, but enlarge the scope of their vision to encompass the half of Wordsworth from which Arnold averted his ken. In these essays, as in Bradley's essay, Wordsworth stands as a complex but integral poet, rather than as a radically divided one whose deepest inclinations, known to the modern critic but not to the poet himself, undercut or annul his repeated affirmations.

Like the recent explorers of the problematic Wordsworth, Lionel Trilling points to an aspect of his poetry that is strange, remote, even chilling to us. His account of it, however, is not psychoanalytic (Wordsworth's unconscious revulsion from life) but historical—Wordsworth's participation in a persistent strain of Hebrew and Christian culture which, at odds with the modern preoccupation with heroic struggle and apocalyptic violence, is committed to quietism, peace, and a wise passiveness. Wordsworth's quietism, however, "is not in the least a negation of life, but . . . an affirmation of life so complete that it needed no saying"; Trilling in fact uses Wordsworth as the positive standard by which to define the negatives of our adversary culture. Wordsworth has an "acute sense of his own being" that sharpens his awareness of other beings, and his intention is "to require us to acknowledge" the being of his narrative personae and so "to bring them within the range of conscience" and of "natural sympathy." It is not Wordsworth, but we moderns who "do not imagine being . . . that it can be a joy" and who "are in love, at least in our literature, with the fantasy of death." Writing also in the affirmative tradition of Arnold, Jonathan Wordsworth nonetheless identifies in *The Ruined Cottage* a dimension of poetic genius that Arnold had denied to Wordsworth: the power to reconcile us imaginatively with an instance of seemingly pointless suffering, futile courage, and meaningless death in a way that manifests both the poet's artistry and his "humanity"—"an insight into emotions not his own"—and with a success that places him "among the very few great English tragic writers."

The position of Harold Bloom in the critical division about Wordsworth's poetry is a complex one. Citing Geoffrey Hartman, he concurs in the latter's distinction between a surface and covert meaning and in the associated claim that, as Bloom puts it, "the inner problem of *The Prelude*, and of all the poetry of Wordsworth's great decade, is that of the autonomy of the poet's creative imagination," hence of a "hidden conflict between Poetry and Nature." But Bloom's reading of Wordsworth, taken overall, is different from Hartman's. He accepts Wordsworth's own statement, most notably in the "Prospectus" to *The Recluse*, that his high argument is the possibility of a union, by means of imagination, between mind and nature, in a reciprocity that redeems the world of ordinary experience. Instead of regarding Wordsworth as an all-but-Blake, he expressly differentiates his poetry from Blake's and parallels it instead to that of Wallace Stevens, as a "naturalistic celebration of the possibilities inherent in our condition here and now." Bloom accordingly reads "Tintern Abbey" as representing the poet in the act of discovering the theme of all his best poetry, a "reciprocity between the external world and his own mind" in which the two agents are equal in initiative and power. "The Old Cumberland Beggar," in Bloom's analysis, registers a correlative aspect of Wordsworth's genius, his reverence for essential human life, seemingly alienated and "stripped to the nakedness of primordial condition," yet "still powerful in dignity, still infinite in value." And though he believes that Wordsworth's confidence in an imaginative communion of mind, nature, and man later weakened and failed, Bloom pays tribute to the novelty and magnitude of the enterprise. Wordsworth "personified a heroic mode of naturalism, which even he then proved unable to sustain." "No poet since," he declares, "has given us more." [8] Such a view is consonant with that of the editor of this volume, whose own essay explores *The Prelude*, and the opening book of *The Recluse* into which it leads, as Wordsworth's attempt to save the traditional design and values of human life, inherited from a Christian past, but to translate them to a naturalistic frame of reference—that is, to represent them as generated by a reciprocity between the natural world and the minds of men, "As natural beings in the strength of nature."

A Note on the Essays

The aim of this book is to reprint critical essays of distinction that will represent: (1) the diversity of recent approaches to Wordsworth; (2) both general comments on Wordsworth's poetic qualities and discussions of specific poems; (3) both detailed analyses of short passages and treatments of the overall design of some longer works; and (4) discussions of as many as possible of Wordsworth's most important poems. Limitation of space and the need to adjust to these multiple criteria have compelled

[8] *The Visionary Company*, rev. ed. (Ithaca, N.Y., 1971), pp. 144–45, 124–28, 198.

the editor to omit many valuable essays. For Wordsworth criticism is in a flourishing condition these days, and its vigorous internal disputes testify to the poet's continuing vitality and pertinence. We are rediscovering what a number of Wordsworth's major contemporaries acknowledged —that he has done what only the greatest poets do. He has transformed the inherited language of poetry into a medium adequate to express new ways of perceiving the world, new modes of experience, and new relations of the individual consciousness to itself, to its past, and to other men. More than all but a very few English writers, Wordsworth has altered not only our poetry, but our sensibility and our culture.

Wordsworth

by A. C. Bradley

There have been greater poets than Wordsworth, but none more original. He saw new things, or he saw things in a new way. Naturally, this would have availed us little if his new things had been private fancies, or if his new perception had been superficial. But that was not so. If it had been, Wordsworth might have won acceptance more quickly, but he would not have gained his lasting hold on poetic minds. As it is, those in whom he creates the taste by which he is relished, those who learn to love him (and in each generation they are not a few), never let him go. Their love for him is of the kind that he himself celebrated, a settled passion, perhaps "slow to begin," but "never ending," and twined around the roots of their being. And the reason is that they find his way of seeing the world, his poetic experience, what Arnold meant by his "criticism of life," to be something deep, and therefore something that will hold. It continues to bring them joy, peace, strength, exaltation. It does not thin out or break beneath them as they grow older and wiser; nor does it fail them, much less repel them, in sadness or even in their sorest need. And yet—to return to our starting-point—it continues to strike them as original, and something more. It is not like Shakespeare's myriad-mindedness; it is, for good or evil or both, peculiar. They can remember, perhaps, the day when first they saw a cloud somewhat as Wordsworth saw it, or first really understood what made him write this poem or that; his unique way of seeing and feeling, though now familiar and beloved, still brings them not only peace, strength, exaltation, but a "shock of mild surprise"; and his paradoxes, long known by heart and found full of truth, still remain paradoxes.

If this is so, the road into Wordsworth's mind must be through his strangeness and his paradoxes, and not round them. I do not mean that they are everywhere in his poetry. Much of it, not to speak of occasional

"Wordsworth." From A. C. Bradley, *Oxford Lectures on Poetry*, 2d ed. (London: Macmillan & Co., Ltd., 1950). Copyright © 1909 by Macmillan & Co., Ltd. Reprinted by permission of St. Martin's Press, The Macmillan Company of Canada, and Macmillan London and Basingstoke. Bradley's entire essay incorporates two lectures given at Oxford in 1903. Reprinted here are part 1, a section of part 3, and the concluding pages.

platitudes, is beautiful without being peculiar or difficult; and some of
this may be as valuable as that which is audacious or strange. But unless
we get hold of that, we remain outside Wordsworth's centre; and, if we
have not a most unusual affinity to him, we cannot get hold of that unless we realise its strangeness, and refuse to blunt the sharpness of its
edge. Consider, for example, two or three of his statements; the statements
of a poet, no doubt, and not of a philosopher, but still evidently statements expressing, intimating, or symbolising, what for him was the
most vital truth. He said that the meanest flower that blows could give
him thoughts that often lie too deep for tears. He said, in a poem not
less solemn, that Nature was the soul of all his moral being; and also
that she can so influence us that nothing will be able to disturb our
faith that all that we behold is full of blessings. After making his
Wanderer tell the heart-rending tale of Margaret, he makes him say that
the beauty and tranquillity of her ruined cottage had once so affected him

> That what we feel of sorrow and despair
> From ruin and from change, and all the grief
> The passing shows of Being leave behind,
> Appeared an idle dream, that could not live
> Where meditation was.
>
> [*The Excursion*, I, 949–53]

He said that this same Wanderer could read in the silent faces of the
clouds unutterable love, and that among the mountains all things for
him breathed immortality. He said to "Almighty God,"

> But thy most dreaded instrument
> For working out a pure intent
> Is Man arrayed for mutual slaughter;
> Yea, Carnage is thy daughter.
>
> [*Ode, 1815*, 106–9]

This last, it will be agreed, is a startling statement; but is it a whit more
extraordinary than the others? It is so only if we assume that we are
familiar with thoughts that lie too deep for tears, or if we translate "the
soul of all my moral being" into "somehow concordant with my moral
feelings," or convert "all that we behold" into "a good deal that we
behold," or transform the Wanderer's reading of the silent faces of the
clouds into an argument from "design." But this is the road round
Wordsworth's mind, not into it.

Again, with all Wordsworth's best poems, it is essential not to miss the
unique tone of his experience. This doubtless holds good of any true
poet, but not in the same way. With many poems there is little risk of
our failing either to feel what is distinctive of the writer, or to appropriate
what he says. What is characteristic, for example, in Byron's lines,

On this day I complete my thirty-sixth year, or in Shelley's *Stanzas written in dejection near Naples,* cannot escape discovery, nor is there any difficulty in understanding the mood expressed. But with Wordsworth, for most readers, this risk is constantly present in some degree. Take, for instance, one of the most popular of his lyrics, the poem about the daffodils by the lake. It is popular partly because it remains a pretty thing even to those who convert it into something quite undistinctive of Wordsworth. And it is comparatively easy, too, to perceive and to reproduce in imagination a good deal that *is* distinctive; for instance, the feeling of the sympathy of the waves and the flowers and the breeze in their glee, and the Wordsworthian "emotion recollected in tranquillity" expressed in the lines (written by his wife),

> They flash upon that inward eye
> Which is the bliss of solitude.

But there remains something still more intimately Wordsworthian:

> I wandered lonely as a Cloud
> That floats on high o'er vales and hills.

It is thrust into the reader's face, for these are the opening lines. But with many readers it passes unheeded, because it is strange and outside their own experience. And yet it is absolutely essential to the effect of the poem.

This poem, however, even when thoroughly conventionalised, would remain, as I said, a pretty thing; and it could scarcely excite derision. Our point is best illustrated from the pieces by which Wordsworth most earned ridicule, the ballad poems. They arose almost always from some incident which, for him, had a novel and arresting character and came on his mind with a certain shock; and if we do not get back to this through the poem, we remain outside it. We may, of course, get back to this and yet consider the poem to be more or less a failure. There is here therefore room for legitimate differences of opinion. Mr. Swinburne sees, no doubt, as clearly as Coleridge did, the intention of *The Idiot Boy* and *The Thorn,* yet he calls them "doleful examples of eccentricity in dullness," while Coleridge's judgement, though he criticised both poems, was very different. I believe (if I may venture into the company of such critics) that I see why Wordsworth wrote *Goody Blake and Harry Gill* and the *Anecdote for Fathers,* and yet I doubt if he has succeeded in either; but a great man, Charles James Fox, selected the former for special praise, and Matthew Arnold included the latter in a selection from which he excluded *The Sailor's Mother.* Indeed, of all the poems at first most ridiculed there is probably not one that has not been praised by some excellent judge. But they were ridiculed by men who judged them without attempting first to get inside them. And this is fatal.

I may bring out the point by referring more fully to one of them. *Alice Fell* was beloved by the best critic of the nineteenth century, Charles Lamb; but the general distaste for it was such that it was excluded "in policy" from edition after edition of Wordsworth's Poems; many still who admire *Lucy Gray* see nothing to admire in *Alice Fell*; and you may still hear the question asked, What could be made of a child crying for the loss of her cloak? And what, I answer, could be made of a man poking his stick into a pond to find leeches? What sense is there in asking questions about the subject of a poem, if you first deprive this subject of all the individuality it possesses in the poem? Let me illustrate this individuality methodically. A child crying for the loss of her cloak is one thing; quite another is a child who has an imagination, and who sees the tattered remnants of her cloak whirling in the wheel-spokes of a post-chaise fiercely driven by strangers on lonesome roads through a night of storm in which the moon is drowned. She was alone, and, having to reach the town she belonged to, she got up behind the chaise, and her cloak was caught in the wheel. And she is fatherless and motherless, and her poverty (the poem is called *Alice Fell, or Poverty*) is so extreme that for the loss of her weather-beaten rag she does not "cry"; she weeps loud and bitterly; weeps as if her innocent heart would break; sits by the stranger who has placed her by his side and is trying to console her, insensible to all relief; sends forth sob after sob as if her grief could never, never have an end; checks herself for a moment to answer a question, and then weeps on as if she had lost her only friend, and the thought would choke her very heart. It was *this* poverty and *this* grief that Wordsworth described with his reiterated hammering blows. Is it not pathetic? And to Wordsworth it was more. To him grief like this is sublime. It is the agony of a soul from which something is torn away that was made one with its very being. What does it matter whether the thing is a woman, or a kingdom, or a tattered cloak? It is the passion that counts. Othello must not agonise for a cloak, but "the little orphan Alice Fell" has nothing else to agonise for. Is all this insignificant? And then—for this poem about a child is right to the last line—next day the storm and the tragedy have vanished, and the new cloak is bought, of duffil grey, as warm a cloak as man can sell; and the child is as pleased as Punch. . . .

Wordsworth's morality is of one piece with his optimism and with his determination to seize and exhibit in everything the element of good. But this is a subject far too large for treatment here, and I can refer to it only in the most summary way. What Arnold precisely meant when he said that Wordsworth "put by" the cloud of human destiny I am not

sure. That Wordsworth saw this cloud and looked at it steadily is beyond all question. I am not building on such famous lines as

> The still sad music of humanity,

or

> the fierce confederate storm
> Of sorrow, barricadoed evermore
> Within the walls of cities;

or

> Amid the groves, under the shadowy hills,
> The generations are prepared; the pangs,
> The internal pangs, are ready; the dread strife
> Of poor humanity's afflicted will
> Struggling in vain with ruthless destiny;[1]

for, although such quotations could be multiplied, isolated expressions, even when not dramatic, would prove little. But I repeat the remark already made, that if we review the subjects of many of Wordsworth's famous poems on human life—the subjects, for example, of *The Thorn*, *The Sailor's Mother*, *Ruth*, *The Brothers*, *Michael*, *The Affliction of Margaret*, *The White Doe of Rylstone*, the story of Margaret in *Excursion*, i., half the stories told in *Excursion*, vi. and vii.—we find ourselves in the presence of poverty, crime, insanity, ruined innocence, torturing hopes doomed to extinction, solitary anguish, even despair. Ignore the manner in which Wordsworth treated his subjects, and you will have to say that his world, so far as humanity is concerned, is a dark world—at least as dark as that of Byron. Unquestionably then he saw the cloud of human destiny, and he did not avert his eyes from it. Nor did he pretend to understand its darkness. The world was to him in the end "this unintelligible world," and the only "adequate support for the calamities of mortal life" was faith.[2] But he was profoundly impressed, through the experience of his own years of crisis, alike by the dangers of despondency, and by the superficiality of the views which it engenders. It was for him (and here, as in other points, he shows his natural affinity to Spinoza) a condition in which the soul, concentrated on its own suffering,

[1] [The quotations are from "Tintern Abbey"; the "Prospectus" to *The Recluse* (in *Poetical Works*, ed. de Selincourt and Darbishire, vol. 5); *The Excursion*, VI, 553 ff. —ED.]
[2] The second half of this sentence, true of the Wordsworth of the *Excursion*, is perhaps not quite true of his earlier mind.

for that very reason loses hold both of its own being and of the reality
of which it forms a part. His experience also made it impossible for him
to doubt that what he grasped

> At times when most existence with herself
> Is satisfied,
>
> [*The Excursion*, IX, 103–4]

—and these are the times when existence is most united in love with
other existence—was, in a special sense or degree, the truth, and therefore that the evils which we suffer, deplore, or condemn, cannot really
be what they seem to us when we merely suffer, deplore, or condemn
them. He set himself to *see* this, as far as he could, and to show it. He
sang of pleasure, joy, glee, blitheness, love, wherever in nature or humanity they assert their indisputable power; and turning to pain and
wrong, and gazing at them steadfastly, and setting himself to present the
facts with a quiet but unsparing truthfulness, he yet endeavoured to
show what he had seen, that sometimes pain and wrong are the conditions of a happiness and good which without them could not have been,
that no limit can be set to the power of the soul to transmute them into
its own substance, and that, in suffering and even in misery, there may
still be such a strength as fills us with awe or with glory. He did not
pretend, I repeat, that what he saw sufficed to solve the riddle of the
painful earth. "Our being rests" on "dark foundations," and "our
haughty life is crowned with darkness." [3] But still what he showed was
what he *saw,* and he saw it in the cloud of human destiny. We are not
here concerned with his faith in the sun behind that cloud; my purpose
is only to insist that he "fronted" it "fearlessly." . . .

Partly because he is the poet of mountains he is, even more pre-
eminently, the poet of solitude. For there are tones in the mountain voice
scarcely audible except in solitude, and the reader whom Wordsworth's
greatest poetry baffles could have no better advice offered him than to
do what he has probably never done in his life—to be on a mountain
alone. But for Wordsworth not this solitude only, but all solitude and
all things solitary had an extraordinary fascination.

> The outward shows of sky and earth,
> Of hill and valley, he has viewed;
> And impulses *of deeper birth*
> Have come to him in solitude.
>
> ["A Poet's Epitaph"]

The sense of solitude, it will readily be found, is essential to nearly all
the poems and passages we have been considering, and to some of quite a

---

[3] [*The Excursion*, IV, 970; "Extempore Effusion upon the death of James Hogg"
—ED.]

different character, such as the Daffodil stanzas. And it is not merely that the poet is alone; what he sees is so too. If the leech-gatherer and the soldier on the moon-lit road had not been solitary figures, they would not have awaked "the visionary power"; and it is scarcely fanciful to add that if the boy who was watching for his father's ponies had had beside him any more than

> The *single* sheep and the *one* blasted tree,
> [*The Prelude* (1850), XII, 319]

the mist would not have advanced along the roads "in such indisputable shapes." With Wordsworth that power seems to have sprung into life at once on the perception of loneliness. What is lonely is a spirit. To call a thing lonely or solitary is, with him, to say that it opens a bright or solemn vista into infinity. He himself "wanders lonely as a cloud": he seeks the "souls of lonely places": he listens in awe to

> One voice, the solitary raven . . .
> An iron knell, with echoes from afar:
> [*The Excursion*, IV, 1178–81]

against the distant sky he descries the shepherd,

> A solitary object and sublime,
> Above all height! like an aerial cross
> Stationed alone upon a spiry rock
> Of the Chartreuse, for worship.
> [*The Prelude* (1850), VIII, 272–75]

But this theme might be pursued for hours, and I will refer only to two poems more. The editor of the *Golden Treasury*, a book never to be thought of without gratitude, changed the title *The Solitary Reaper* into *The Highland Reaper*. He may have had his reasons. Perhaps he had met some one who thought that the Reaper belonged to Surrey. Still the change was a mistake: the "solitary" in Wordsworth's title gave the keynote. The other poem is *Lucy Gray*. "When I was little," a lover of Wordsworth once said, "I could hardly bear to read *Lucy Gray*, it made me feel so lonely." Wordsworth called it *Lucy Gray, or Solitude*, and this young reader understood him. But there is too much reason to fear that for half his readers his "solitary child" is generalised into a mere "little girl," and that they never receive the main impression he wished to produce. Yet his intention is announced in the opening lines, and as clearly shown in the lovely final stanzas, which give even to this ballad the visionary touch which distinguishes it from *Alice Fell*:

> Yet some maintain that to this day
> She is a living child;

That you may see sweet Lucy Gray
Upon the lonesome wild.

O'er rough and smooth she trips along,
And never looks behind;
And sings a solitary song
That whistles in the wind.

The solitariness which exerted so potent a spell on Wordsworth had in it nothing "Byronic." He preached in the *Excursion* against the solitude of "self-indulging spleen." He was even aware that he himself, though free from that weakness, had felt

perhaps too much
The self-sufficing power of Solitude.
[*The Prelude* (1850), II, 76–77]

No poet is more emphatically the poet of community. A great part of his verse—a part as characteristic and as precious as the part on which I have been dwelling—is dedicated to the affections of home and neighbourhood and country, and to that soul of joy and love which links together all Nature's children, and "steals from earth to man, from man to earth." And this soul is for him as truly the presence of "the Being that is in the clouds and air" and in the mind of man as are the power, the darkness, the silence, the strange gleams and mysterious visitations which startle and confuse with intimations of infinity. But solitude and solitariness were to him, in the main, one of these intimations. They had not for him merely the "eeriness" which they have at times for everyone, though that was essential to some of the poems we have reviewed. They were the symbol of power to stand alone, to be "self-sufficing," to dispense with custom and surroundings and aid and sympathy—a self-dependence at once the image and the communication of "the soul of all the worlds." Even when they were full of "sounds and sweet airs that give delight and hurt not," the solitude of the Reaper or of Lucy, they so appealed to him. But they appealed also to that austerer strain which led him to love "bare trees and mountains bare," and lonely places, and the bleak music of the old stone wall, and to dwell with awe, and yet with exultation, on the majesty of that "unconquerable mind" which through long years holds its solitary purpose, sustains its solitary passion, feeds upon its solitary anguish. For this mind, as for the blind beggar or the leech-gatherer, the "light of sense" and the sweetness of life have faded or "gone out"; but in it "greatness makes abode," and it "retains its station proud," "by form or image unprofaned." Thus, in whatever guise it might present itself, solitariness "carried far into his heart" the haunting sense of an "invisible world";

of some Life beyond this "transitory being" and "unapproachable by death";

> Of Life continuous, Being unimpaired;
> That hath been, is, and where it was and is
> There shall endure,—existence unexposed
> To the blind walk of mortal accident;
> From diminution safe and weakening age;
> While man grows old, and dwindles, and decays;
> And countless generations of mankind
> Depart; and leave no vestige where they trod.
>   [*The Excursion*, IV, 755–62]

For me, I confess, all this is far from being "mere poetry"—partly because I do not believe that any such thing as "mere poetry" exists. But whatever kind or degree of truth we may find in all this, everything in Wordsworth that is sublime or approaches sublimity has, directly or more remotely, to do with it. And without this part of his poetry Wordsworth would be "shorn of his strength," and would no longer stand, as he does stand, nearer than any other poet of the Nineteenth Century to Milton.

Wordsworth and the Revolt
against Abstractions

by A. N. Whitehead

So far as concerns English literature we find, as might be anticipated, the most interesting criticism of the thoughts of science among the leaders of the romantic reaction which accompanied and succeeded the epoch of the French Revolution. In English literature, the deepest thinkers of this school were Coleridge, Wordsworth, and Shelley. Keats is an example of literature untouched by science. We may neglect Coleridge's attempt at an explicit philosophical formulation. It was influential in his own generation; but in these lectures it is my object only to mention those elements of the thought of the past which stand for all time. Even with this limitation, only a selection is possible. For our purposes Coleridge is only important by his influence on Wordsworth. Thus Wordsworth and Shelley remain.

Wordsworth was passionately absorbed in nature. It has been said of Spinoza, that he was drunk with God. It is equally true that Wordsworth was drunk with nature. But he was a thoughtful, well-read man, with philosophical interests, and sane even to the point of prosiness. In addition, he was a genius. He weakens his evidence by his dislike of science. We all remember his scorn of the poor man whom he somewhat hastily accuses of peeping and botanising on his mother's grave. Passage after passage could be quoted from him, expressing this repulsion. In this respect, his characteristic thought can be summed up in his phrase, "We murder to dissect."

In this latter passage, he discloses the intellectual basis of his criticism of science. He alleges against science its absorption in abstractions. His consistent theme is that the important facts of nature elude the scientific

"Wordsworth and the Revolt against Abstractions" (editor's title). From Alfred North Whitehead, *Science and the Modern World* (Cambridge: Cambridge University Press, 1926). Copyright © 1925 by The Macmillan Company; copyright renewed 1953 by Evelyn Whitehead. Reprinted by permission of Cambridge University Press and The Macmillan Company. The selection is from chapter 5, "The Romantic Reaction."

method. It is important therefore to ask, what Wordsworth found in nature that failed to receive expression in science. I ask this question in the interest of science itself; for one main position in these lectures is a protest against the idea that the abstractions of science are irreformable and unalterable. Now it is emphatically not the case that Wordsworth hands over inorganic matter to the mercy of science, and concentrates on the faith that in the living organism there is some element that science cannot analyse. Of course he recognises, what no one doubts, that in some sense living things are different from lifeless things. But that is not his main point. It is the brooding presence of the hills which haunts him. His theme is nature *in solido,* that is to say, he dwells on that mysterious presence of surrounding things, which imposes itself on any separate element that we set up as an individual for its own sake. He always grasps the whole of nature as involved in the tonality of the particular instance. That is why he laughs with the daffodils, and finds in the primrose "thoughts too deep for tears."

Wordsworth's greatest poem is, by far, the first book of *The Prelude.* It is pervaded by this sense of the haunting presences of nature. A series of magnificent passages, too long for quotation, express this idea. Of course, Wordsworth is a poet writing a poem, and is not concerned with dry philosophical statements. But it would hardly be possible to express more clearly a feeling for nature, as exhibiting entwined prehensive unities, each suffused with modal presences of others:

> Ye Presences of Nature in the sky
> And on the earth! Ye Visions of the hills!
> And Souls of lonely places! can I think
> A vulgar hope was yours when ye employed
> Such ministry, when ye through many a year
> Haunting me thus among my boyish sports,
> On caves and trees, upon the woods and hills,
> Impressed upon all forms the characters
> Of danger or desire; and thus did make
> The surface of the universal earth
> With triumph and delight, with hope and fear,
> Work like a sea? . . .
> [*The Prelude,* 1850 ed., I, 464–75]

In thus citing Wordsworth, the point which I wish to make is that we forget how strained and paradoxical is the view of nature which modern science imposes on our thoughts. Wordsworth, to the height of genius, expresses the concrete facts of our apprehension, facts which are distorted in the scientific analysis. Is it not possible that the standardised concepts of science are only valid within narrow limitations, perhaps too narrow for science itself?

Shelley's attitude to science was at the opposite pole to that of Words-worth. He loved it, and is never tired of expressing in poetry the thoughts which it suggests. It symbolises to him joy, and peace, and illumination. What the hills were to the youth of Wordsworth, a chemical laboratory was to Shelley. It is unfortunate that Shelley's literary critics have, in this respect, so little of Shelley in their own mentality. They tend to treat as a casual oddity of Shelley's nature what was, in fact, part of the main structure of his mind, permeating his poetry through and through. If Shelley had been born a hundred years later, the twentieth century would have seen a Newton among chemists.

For the sake of estimating the value of Shelley's evidence it is important to realise this absorption of his mind in scientific ideas. It can be illustrated by lyric after lyric. I will choose one poem only, the fourth act of his *Prometheus Unbound*. The Earth and the Moon converse together in the language of accurate science. Physical experiments guide his imagery. For example, the Earth's exclamation,

> The vaporous exultation not to be confined!

is the poetic transcript of "the expansive force of gases," as it is termed in books on science. Again, take the Earth's stanza,

> I spin beneath my pyramid of night,
> Which points into the heavens,—dreaming delight,
> Murmuring victorious joy in my enchanted sleep;
> As a youth lulled in love-dreams faintly sighing,
> Under the shadow of his beauty lying,
> Which round his rest a watch of light and warmth doth keep.

This stanza could only have been written by someone with a definite geometrical diagram before his inward eye—a diagram which it has often been my business to demonstrate to mathematical classes. As evidence, note especially the last line which gives poetical imagery to the light surrounding night's pyramid. This idea could not occur to anyone with-out the diagram. But the whole poem and other poems are permeated with touches of this kind.

Now the poet, so sympathetic with science, so absorbed in its ideas, can simply make nothing of the doctrine of secondary qualities which is fundamental to its concepts. For Shelley nature retains its beauty and its colour. Shelley's nature is in its essence a nature of organisms, function-ing with the full content of our perceptual experience. We are so used to ignoring the implication of orthodox scientific doctrine, that it is dif-ficult to make evident the criticism upon it which is thereby implied. If anybody could have treated it seriously, Shelley would have done so.

Furthermore Shelley is entirely at one with Wordsworth as to the interfusing of the Presence in nature. Here is the opening stanza of his poem entitled *Mont Blanc*:

> The everlasting universe of Things
> Flows through the Mind, and rolls its rapid waves,
> Now dark—now glittering—now reflecting gloom—
> Now lending splendour, where from secret springs
> The source of human thought its tribute brings
> Of waters,—with a sound but half its own,
> Such as a feeble brook will oft assume
> In the wild woods, among the Mountains lone,
> Where waterfalls around it leap for ever,
> Where woods and winds contend, and a vast river
> Over its rocks ceaselessly bursts and raves.

Shelley has written these lines with explicit reference to some form of idealism, Kantian or Berkeleyan or Platonic. But however you construe him, he is here an emphatic witness to a prehensive unification as constituting the very being of nature.

Berkeley, Wordsworth, Shelley are representative of the intuitive refusal seriously to accept the abstract materialism of science.

There is an interesting difference in the treatment of nature by Wordsworth and by Shelley, which brings forward the exact questions we have got to think about. Shelley thinks of nature as changing, dissolving, transforming as it were at a fairy's touch. The leaves fly before the West Wind

> Like ghosts from an enchanter fleeing.

In his poem *The Cloud* it is the transformations of water which excite his imagination. The subject of the poem is the endless, eternal, elusive change of things:

> I change but I cannot die.

This is one aspect of nature, its elusive change: a change not merely to be expressed by locomotion, but a change of inward character. This is where Shelley places his emphasis, on the change of what cannot die.

Wordsworth was born among hills; hills mostly barren of trees, and thus showing the minimum of change with the seasons. He was haunted by the enormous permanences of nature. For him change is an incident which shoots across a background of endurance,

> Breaking the silence of the seas
> Among the farthest Hebrides.
> ["The Solitary Reaper"]

Every scheme for the analysis of nature has to face these two facts, *change* and *endurance*. There is yet a third fact to be placed by it, *eternality*, I will call it. The mountain endures. But when after ages it has been worn away, it has gone. If a replica arises, it is yet a new mountain. A colour is eternal. It haunts time like a spirit. It comes and it goes. But where it comes, it is the same colour. It neither survives nor does it live. It appears when it is wanted. The mountain has to time and space a different relation from that which colour has. In the previous lecture, I was chiefly considering the relation to space-time of things which, in my sense of the term, are eternal. It was necessary to do so before we can pass to the consideration of the things which endure.

Also we must recollect the basis of our procedure. I hold that philosophy is the critic of abstractions. Its function is the double one, first of harmonising them by assigning to them their right relative status as abstractions, and secondly of completing them by direct comparison with more concrete intuitions of the universe, and thereby promoting the formation of more complete schemes of thought. It is in respect to this comparison that the testimony of great poets is of such importance. Their survival is evidence that they express deep intuitions of mankind penetrating into what is universal in concrete fact. Philosophy is not one among the sciences with its own little scheme of abstractions which it works away at perfecting and improving. It is the survey of sciences, with the special objects of their harmony, and of their completion. It brings to this task, not only the evidence of the separate sciences, but also its own appeal to concrete experience. It confronts the sciences with concrete fact.

The literature of the nineteenth century, especially its English poetic literature, is a witness to the discord between the aesthetic intuitions of mankind and the mechanism of science. Shelley brings vividly before us the elusiveness of the eternal objects of sense as they haunt the change which infects underlying organisms. Wordsworth is the poet of nature as being the field of enduring permanences carrying within themselves a message of tremendous significance. The eternal objects are also there for him,

> The light that never was, on sea or land.
> ["Elegiac Stanzas"]

Both Shelley and Wordsworth emphatically bear witness that nature cannot be divorced from its aesthetic values; and that these values arise from the cumulation, in some sense, of the brooding presence of the whole onto its various parts. Thus we gain from the poets the doctrine that a philosophy of nature must concern itself at least with these five notions: change, value, eternal objects, endurance, organism, interfusion. . . .

. . . But conversely, nothing must be left out. Remembering the poetic rendering of our concrete experience, we see at once that the element of value, of being valuable, of having value, of being an end in itself, of being something which is for its own sake, must not be omitted in any account of an event as the most concrete actual something. "Value" is the word I use for the intrinsic reality of an event. Value is an element which permeates through and through the poetic view of nature. We have only to transfer to the very texture of realisation in itself that value which we recognise so readily in terms of human life. This is the secret of Wordsworth's worship of nature. Realisation therefore is in itself the attainment of value. But there is no such thing as mere value. Value is the outcome of limitation. The definite finite entity is the selected mode which is the shaping of attainment; apart from such shaping into individual matter of fact there is no attainment. The mere fusion of all that there is would be the nonentity of indefiniteness. The salvation of reality is its obstinate, irreducible, matter-of-fact entities, which are limited to be no other than themselves. Neither science, nor art, nor creative action can tear itself away from obstinate, irreducible, limited facts. The endurance of things has its significance in the self-retention of that which imposes itself as a definite attainment for its own sake. That which endures is limited, obstructive, intolerant, infecting its environment with its own aspects. But it is not self-sufficient. The aspects of all things enter into its very nature. It is only itself as drawing together into its own limitation the larger whole in which it finds itself. Conversely it is only itself by lending its aspects to this same environment in which it finds itself. The problem of evolution is the development of enduring harmonies of en- during shapes of value, which merge into higher attainments of things beyond themselves. Aesthetic attainment is interwoven in the texture of realisation. The endurance of an entity represents the attainment of a limited aesthetic success, though if we look beyond it to its external effects, it may represent an aesthetic failure. Even within itself, it may represent the conflict between a lower success and a higher failure. The conflict is the presage of disruption.

The further discussion of the nature of enduring objects and of the conditions they require will be relevant to the consideration of the doc- trine of evolution which dominated the latter half of the nineteenth century. The point which . . . I have endeavoured to make clear is that the nature-poetry of the romantic revival was a protest on behalf of the organic view of nature, and also a protest against the exclusion of value from the essence of matter of fact. In this aspect of it, the romantic move- ment may be conceived as a revival of Berkeley's protest which had been launched a hundred years earlier. The romantic reaction was a protest on behalf of value.

The Isolation of the Human Mind

by David Perkins

What is written largest in Wordsworth as a prototype for modern poetry is not his solution (if it is a solution). Rather it is his sense of the gulf between human nature, with all of its greedy demands, its turbulent assertions, its often chaotic passions, and the rest of nature. Few critics have paid much attention to this side of Wordsworth, for Wordsworth differs from most modern poets in that he does not accept the split as final or necessary. Hence there has been a natural tendency to follow Wordsworth himself, and to stress his hope that the human mind can be formatively infused with the life of nature. But if one asks what motivates and gives urgency to this hope, and if one turns to Wordsworth's poetry without being controlled by his own overt emphasis, one finds that he was seeking to ease a suffocating, almost panicky fear that man is doomed to isolation from the healthful influence of his natural surroundings. In the poetry, this fear expresses itself, first of all, in situations where man is pictured as an actual intruder, whose "restless thoughts" and impulsive actions violate the harmonious "calm of nature."

In one instance the *Prelude* speaks of a "month of calm and glassy days" spent on an island during the war with France. "Each evening, pacing by the still sea-shore," Wordsworth heard the "monitory sound" of the "sunset cannon" (X, 320–325).[1] While the sun

> went down
> In the tranquillity of nature, came
> That voice, ill requiem! seldom heard by me
> Without a spirit overcast by dark
> Imaginations, sense of woes to come,
> Sorrow for human kind, and pain of heart.
> [1850 ed., X, 325–330]

"The Isolation of the Human Mind." From David Perkins, *The Quest for Permanence: The Symbolism of Wordsworth, Shelley and Keats* (Cambridge: Harvard University Press, 1959). Copyright © 1959 by the President and Fellows of Harvard College. Reprinted by permission of the author and the publisher. This essay is part 3 of chapter 1.

[1] [All quotations are from *The Prelude* of 1850. —ED.]

A key word here is the preposition "in." It implies that the sun went down in accordance with the tranquil order of nature proceeding without relation to human activities. But it also suggests that the cannon breaks in upon the "tranquillity of nature," shattering its "glassy" calm, or at least the calm it momentarily imposes on the human observer. The cannon calls to mind the bloody passions associated with war, and the dark imaginations it evokes suggest that the observer himself is all too precarious in his composure. He seems fearfully receptive to the "voice" of the cannon, and as it intrudes it vitiates his response to the natural scene.

Another example would be the poem "Nutting," which describes a boyhood trip to the woods to gather hazelnuts. The child came to a nook which had not previously been visited. Here

> the hazels rose
> Tall and erect, with tempting clusters hung,
> A virgin scene!
>
> [lines 19–21]

He stood still for a while

> Breathing with such suppression of the heart
> As joy delights in; and with wise restraint
> Voluptuous, fearless of a rival, eyed
> The banquet.
>
> [lines 22–25]

After dallying beneath the tree, he rose

> And dragged to earth both branch and bough, with crash
> And merciless ravage; and the shady nook
> Of hazels, and the green and mossy bower,
> Deformed and sullied, patiently gave up
> Their quiet being.
>
> [lines 44–48]

As he turned away from "the mutilated bower," he was "Exulting, rich beyond the wealth of kings"; yet he also "felt a sense of pain when" he "beheld / The silent trees." In this poem, the phrasing carries obvious sexual implications, and the emotions expressed—the joy of anticipated possession, the dallying, the "merciless ravage" and the remorse—affirm the root metaphor. To have felt and described the experience in these terms suggests not only how strongly he was affected but why. For although the remorse, which may be directly related to the patience of nature in enduring the attack, implies some chastening of the child's feelings, the incident revealed a chasm separating nature from the mind and habits of man. The shady nook does not infuse its calm into the human soul. The state of mind in which the grove is entered is the opposite of receptive. Guilty and assertive feeling blots out almost all sensitivity to the scene except the "voluptuous" temptation to take and mar. In other words, we do not discover here an approach to nature with the receptivity Wordsworth would have conceived formative. Instead, it is a misuse, an onslaught; and the place is accordingly left "deformed and sullied."

"Nutting" provides something of a prototype for recurring episodes in the *Prelude.* Among the most marked is the account of stealing out at night, as a child, to snare woodcocks:

> Through half the night,
> Scudding away from snare to snare, I plied
> That anxious visitation;—moon and stars
> Were shining o'er my head. I was alone,
> And seemed to be a trouble to the peace
>   [*Prelude,* I, 312–316]

of the surroundings. A passage from an earlier version had related

> How my heart
> Panted among the scattered yew-trees, and the crags
> That look'd upon me, how my bosom beat
> With expectation.

Both versions then relate how "strong desire / O'erpowered" him and he took a bird from someone else's snare:

> and when the deed was done
> I heard among the solitary hills
> Low breathings coming after me, and sounds
> Of undistinguishable motion, steps
> Almost as silent as the turf they trod.
>   [*Prelude,* I, 321–325]

As in "Nutting," there is at first a strange, excited expectation. There is also a sense of guilt projected in the "low breathings" and "steps" he hears. But the guilt does not arise primarily from the theft. Significantly, he felt it before he took the bird "Which was the captive of another's toil." As soon as he came among the mountains he felt himself "to be a trouble to the peace / That dwelt among them," and a sense of guilt objectified itself in his consciousness of the "crags / That look'd upon" him. Like Gulliver among the Houyhnhnms, he was the only passionate, desiring intelligence in a harmonious and tranquil world. Similarly, when Wordsworth and his companions came as "plunderers" among the rocks or when he took the boat, "an act of stealth / And troubled pleasure," and rowed swiftly out on the "silent lake," the experience is again construed as guilty desire amid the surrounding tranquillity (I, 326–400).

Boyhood episodes which involve his own personal acts provide particularly clear-cut illustrations of the sense of man as intruder, and the association of this intrusion with guilt. But analogous feelings appear in a reaction to other people—a reaction which may be less immediately vivid but which goes further in explaining the alternating blandness and deep uneasy disturbance with which Wordsworth's poetry treats actual human beings encountered within the setting of nature. Here one must not think of poems with an openly didactic theme, like *Peter Bell*, which is concerned with a human being who is unresponsive to nature, and who is automatically supposed to be guilty. This can be taken for granted. Less obvious, but more general and disturbing, is the feeling that the mere presence of human beings may bring a certain stain, an uneasy ripple, upon the calm surface of nature. A singularly apt example occurs in an episode in the *Prelude* (V, 435 ff.) where the body of a drowned man is recovered from a lake. The setting as a whole is one of complete tranquillity. The man himself, as he rises "bolt upright" with a "ghastly face" is dead. In a real sense, the drowned man has about as much or more repose than human nature would ever wish. But the point is that Wordsworth tacks on to the incident a rather prosaic statement that he was able to tamp down his reaction to it, that it did not unduly affect him. There is surely some significance in this need to reassure himself. It is also suggestive that the actual presentation of the occurrence is far more impressive than the attempt to state that he was capable of taking it in his stride. The "anxious crowd" that huddles in the twilight about the lake, the people in the boat, "sounding with grappling irons," are not themselves an intrusion. They are associations brought in as mere planetary actions gravitating about the rising of the human corpse. What does intrude is the corpse itself, "ghastly" and "bolt upright" in the very midst of the tranquil lake—"mid that beauteous scene / Of trees and hills and water." It is "a spectre shape / Of terror," frightening in itself and possibly the more disturbing because it symbolizes the poet's own fears concerning human nature. And the very violence of these fears may be what compels Wordsworth to assert that the incident could be blunted, the fears managed.

So, in the encounter with the veteran soldier, earlier in the *Prelude* (IV, 353–469), we have a projection of the profound sense of man as alien or intruder, though in this case a temporary or *ad hoc* resolution is found. And the resolution presents, in miniature, what Wordsworth was trying to conceive as a possibility. At the end of the episode, the veteran fades into the context of nature, just as (in a very different way) the dead maiden in "A slumber did my spirit seal" is made one with nature's "diurnal course," caught up in a solemn and inevitable absorption into "rocks, and stones, and trees." In this particular instance, the veteran finally proves, like the leech gatherer, Michael, and other characters who represent Wordsworth's hope for human nature, to have a "demeanour calm," to come close to being "solemn and sublime." In other words, he possesses all the qualities usually located in nature and none that Wordsworth usually associates with man. Hence at the end of the incident the poet finds himself able to continue on his way "with quiet heart."

But the background of the encounter, however it may have been resolved, and the poet's first impressions, are extraordinarily revealing. Wordsworth, to begin with, is returning home, late at night, from a visit with friends. The contrast that this solitary walk presents with the earlier part of the evening is sharp. Certainly there is no conscious intention to refer back to the particular visit or evening-party, but there is still the brooding reflection that we are "parted," as he says, "from our better selves" by

> the hurrying world, and droop,
> Sick of its business, of its pleasures tired.
>   [IV, 355–356]

This thought leads immediately to a passage in direct praise of "Solitude" —"How gracious, how benign"—and even of a "mere image of her sway" such as

>   a public road,
> When, for the night deserted, it assumes
> A character of quiet more profound
> Than pathless wastes.
>   [IV, 367–370]

But Wordsworth also remarks that an image of "Solitude" becomes "Most potent when impressed upon the mind / With an appropriate human centre," a "hermit, / Deep in the bosom of the wilderness," or a "Votary . . . Kneeling at prayers" alone in some "vast cathedral." He goes on to suggest that the lonely veteran standing in the road was also a "human centre" embodying the "soul" of "Solitude." These lines represent Wordsworth's own effort to account for the deep impression made by the encounter. What is striking about them is that the explanation does not seem to accord with the experience, as though Wordsworth himself could not recognize or admit what was involved. At least, when first seen the veteran is felt to be anything but "gracious" or "benign."

Before the encounter, the quiet and calm of the scene is emphasized. Except for the sound of a brook, there is complete silence:

No living thing appeared in earth or air,
And, save the flowing water's peaceful voice,
Sound there was none.

[IV, 385-387]

Then suddenly there is the meeting with another person. At once the tranquil peace of the scene, and of Wordsworth's corresponding mood, is shattered. Instead of blending into the natural scene, the man intrudes upon it. He appears as an "uncouth shape," assertively "stiff, lank, and upright" (we may remember that the corpse emerges from the bosom of the lake "bolt upright"). Moreover, this innocent and solitary human being is seen as "ghastly in the moonlight." Even later on, after the meeting, his is a "ghostly figure." Also, when Wordsworth, still unperceived, first notices him,

From his lips . . .
Issued low muttered sounds, as if of pain
Or some uneasy thought.

[IV, 404-406]

The intrusion, in other words, is more than physical. It involves the presence of human pain and guilt in the natural world. Moreover, the guilt imputed may be something more than what Wordsworth usually associated with human nature. The first reaction may have been to see the man as guilty because he intrudes. Nor do later developments completely belie these impressions. He is, as Wordsworth learns, a veteran soldier, a reminder of the violent emotions unleashed in war. By association, he arouses a disturbing train of images in the poet's mind, yet, at the same time, being solitary and surrounded by the "vast cathedral" of nature, he gradually permits these images and associations to be managed. In fact, as it turns out, he has certain traits of character which offer a kind of catharsis; for when Wordsworth, learning that he is a veteran, is led to broach the subject of

war, battle, and pestilence,
Sprinkling this talk with questions, better spared,
On what he might himself have seen or felt,

[IV, 437-439]

the veteran answers calmly, with

a strange half-absence, as of one
Knowing too well the importance of his theme,
But feeling it no longer.

[IV, 443-445]

It is partly this lack of feeling in the veteran which calms and subdues the agitations he had roused. Indeed, this "half-absence" suggests exactly what Wordsworth sought when faced with situations of emotional stress. But however the catharsis or resolution may have been achieved, the poet's immediate reaction may remind us of Robinson Crusoe's sudden fear when, after so many years of solitude, he suddenly discovered a human footprint in the sand.

Some Characteristics of Wordsworth's Style

by David Ferry

It is the main function of the critic of any poet to discover in him ideas and feelings which can in some way be related to our own deepest feelings and ideas, and which are able to make their appeal ultimately outside the limits of their own time. These are the truly formative contents of any good poem, since all its other evidences of unity proceed from them and since all its other, lesser meanings must subsist in them or else be considered irrelevant. Thus, if one should decide that *Lycidas* is merely a poem about the death of Edward King, or merely about the social and spiritual condition of England in Milton's time, then two conclusions are possible—*Lycidas* is minor, or else the critic has not gone far enough to discover its truly formative subject matter, by which alone the poem can be finally judged. Wordsworth says:

> Aristotle, I have been told, has said, that Poetry is the most philosophic of all writing: it is so: its object is truth, not individual and local, but general and operative; not standing upon external testimony, but carried alive into the heart by passion; truth which is its own testimony, which gives competence and confidence to the tribunal to which it appeals, and receives them from the same tribunal.[1]

This kind of truth, as it exists in poetry, is what the critic has to find, and he will know it when he has found it, because it will be its own testimony that he has done so. This kind of truth, I believe, can be found along the line where the critic's insights into content and his insights into style join and become one.

My general conclusion, after an attempt to perform this critical function, is that the ideas and feelings in Wordsworth's best poems are indeed "in some way" related to the ideas and feelings we are accustomed to find

[1] "Preface to . . . Lyrical Ballads," [in] *Poetical Works*, ed. de Selincourt and Darbishire, II, 394–395.

in a more humane poetry, but related as a great enemy, say, is related to a great hero—as an enemy almost equal in strength to that hero, and loving him almost, but an enemy nevertheless. The ideas and feelings in Wordsworth's most important poems are lovingly hostile to the humane world. I shall try to show how this is true by concentrating on one central subject matter: man's relations to nature with respect to his mortality. For it is the limits of mortality that define man as what he is, individual, idiosyncratic, circumscribed; and it is against the mortal limitations of man that Wordsworth, in my view of him, conceived such a hatred.

To say the very least, this is not the usual view of Wordsworth. That is why I have chosen for the most part to develop my argument through the patient reading of whole poems, rather than more generally and topically and by the quotation of selected passages merely. My case can be argued most effectively by demonstrating how such meanings emerge from their fullest poetic context.

My view of Wordsworth derives from a special way of reading his poems—a way of reading which of course I think is the right one. A poet's style is in the last analysis the habit of reading he trains us in— Wordsworth himself said that an original poet must create "the taste by which he is relished." But Wordsworth has often in the past been read without regard to the special sorts of demands the poems make on us, and this resistance to his training has led to a good deal of distortion. . . . Therefore, I shall try to define some of the special qualities of Wordsworth's style and consequently to describe the habits of reading with which I have read him.

For this purpose it is useful to examine some criticisms Coleridge made of Wordsworth, because in them Coleridge himself (surprisingly enough) demonstrates how the poetry can be misunderstood if it is read with the wrong assumptions in mind. Coleridge, to be sure, thought the criticisms trifling and minor, but I think we will be able to see that their implications are very far from being so.

In the *Biographia Literaria,* Coleridge cites as one of Wordsworth's characteristic defects that of employing "thoughts and images too great for the subject." This, he says,

> . . . is an approximation to what might be called *mental* bombast, as distinguished from verbal: for, as in the latter there is a disproportion of the expressions to the thoughts, so in this there is a disproportion of thought to the circumstances and occasion.

One of his examples of this fault is the poem *Gipsies,* in which

> . . . the poet, having gone out for a day's tour of pleasure, meets early in the morning with a knot of *gipsies,* who had pitched their blanket-tents and straw-beds, together with their children and asses, in some field

by the road-side. At the close of day on his return our tourist found them in the same place. "Twelve hours," says he,

"Twelve hours, twelve bounteous hours are gone, while I
Have been a traveller under open sky,
Much witnessing of change and cheer,
Yet as I left I find them here."

Whereat the poet, without seeming to reflect that the poor tawny wanderers might probably have been tramping for weeks together through road and lane, over moor and mountain, and consequently must have been right glad to rest themselves, their children and cattle for one whole day; and overlooking the obvious truth, that such repose might be quite as necessary for *them,* as a walk of the same continuance was pleasing or healthful for the more fortunate poet; expresses his indignation in a series of lines, the diction and imagery of which would have been rather above, than below the mark, had they been applied to the immense empire of China improgressive for thirty centuries:

"The weary SUN betook himself to rest:—
Outshining, like a visible God,
The glorious path, in which he trod!
And now, ascending, after one dark hour,
And one night's diminution of her power,
Behold the mighty MOON! this way
She looks, as if at them—but they
Regard not her:—oh better wrong and strife,
Better vain deeds or evil than such life!
The silent HEAVENS have goings on:
The STARS have tasks!—but *these* have none!" [2]

This passage calls on us to judge the verses by the touchstone of our most humane and sympathetic reactions to things. For Coleridge the main point is the actual condition of the gipsies themselves, and in order to judge the poem he draws on his own knowledge, as a human being aware of the fortunes of other human beings, of how tired and how glad to rest the gipsies must often be. He accuses the poet of having overlooked an obvious truth about these "poor tawny wanderers" which he should not have overlooked, of having in his own good fortune lorded it over creatures less fortunate than himself. Furthermore, he says that the diction and imagery expended on these objects are too elevated and would have been so even if they had been expended on something far more imposing, say the immense torpid empire of China.

The common-sense foundation of this criticism, the confidence that the gipsies should be "placed" properly in relation to the world around

[2] *Biographia Literaria,* ed. J. Shawcross (2 vols.; London, 1907), II, 109-111.

them, might in a very simple way be called "classicist": the poet's function is to be a more or less disinterested but always humane observer of the world outside himself, whose objects have inherent values from which the poet draws the conclusions which propel and direct his sympathies and antipathies. He looks out on the world, and because his awareness of the human condition is large and sympathetic, he misses no obvious truths which call for his pity and tolerance. But at the same time he is able to see things within the grander frame or structure of values which obtains in the world, and so is never impelled to use impertinent or grandiose language about things whose claims are humble. To such a poet, every object is the meeting ground of two noncontradictory systems of values, those they contain "within themselves" and those they have within the total scheme. It is the poet's duty and special privilege to know both kinds of values and to express their coming together in his language.

Judged by such criteria, it is plain enough that the poem is silly and intolerant, full of a propertied self-content. Gipsies do obviously get tired and need to rest; to cavil at them for it seems mere uninteresting peevishness. And the reader is after all likely to be both puzzled and irritated when the poet calls on sun, moon, and stars to support his caviling. It is shooting a mouse with an elephant gun.

But perhaps such criteria do not really apply. Perhaps it is of the nature of this imagination to overlook "obvious truths" and to treat a band of gipsies like the empire of China. Wordsworth says that the poet is a man "pleased with his own passions and volitions as manifested in the goings-on of the Universe, and habitually impelled to create them where he does not find them." [3] His tenderness is to be lavished on these passions and volitions, not on the outside world, and whatever attention he pays to that world is in the search for versions of those passions and volitions in other things. If the search should fail, the poet is even compelled to make it a success by creating them where he does not find them. Where Coleridge asserts that the poet has obligations to the actual circumstances and conditions of what he sees, that the poet is bound to a sane and just response to what is true of them "in themselves," Wordsworth asserts an extraordinary freedom for the poet from such obligations, the freedom to ignore whatever is irrelevant to his sublime egotism. It is a freedom which upsets the hierarchical system of values within which the empire of China is thought more than a band of gipsies, and which radically alters the way the poet will regard the band of gipsies in itself. The difference is the difference between a poetry which *evaluates* the world according to a reasonable and common-sense set of attitudes, and a poetry which *makes use of* the world for other purposes.

[3] Preface to *Lyrical Ballads, Poetical Works*, II, 393.

We are misled if we understand by "passions and volitions" simply the ordinary complex and multifoliate responses and desires of most men's inner lives. Wordsworth's passions and volitions are specifically religious and metaphysical, and their nature is such as to obliterate all others insofar as possible. Spinoza, whose mind in this respect was very similar to Wordsworth's, provides us with a useful vocabulary here. He says:

> From all this we easily conceive what is the power which clear and distinct knowledge, and especially that . . . kind of knowledge . . . whose foundation is the knowledge itself of God, possesses over the affects; the power, namely, by which it is able, in so far as they are passions, if not actually to destroy them . . . , at least to make them constitute the smallest part of the mind. . . . Moreover, it begets a love towards an immutable and eternal object . . . , of which we are really partakers . . . ; a love which therefore cannot be vitiated by the defects which are in common love, but which can always become greater and greater . . . occupy the largest part of the mind . . . , and thoroughly affect it.

He also says:

> Everything which the mind understands under the form of eternity, it understands not because it conceives the present actual existence of the body, but because it conceives the essence of the body under the form of eternity.

And he explains this further by saying:

> Things are conceived by us as actual in two ways: either in so far as we conceive them to exist with relation to a fixed time and place, or in so far as we conceive them to be contained in God, and to follow from the necessity of the divine nature. But those things which are conceived in this second way as true or real we conceive under the form of eternity, and their ideas involve the eternal and infinite essence of God.[4]

Coleridge's criticism of Wordsworth essentially means, then, that the poet failed to take sufficient account of the gipsies conceived as existing "with relation to a fixed time and place." But if we think of the poet as interested in his own passions and volitions "as manifested in the goings-on of the Universe"—that is, as "contained within God"—we see that he has the authority of Spinoza for reducing to "the smallest part of the mind," for destroying as far as possible, that "common love" which might have seen that the gipsies were tired.

Indeed, Wordsworth would be true to himself if he were to blame the gipsies precisely *because* they are tired, for their weariness is the symptom of their condition with relation to a fixed time and place, the symptom of a stubborn particularity which resists and denies the eternal. Wordsworth blames the gipsies for their mortality, for not participating suffi-

---

⁴ Baruch Spinoza, *Selections*, ed. John Wild (New York, 1930), pp. 383, 387.

ciently in the eternal. He himself participates by imitating the immense
courteous interchanges of sun, moon, and stars, emblems of the eternal
nature of things, and the tone he takes toward the gipsies is to be
thought of not as some glum trivial irritability, but as a sublime arro-
gance which is almost identified with his joy in the processes of the
universe and takes its justification from that joy. And the magnificent
imagery with which he bombards the gipsies is not inappropriate, since
he is judging them "under the form of eternity" and by contrast to the
mighty creatures of the cosmos, sun, moon, and stars. In the freedom of
his sublime egotism, the gipsies are a mere convenience for the poet, to
express his feelings about eternity. And for this he sacrifices the humane
and common-sense considerations which Coleridge has to take into
account.

Coleridge also criticized a more famous poem, *I wandered lonely as
a cloud,* as exhibiting this same "defect" of "thoughts and images too
great for the subject." This poem presents a more intricate problem.

Here again, Coleridge read the poem as if the poet were looking at the
daffodils "with relation to a fixed time and place," and of course from
one point of view we do respond to it in that way. Coleridge thought
Wordsworth had an experience of a particular event, "a vivid image or
visual spectrum," and that he had an excessive response to that experience. Daffodils are really too trivial for the attentions of the "inward eye,"
which might better be reserved for a moral experience of a much higher
order, "the joy of retrospection, when the images and virtuous actions of
a whole well-spent life, pass before that conscience which is indeed 'the
bliss of solitude.' " [5] Even if we grant his assumptions in this case, we
do not go along with his strictures quite as readily in this poem as in
Gipsies. We are all familiar with the pleasures a pretty scene can afford,
and the scene of daffodils by a lake is a very pretty one indeed. And we
are willing to admit that there are considerable emotional possibilities
in such a scene, whose effects are ultimately therapeutic. So Coleridge's
demand for a more profound and moral subject matter may perhaps
seem captious, too solemn for the charming occasion. But on further
reflection there *does* seem to be something more here than the occasion
warrants, something which Coleridge's moral vocabulary of "conscience"
and of a "well-spent life" cannot tell us much about.

Under the aspect of eternity, daffodils, in their joyous organization, in
their dancing, represent as well as anything else the divine organization
of things, the "goings-on of the Universe." And it is even a rhetorical
advantage to the poet that daffodils, such mere pretty flowers, so humble
and modest in the great scheme of things, can represent such grandeur.
In the beginning the poet is what the gipsies were, emblem of that which

[5] *Biographia Literaria,* II, 109.

does not participate in the eternal. But in his case, by a process of abstraction, by removing himself from the actual scene, and by a process of imagination, by seeing what the daffodils mean as "contained in God," he is able at last to join them, to perceive in them those passions and volitions which in his loneliness he had temporarily lost. And his loneliness has nothing to do with a separation from the world of men. It is a separation from the harmony of things and the aspect of eternity. The whole action of the poem is the symbol of the poet's relation to eternity (and the difficulty of perfecting that relation), of which his experience of daffodils is merely an example.

Certain "obvious truths" about a band of gipsies are ignored in order that they may be used as part of a symbolic design that figures forth the relations of the poet's mind to the universe; a degree of emotion is invested in a field of daffodils which seems excessive if we consider them "with relation to a fixed time and place." The Romantic metaphysical poet of this sort is likely to view nature, then, not as a set of objects, events, conditions which are in themselves his final interest, his final subject matter, but as a *language to be read,* signposts to that metaphysical place to which he wants to go. Insofar as those signposts appear to give him right directions, he will celebrate them, they will seem to him to be holy. And what the objects of physical nature are to the metaphysical nature of which he wants to have experience, the "surface" of his poems— its imagery and its feelings as expressed in tone and attitude—are to its "deeper meanings," its ultimate subject matter, which is the celebration of the metaphysical, the eternal and one. Thus, if we read the poems from a more or less "classicist" and common-sense point of view, as evaluations of this world seen with respect to time and place, we are likely to feel some dissatisfaction, to think that some obvious things about the condition of gipsies have been overlooked or that an excessive response is being made to mere daffodils. But if we read them as symbols of man's relations to the eternal, many of these dissatisfactions disappear. This is the principal habit of reading in which Wordsworth trains us.

But there are further considerations. If the natural world is for such a poet a system of signposts telling him the way to the place he wants to go to, he is likely to feel the sort of impatience with them that we often feel with signposts: if they tell us the way to get there, they also tell us that we have not gotten there yet. They are the sign of the incompleteness of our mission. And if the objects of this world are for Wordsworth signposts to eternity, they are more than that too, they necessarily have particular and individual complexities—he must to some degree see them with relation to a fixed time and place—and this is a cause of impatience too. This impatience is likely to be reflected, for example, in the poet's use of metaphor. The goldenness of the daffodils is first of all a quality

which tells us that they are charming, but it is only after the poet has
abstracted himself from that golden scene that the physical gold can be
converted into a much more valuable gold, "the wealth the show to
[him] had brought." In one sense the wealth is the same as the gold
he saw in the daffodils at first, but in another it is what that mere physical
prettiness had to be *transformed into,* after a rather complex abstractive
and imaginative process. If the classical poet is like a miner, sifting
through the ore of his experience for its real gold, the Romantic metaphysical poet of this sort is like an alchemist, transforming petty substance into gold. He is unlike most alchemists only in that the gold he
achieves may be real gold, but he is like most alchemists in that the
splendor of his achievement depends on the pettiness of what he begins
with. And the word "show," in the daffodils poem, illustrates this complexity too. The scene was a "show" in the sense that it was the concrete
embodiment of the metaphysical joy he was looking for; but it was
"only a show" in the sense that the physical scene was the appearance
whose reality he was seeking and which he could find only after he had
removed himself from that scene. The "inward eye" with which at last
he so truly sees is in one sense the outward eye functioning at its most
profound, but in another sense it is the opposite of the outward eye and
depends on its closing. The "inward eye" sees at that moment when
"we are laid asleep / In body, and become a living soul."

Such details illustrate very well the tension and in some respects the
hostility between "surface" and "deeper" meanings in Wordsworth's
poems, between symbols and what the symbols refer to, even as they
illustrate the tension and in some ways the hostility between the physical
and the metaphysical natures. An artist can never do entirely without the
physical world, and a poet perhaps least of all. It is a condition of language that it involves willy-nilly all sorts of references and appeals not
only to particular objects but to highly particularized emotions, and the
complex ramifications of these are impossible for the poet utterly to
resist. (Music and abstract painting, of course, have this referential quality, this tendency to concreteness, to a far lesser degree.) In later chapters
we shall see some larger consequences of this problem for Wordsworth.

Our main point here is the special way in which all these considerations
have led us to read the poems. It is often as if the "surface" meanings of
the poems were a beautiful and intelligible message, apparent at once,
and as if hidden in that message there were clues to a "deeper" meaning,
still more beautiful though in some ways at odds with the message one
had read at first.

Wordsworth's celebrated sonnet on Westminster Bridge is a mar-
velous illustration of the sort of poem which has a satisfactory meaning
"with relation to a fixed time and place" and an equally wonderful,
quite different meaning when understood "under the aspect of eternity":

> Earth has not anything to show more fair:
> Dull would he be of soul who could pass by
> A sight so touching in its majesty:
> This City now doth, like a garment, wear
> The beauty of the morning; silent, bare,
> Ships, towers, domes, theatres, and temples lie
> Open unto the fields, and to the sky;
> All bright and glittering in the smokeless air.
> Never did sun more beautifully steep
> In his first splendour, valley, rock, or hill;
> Ne'er saw I, never felt, a calm so deep!
> The river glideth at his own sweet will:
> Dear God! the very houses seem asleep;
> And all that mighty heart is lying still!

The poem is justly famous. It is a kind of dramatic monologue, in the present tense, and it seems very directly to express immediate pleasure in the eye and ear and to celebrate qualities of a particular, immediate, and personal experience, and to leave it at that, without moralizing or in any way shaking its finger at us. It is solemn without being heavy, and we are at once enchanted by the picture of London in the early morning, with its "ships, towers, domes, theatres, and temples" glittering "in the smokeless air."

The speaker is admiring London at the moment when it is least characteristic of itself, and admiring it because it is at that moment so uncharacteristic of itself. The city wears its beauty "like a garment" which covers its essential, its naked ugliness, as Duessa's ugliness was covered. There is now none of the usual smoke in the air, and the buildings lie open to the fields and sky as if they were ruins of their usual selves. A good deal of the emphasis is given not to what the city looks like but to scenes of an opposite sort, of natural country beauty, "valley, rock, and hill" at sunrise, and of a river uncluttered by the Thames' usual barges. The speaker's attitudes toward country and city, then, are the organizing notions which permit his poem to display its beautiful qualities of pathos and pleasure, the bated breath which characterizes his mood, as if his eye went on tiptoe over the scene, anxious not to awaken the city into the ugliness and confusion he hates. The speaker is a man who likes the calm and quiet of the country and dislikes the bustle of the city. His *opinions* are, in that sense, only the means by which we share his pathos and wonder at this moment, and we do not feel it necessary to agree or disagree with them. The "real subject" of the poem, by this reading, is its qualities of tone and its tactful imagery, the rendering of the particular experience, "conceived as existing with relation to a fixed time and place."

But the poem is queerer than it looks at first, and it expresses doctrines which are the antithesis, in certain ways, of the values of this particularized experience. Read in the context of his poetry as a whole, and with Wordsworth's passion for eternity in mind, the sonnet is a statement about man's essential relations to his experience and to the real, the metaphysical, nature which devaluates his temporal experience. Wordsworth's poems are major documents in the history of symbolism, which is to say that they belong to the history of an art whose "inner" or "final" or "deeper" meanings are not mere extensions or generalizations of the implications of its surface. The surface is an organization of clues to such meanings and is always to a degree depreciated by them, just as a code is in a sense depreciated by its deciphering.

This is not to say that the surface in these poems has no significance in itself. It has the significance that it has. But it is also the means to another end. The dramatic and highly particularized "surface" of the Westminster Bridge sonnet is interesting in itself, but from another point of view it is only a symbol for another set of meanings, which in themselves deny the source of values of the dramatic and the particular. Thus the last line of Wordsworth's sonnet suggests that the city is not merely sleeping but dead, its heart stilled. The poet looks at London and sees it as a sort of corpse and admires it as such, welcomes a death which is the death of what the city has come to stand for in his symbolic world. The city is a collection of men and of all their ordinary experiences, their common loves and attachments, and it therefore represents all the involvements in temporal experience from which the poet would like to escape. London awake would be the rising up of all those passions which Spinoza and Wordsworth would like to destroy or to relegate to "the smallest part of the mind." What is so beautiful to the poet about this moment early in the morning is that these passions seem for the moment to be quieted, even to be expunged. What is so full of pathos, from this point of view, is that it *is* so early in the morning, that London will inevitably awaken, that we are creatures of time, and that we have our pleasures and our pains within the limits of mortality.

The hostility between the dramatic and the symbolic readings of the poem expresses itself here in a curious observation: the "death" the poet is so pleased to witness is the death even of those properties in himself by which he responds so wonderfully to the city at this particular moment. It must always be so in the conflict between the love of eternity and the loves of time, but it is especially poignant that it should be so for a poet. It is especially moving that one of the great representatives of our human powers of articulation should be himself a lover of silence. . . .

Wordsworth and the Iron Time

by Lionel Trilling

Our commemoration of the hundredth anniversary of Wordsworth's death must inevitably be charged with the consciousness that if Wordsworth were not kept in mind by the universities he would scarcely be remembered at all.[1] In our culture it is not the common habit to read the books of a century ago, and very likely all that we can mean when we say that a writer of the past is "alive" in people's minds is that, to those who once read him as a college assignment or who have formed an image of him from what they have heard about him, he exists as an attractive idea, as an intellectual possibility. And if we think of the three poets whom Matthew Arnold celebrated in his "Memorial Verses," we know that Byron is still attractive and possible, and so is Goethe. But Wordsworth is not attractive and not an intellectual possibility. He was once the great, the speaking poet for all who read English. He spoke both to the ordinary reader and to the literary man. But now the literary man outside the university will scarcely think of referring to Wordsworth as one of the important events of modern literature; and to the ordinary reader he is likely to exist as the very type of the poet whom life has passed by, presumably for the good reason that he passed life by.[2]

If we ask why Wordsworth is no longer the loved poet he once was, why, indeed, he is often thought to be rather absurd and even a little despicable, one answer that suggests itself is that for modern taste he is too Christian a poet. He is certainly not to be wholly characterized by the Christian element of his poetry. Nor can we say of him that he is a

"Wordsworth and the Iron Time" by Lionel Trilling. First printed with this title in *Wordsworth: Centenary Studies Presented at Cornell and Princeton Universities* (Princeton: Princeton University Press, 1951). Revised, and printed with the title "Wordsworth and the Rabbis," in Lionel Trilling, *The Opposing Self* (New York: The Viking Press, 1955). Copyright © 1950 by Lionel Trilling. The revised version is reprinted here with a few additions, and with the original title restored, by permission of The Viking Press, Martin Secker & Warburg Ltd., London, and the author.

[1] The Centenary was celebrated in America at Cornell and Princeton Universities on April 21 and 22, 1950.
[2] 1971: Wordsworth's standing as a poet would seem to be considerably higher at the present time than it was when I gave this account of it in 1950.

Christian poet in the same sense that Dante is, or Donne, or Hopkins.
With them the specific Christian feeling and doctrine is of the essence
of their matter and their conscious intention, as it is not with Wordsworth. Yet at the present time, the doctrinal tendency of the world at
large being what it is, that which *is* Christian in Wordsworth may well
seem to be more prominent than it ever was before, and more decisive.
I have in mind his concern for the life of humbleness and quiet, his
search for peace, his sense of the burdens of this life, those which are
inherent in the flesh and spirit of man. Then there is his belief that the
bonds of society ought to be inner and habitual, not merely external and
formal, and that the strengthening of these bonds by the acts and attitudes
of charity is a great and charming duty. Christian too seems his responsiveness to the idea that there is virtue in the discharge of duties
which are of the great world and therefore dangerous to simple peace—
his sense of affinity with Milton was as much with Milton's political as
with his poetical career, and the Happy Warrior is the man who has,
as it were, sacrificed the virtuous peace of the poet to the necessities of
public life. There is his impulse to submit to the conditions of life under
a guidance that is at once certain and mysterious; his sense of the possibility and actuality of enlightenment, it need scarcely be said, is one
of the characteristic things about him. It was not he who said that the
world was a vale of soul-making, but the poet who did make this striking
paraphrase of the Christian sentiment could not have uttered it had
not Wordsworth made it possible for him to do so.[3] And then, above all,
there is his consciousness of the *neighbor,* his impulse to bring into the
circle of significant life those of the neighbors who are simple and outside the circle of social pride, and also those who in the judgment of the
world are queer and strange and useless: faith and hope were to him
very great virtues, but he conceived that they rested upon the still
greater virtue, charity.

Certainly what I have called Christian in Wordsworth scarcely approaches, let alone makes up, the sum of Christianity. But then no personal document or canon can do that, not even the work of a poet who
is specifically Christian in the way of Dante, or of Donne, or of Hopkins.
When we speak of a poet as being of a particular religion, we do not
imply in him completeness or orthodoxy, or even explicitness of doctrine,
but only that his secular utterance has the decisive mark of the religion
upon it. And if a religion is manifold in its aspects and extensive in time,
the marks that are to be found on the poets who are in a relation to it will
be various in kind. It seems to me that the marks of Christianity on
Wordsworth are clear and indelible. It is therefore worth trying the

<hr>

[3] It is of some relevance to our argument that when Keats wrote the famous phrase
he believed that he was controverting, not affirming, a tendency of Christian thought.

hypothesis that the world today does not like him because it does not like the Christian quality and virtues.

But the question at once arises whether this hypothesis is actually available to us. Professor Hoxie Neal Fairchild says that it is not. In the chapter on Wordsworth in the third volume of his *Religious Trends in English Poetry,* he tells us that Wordsworth was *not* a Christian poet and goes on to express his doubt that Wordsworth was ever properly to be called a Christian person even when he became a communicant of the Church and its defender. And Professor Fairchild goes so far as to tell us that as a poet Wordsworth is actually dangerous to the Christian faith. He is dangerous in the degree that he may be called religious at all, for his religion is said to be mere religiosity, the religion of nothing more than the religious emotion, beginning and ending in the mere sense of transcendence. Naked of dogma, bare of precise predication of God and the nature of man, this religiosity of Wordsworth's is to be understood as a pretentious and seductive rival of Christianity. It is the more dangerous because it gives license to man's pretensions—Professor Fairchild subscribes to the belief that romanticism must bear a large part of the responsibility for our present ills, especially for those which involve man's direct and conscious inhumanity to man.

We can surely admit the cogency of Professor Fairchild's argument within the terms of its intention. The nineteenth century was in many respects a very Christian century, but in the aspect of it which bulks largest in our minds it developed chiefly the ethical and social aspects of Christian belief, no doubt at the cost of the dogmatic aspect, which had already been weakened by the latitudinarian tendency of the eighteenth century. And it is probably true that when the dogmatic principle in religion is slighted, religion goes along for a while on generalized emotion and ethical intention—"morality touched by emotion"—and then loses the force of its impulse, even the essence of its being. In this sort of attenuation of religion, romanticism in general, and Wordsworth in particular, did indeed play a part by making the sense of transcendence and immanence so real and so attractive. During the most interesting and important period of his career, Wordsworth seems to have been scarcely aware of the doctrines of the Church in which he had been reared. He spoke of faith, hope, and charity without reference to the specifically Christian source and end of these virtues. His sense of the need for salvation did not take the least account of the Christian means of salvation. Of evil in the Christian sense of the word, of sin as an element of the nature of man, he also took no account.

And yet, all this being true, as we look at Wordsworth in the context of his own time and in the context of our time, what may properly be called the Christian element of his poetry can be made to speak to us, as it spoke to so many Christians in the nineteenth century, as it spoke to so many who were not Christians and made them in one degree or another accessible to Christianity.

"Any religious movement," says Christopher Dawson, an orthodox Christian scholar, "which adopts a purely critical and negative attitude to culture is . . . a force of destruction and disintegration which mobilizes against it the healthiest and most constructive elements in society— elements which can by no means be dismissed as worthless from the religious point of view." Romanticism in general was far from worthless to Christianity, far from worthless to that very Anglo-Catholicism which inclines to be so strict with it. And this is true of Wordsworth in particular. He certainly did not in his great period accept as adequate what the Church taught about the nature of man. But he was one of the few poets who really discovered something about the nature of man. What he discovered can perhaps be shown, if the argument be conducted by a comparison of formulas and doctrine, to be at variance with the teachings of Christianity. Yet I think it can also be shown that Wordsworth discovered much that a strong Christianity must take account of, and be easy with, and make use of. It can be shown too, I believe, that the Church has found advantage in what Wordsworth has told us of the nature of man.

Professor Fairchild, I need scarcely say, understands Christianity far better than I do, through his having studied it ever so much more than I have; and of course he understands it far better than I might ever hope to, because he has experienced it as a communicant. He has also, I am sure, tested his conclusions by the whole tendency of the Church to which he gives so strong and thoughtful an allegiance. My own reading of this tendency, at least as it appears in literature and in literary criticism, where it has been so influential, is that it is not inclined to accept Wordsworth as a Christian poet. And still, even against the force of Professor Fairchild's judgment, I cannot help feeling that there is an important element of Christianity with which Wordsworth has a significant affinity, even though this element is not at the present time of chief importance to Christian intellectuals.

But this is not an occasion for anything like contentiousness, and I ought not to seem to be forcing even a great poet into a faith whose members do not want him there. I am not, in any case, so much concerned to prove that Wordsworth is a Christian poet as to account for a certain quality in him which makes him unacceptable to the modern world. And so, without repudiating my first hypothesis, I shall abandon it for this fresh one: that the quality in Wordsworth that now makes him unacceptable is a Judaic quality.

My knowledge of the Jewish tradition is, I fear, all too slight to permit me to hope that I can develop this new hypothesis in any very enlightening way. Yet there is one Jewish work of traditional importance which I happen to know with some intimacy, and it lends a certain color of accuracy to my notion. This is the work called *Pirke Aboth,* that is, the sayings, the *sententiae,* of the Fathers. It was edited in the second century of the present era by the scholar and teacher who bore the magnificent name of Rabbi Jehudah the Prince, and who is traditionally referred to by the even more magnificent name of *Rabbi*—that is to say, *the* rabbi, the master teacher, the greatest of all. In its first intention *Pirke Aboth,* under the name *Aboth,* "Fathers," was one of the tractates of the Mishnah, which is the traditional Jewish doctrine represented chiefly by rabbinical decisions. But *Aboth* itself, the last of the tractates, does not deal with decisions; nor is it what a common English rendering of the longer title, "Ethics of the Fathers," would seem to imply, for it is not a system of ethics at all but simply a collection of maxims and *pensées,* some of them very fine and some of them very dull, which praise the life of study and give advice on how to live it.

In speaking of Wordsworth a recollection of boyhood cannot be amiss— my intimacy with *Pirke Aboth* comes from my having read it many times in boyhood. It certainly is not the kind of book a boy is easily drawn to read, and certainly I did not read it out of piety. On the contrary, indeed: for when I was supposed to be reading my prayers—very long, and in the Hebrew language, which I never mastered—I spent the required time and made it seem that I was doing my duty by reading the English translation of the *Pirke Aboth,* which, although it is not a devotional work, had long ago been thought of as an aid to devotion and included in the prayer book. It was more attractive to me than psalms, meditations, and supplications; it seemed more humane, and the Fathers had a curious substantiality. Just where they lived I did not know, nor just when, and certainly the rule of life they recommended had a very quaint difference from the life I knew, or, indeed, from any life that I wanted to know. Yet they were real, their way of life had the charm of coherence. And when I went back to them, using R. Travers Herford's scholarly edition and translation of their sayings,[4] I could entertain the notion that my early illicit intimacy with them had had its part in preparing the way for my responsiveness to Wordsworth, that between the Rabbis and Wordsworth an affinity existed.

But I must at once admit that a large difficulty stands in the way of the affinity I suggest. The *Aboth* is a collection of the sayings of masters of the written word. The ethical life it recommends has study as both its means and its end, the study of Torah, of the Law, which alone can give

[4] *Pirke Aboth,* edited with introduction, translation and commentary, third edition (New York: 1945). I have also consulted the edition and translation of the Very Rev. Dr. Joseph H. Hertz, Chief Rabbi of the British Empire, and in my quotations I have drawn upon both versions, and sometimes, when it suited my point, I have combined two versions in a single quotation.

blessedness. So that from the start I am at the disadvantage of trying
to make a conjunction between scholars living for the perpetual interpretation of a text and a poet for whom the natural world was at the
heart of his doctrine and for whom books were barren leaves. The Rabbis
expressed a suspiciousness of the natural world which was as extreme as
Wordsworth's suspiciousness of study. That the warning was given at
all seems to hint that it was possible for the Rabbis to experience the
natural world as a charm and a temptation: still, the *Aboth* does warn
us that whoever interrupts his study to observe the beauty of a fine tree
or a fine meadow is guilty of sin. And yet I think it can be said without
more extravagance than marks my whole comparison that it is precisely
here, where they seem most to differ, that the Rabbis and Wordsworth
are most at one. For between the Law as the Rabbis understood it and
Nature as Wordsworth understood that, there is a pregnant similarity.

The Rabbis of the *Aboth* were Pharisees. I shall assume that the long
scholarly efforts of Mr. Herford, as well as those of George Foot Moore,
have by now made it generally known that the Pharisees were not in
actual fact what tradition represents them to have been. They were
anything but mere formalists, and of course they were not the hypocrites
of popular conception. Here is Mr. Herford's statement of the defining
principle of Pharisaism: "The central conception of Pharisaism is Torah,
the divine Teaching, the full and inexhaustible revelation which God had
made. The knowledge of what was revealed was to be sought, and would
be found, in the first instance in the written text of the Pentateuch; but
the revelation, the real Torah, was the meaning of what was there
written, the meaning as interpreted by all the recognized and accepted
methods of the schools, and unfolded in ever greater fullness of detail
by successive generations of devoted teachers. The written text of the
Pentateuch might be compared to the mouth of a well; the Torah was the
water which was drawn from it. He who wished to draw the water must
needs go to the well, but there was no limit to the water which was
there for him to draw. . . . The study of Torah . . . means therefore
much more than the study of the Pentateuch, or even of the whole
Scripture, regarded as mere literature, written documents. It means the
study of the revelation made through those documents, the divine teaching therein imparted, the divine thought therein disclosed. Apart from
the direct intercourse of prayer, the study of Torah was the way of closest
approach to God; it might be called the Pharisaic form of the Beatific
Vision. To study Torah was, to the devout Pharisee, to 'think God's
thoughts after him,' as Kepler said." The Rabbis, that is, found sermons
in texts, tongues in the running commentary.

And Mr. Herford goes on to say that it might be observed of the
Aboth that it makes very few direct references to God. "This is true," he
says, "but it is beside the mark. Wherever Torah is mentioned, there God

is implied. He is behind the Torah, the Revealer of what is Revealed."
What I am trying to suggest is that, different as the immediately present
objects were in each case, Torah for the Rabbis, Nature for Wordsworth,
there existed for the Rabbis and for Wordsworth a great object, which
is from God and might be said to represent Him as a sort of surrogate,
a divine object to which one can be in an intimate passionate relationship,
an active relationship—for Wordsworth's "wise passiveness" is of course
an activity—which one can, as it were, handle, and in a sense create,
drawing from it inexhaustible meaning by desire, intuition, and attention.

And when we turn to the particulars of the *Aboth* we see that the
affinity continues. In Jewish tradition the great Hillel has a peculiarly
Wordsworthian personality, being the type of gentleness and peace, and
having about him a kind of *joy* which has always been found wonderfully attractive; and Hillel said—was, indeed, in the habit of saying: he
"used to say"—"If I am not for myself, who, then, is for me? And if I am
for myself, what then am I?" Mr. Herford implies that this is a difficult
utterance. But it is not difficult for the reader of Wordsworth, who finds
the Wordsworthian moral essence here, the interplay between individ-
ualism and the sense of community, between an awareness of the self that
must be saved and developed, and an awareness that the self is yet ful-
filled only in community.

Then there is this saying of Akiba's: "All is foreseen, and yet free will
is given; and the world is judged by grace, and yet all is according to the
work." With how handsome a boldness it handles the problem of fate
and free will, or "grace" and "works," handles the problem by stating
it as an antinomy, escaping the woeful claustral preoccupation with the
alternatives, but not their grandeur. This refusal to be fixed either in
fate or in free will, either in grace or in works, and the recognition of
both, are characteristic of Wordsworth.

There are other parallels to be drawn. For example, one finds in the
Aboth certain remarks which have a notable wit and daring because they
go against the whole tendency of the work in telling us that the multiplica-
tion of words is an occasion for sin, and the chief thing is not study but
action. One finds the injunction to the scholar to divide his time between
study and a trade, presumably in the interest of humility. And the
scholar is warned that the world must not be too much with him, that,
getting and spending, he lays waste his powers. There is the concern, so
typical of Wordsworth, with the "ages of man," with the right time in
the individual's development for each of life's activities. But it is need-
less to multiply the details of the affinity, which in any case must not be
insisted on too far. All that I want to suggest is the community of ideal
and sensibility between the *Aboth* and the canon of Wordsworth's work
—the passionate contemplation and experience of the great object which
is proximate to Deity; then the plain living that goes with the high

thinking, the desire for the humble life and the discharge of duty; and last, but not least important, a certain insouciant acquiescence in the anomalies of the moral order of the universe, a respectful indifference to, or graceful surrender before, the mysteries of the moral relation of God to man.

This last element, as it is expressed in the *pensée* of Akiba which I have quoted, has its connection with something in the *Aboth* which for me is definitive of its quality. Actually it is something not in the *Aboth* but left out—we find in the tractate no implication of moral struggle. We find the energy of assiduity but not the energy of resistance. We hear about sin, but we do not hear of the sinful nature of man. Man in the *Aboth* guards against sin but he does not struggle against it, and of evil we hear nothing at all.

When we have observed this, it is natural to observe next that there is no mention in the *Aboth* of courage or heroism. In our culture we connect the notion of courage or heroism with the religious life. We conceive of the perpetual enemy within and the perpetual enemy without, which must be "withstood," "overcome," "conquered"—the language of religion and the language of fighting are in our culture assimilated to each other. Not so in the *Aboth*. The enemy within seems not to be conceived of at all. The enemy without is never mentioned, although the *Aboth* was compiled after the Dispersion, after the Temple and the nation had been destroyed—with what heroism in the face of suffering we know from Josephus. Of the men whose words are cited in the *Aboth*, many met martyrdom for their religion, and the martyrology records their calm and fortitude in torture and death; of Akiba it records his heroic joy. And yet in their maxims they never speak of courage. There is not a word to suggest that the life of virtue and religious devotion requires the heroic quality.

As much as anything else in my boyhood experience of the *Aboth* it was this that fascinated me. It also repelled me. It had this double effect because it went so clearly against the militancy of spirit which in our culture is normally assumed. And even now, as I consider this indifference to heroism of the *Aboth,* I have the old ambiguous response to it, so that I think I can understand the feelings that readers have when they encounter something similar in Wordsworth. It is what Matthew Arnold noted when in the "Memorial Verses" he compared Wordsworth with Byron, who was for Arnold the embodiment of militancy of spirit. Arnold said of Wordsworth that part of his peculiar value to us arose from his indifference to "man's fiery might," to the Byronic courage in fronting human destiny.

> The cloud of mortal destiny,
> Others will front it fearlessly—
> But who, like him, will put it by?

Arnold certainly did not mean that Wordsworth lacked courage or took no account of it. Wordsworth liked nothing better, indeed, than to recite examples of courage, but the Wordsworthian courage is different in kind from the Byronic. For one thing, it is never aware of itself, it is scarcely personal. It is the courage of mute, insensate things, and it is often associated with such things, "with rocks, and stones, and trees," or with stars. Michael on his hilltop, whose character is defined by the light of his cottage, which was called "The Evening Star," and by the stones of his sheepfold; or the Leech Gatherer, who is like some old, great rock; or Margaret, who, like a tree, endured as long as she might after she was blasted—of the Lesser Celandine it is said that its fortitude in meeting the rage of the storm is neither its courage nor its choice but "its necessity in being old," and the same thing is to be said of all Wordsworth's exemplars of courage: they endure because they are what they are, and we might almost say that they survive out of a kind of biological faith, which is not the less human because it is nearly an animal or vegetable faith; and, indeed, as I have suggested, it is sometimes nearly mineral. Even the Happy Warrior, the man in arms, derives his courage not from his militancy of spirit but from his calm submission to the law of things.

In Wordsworth's vision of life, then, the element of quietude approaches passivity, even insentience, and the dizzy raptures of youth have their issue in the elemental existence of which I have spoken. The scholars of the *Aboth* certainly had no such notion; they lived for intellectual sentience. But where the scholars and Wordsworth are at one is in the quietism, which is not in the least a negation of life, but, on the contrary, an affirmation of life so complete that it needed no saying. To the Rabbis, as I read them, there life was, unquestionable because committed to a divine object. There life was—in our view rather stuffy and airless, or circumscribed and thin, but very intense and absolutely and utterly real, not needing to be affirmed by force or assertion, real because the object of its regard was unquestioned, and because the object was unquestionably more important than the individual person who regarded it and lived by it. To Wordsworth, as I read him, a similar thing was true in its own way. Much as he loved to affirm the dizzy raptures of sentience, of the ear and the eye and the mind, he also loved to move down the scale of being, to say that when the sentient spirit was sealed by slumber, when it was without motion and force, when it was like a rock or a stone or a tree, not hearing or seeing, and passive in the cosmic motion— that even then, perhaps especially then, existence was blessed.

Nothing could be further from the tendency of our Western culture, which is committed to an idea of consciousness and activity, of motion and force. With us the basis of spiritual prestige is some form of aggressive action directed outward upon the world, or inward upon ourselves.

During the last century and a half this ideal has been especially strong in literature. If the religious personality of preceding times took to itself certain of the marks of military prestige, the literary personality now takes to itself certain of the marks of religious prestige, in particular the capacity for militant suffering.

A peculiarly relevant example of this lies to hand in T. S. Eliot's explanation of the decline of Wordsworth's genius from its greatness to what Mr. Eliot calls the "still sad music of infirmity." The small joke, so little characteristic of Mr. Eliot's humor, suggests something of the hostile uneasiness that Wordsworth can arouse in us. And Mr. Eliot's theory of the decline suggests the depth of our belief in the value of militancy, of militant suffering, for Mr. Eliot tells us that the trouble with Wordsworth was that he didn't have an eagle: it is that eagle which André Gide's Prometheus said was necessary for success in the spiritual or poetic life—"*Il faut avoir un aigle.*" As an explanation of Wordsworth's poetic career this is, we perceive, merely a change rung on the weary idea that Wordsworth destroyed his poetic genius by reversing his position on the French Revolution or by terminating his connection with Annette Vallon. Wordsworth had no need of an eagle for his greatness, and its presence or absence had nothing to do with the decline of his genius. His pain, when he suffered, was not of the kind that eagles inflict, and his power did not have its source in his pain. But we are disturbed by the absence of the validating, the poetically respectable bird, that *aigle obligatoire*. We like the fiercer animals. Nothing is better established in our literary life than the knowledge that the tigers of wrath are to be preferred to the horses of instruction, a striking remark which is indeed sometimes very true, although not always. We know that we ought to prefer the bulls in the ring to the horses, and when we choose between the two kinds of horses of Plato's chariot we all know that Plato was wrong, that it is the blacks, not the whites, which are to be preferred. We do not, to be sure, live in the fashion of the beasts we admire in our literary lives, but we cherish them as representing something that we all seek. They are the emblems of the *charisma*—to borrow from the sociologists a word they have borrowed from the theologians—which is the hot, direct relationship with Godhead, or with the sources of life, upon which depend our notions of what I have called spiritual prestige.

The predilection for the powerful, the fierce, the assertive, the personally militant, is very strong in our culture. We find it in the liberal-bourgeois admiration of the novels of Thomas Wolfe and Theodore Dreiser. On a lower intellectual level we find it in the long popularity of that curious underground work *The Fountainhead*. On a higher intellectual level we find it in certain aspects of the work of Yeats and Lawrence. We find it too, if not in our religion itself, then at least in one of our dominant conceptions of religion—to many intellectuals the violence of Dostoevski represents the natural form of the religious life, to many gentle spirits the ferocity of Léon Bloy seems quite appropriate to the way of faith; and although some years ago Mr. Eliot reprobated D. H. Lawrence, in the name of religion, for his addiction to this characteristic violence, yet for Mr. Eliot the equally violent Baudelaire is pre-eminently a Christian poet.[5]

I cannot give a better description of the quality of our literature with which I am concerned than by quoting the characterization of it which Richard Chase found occasion to make in the course of a review of a work on the nineteenth century by a notable English scholar, Professor Basil Willey. It is relevant to remark that Professor Willey deals with the nineteenth century from the point of view of the Anglican form of Christianity, and Mr. Chase is commenting on Professor Willey's hostility to a certain Victorian figure who, in any discussion of Wordsworth, must inevitably be in our minds—John Stuart Mill. His name seems very queer and shocking when it is spoken together with the names of the great figures of modern literature. Yet Mr. Chase is right when he says that "among the Victorians, it is Mill who tests the modern mind," and goes on to say that "in relation to him at least two of its weaknesses come quickly to light. The first is its morose desire for dogmatic certainty. The second is its hyperaesthesia: its feeling that no thought is permissible except an extreme thought: that every idea must be directly emblematic of concentration camps, alienation, madness, hell, history, and God; that every word must bristle and explode with the magic potency of our plight."

I must be careful not to seem to speak, as certainly Mr. Chase is not speaking, against the sense of urgency or immediacy, or against power or passion. Nor would I be taken to mean that the Wordsworthian quietism I have described is the whole desideratum of the emotional life. It obviously wasn't that for Wordsworth himself—he may be said to be the first poet who praised movement and speed for their own sakes, and dizziness and danger; he is the poet of rapture. No one can read Book Five of *The Prelude* and remain unaware of Wordsworth's conception of literature as urgency and immediacy, as power and passion. Book Five, which is about literature and the place of reading in our spiritual development, opens with an impressive eschatological vision, a vision of final events—Wordsworth shared in his own way our present sense of the possible end of man and of all the works of man's spirit, and it is important to observe that in the great dream of the Arab who hastens

---

[5] In his brief introduction to Father Tiverton's *D. H. Lawrence and Human Existence*, Mr. Eliot has indicated that he has changed his mind about Lawrence's relation to the religious life. I think he was right to do so. The revision of his opinion confirms, if anything, what I say of the place of violence in our conception of the religious life.

before the advancing flood to rescue Science and Poetry, represented by
the Stone and the Shell he carries, the prophecy of the world destroyed
is made to seem the expression of the very essence of literature. It is in
this book that Wordsworth defends the violence and fearfulness of literature from the "progressive" ideas of his day; it is here that he speaks of
the poet as "crazed / By love and feeling, and internal thought / Pro-
tracted among endless solitude," and of the "reason" that lies couched
"in the blind and awful lair" of the poet's madness; and it is here that he
defends the "maniac's" dedication at the cost of the domestic affections:

> Enow there are on earth to take in charge
> Their wives, their children, and their virgin loves,
> Or whatsoever else the heart holds dear;
> Enow to stir for these. . . .
>   [*The Prelude* (1850), V, 153–56]

As we speak of Wordsworth's quietism this opposite element of his poetry
must be borne in mind. Then too, if we speak in anything like praise of
his quietism, we must be conscious of the connection of his quietism with
an aspect of his poetry that we rightly dread. When, in *The Excursion*,
the Wanderer and the Poet and the Pastor sit upon the gravestones and
tell sad stories of the deaths of other mild old men, for the benefit of the
Solitary, who has had his fling at life and is understandably a little bitter,
we know that something wrong is being done to us; we long for the
winding of a horn or the drawing of a sword; we want someone to dash
in on a horse—I think we want exactly a stallion, St. Mawr or another; for
there can be no doubt about it, Wordsworth, at the extreme or perversion
of himself, carries the element of quietude to the point of the denial of
sexuality. And this is what makes the *Aboth* eventually seem to us
quaint and oppressive, what, I suppose, makes a modern reader uneasy
under any of the philosophies which urge us to the contemplative accord
with a unitary reality and warn us that the accord will infallibly be
disturbed and destroyed by the desires. Whether it be the Torah of the
Rabbis, or the Cosmos of Marcus Aurelius, or the Nature of Spinoza or
of Wordsworth, the accord with the unitary reality seems to depend upon
the suppression not only of the sexual emotions but also of the qualities
that are associated with sexuality: high-heartedness, wit, creative innova-
tion, will.

But now, when we have touched upon the Wordsworthian quality that
is very close to the Stoic *apatheia,* to not-feeling, let us remember what
great particular thing Wordsworth is said to have accomplished. Matthew
Arnold said that in a wintry clime, in an iron time, Wordsworth taught
us to *feel.* This statement, extreme as it is, will be seen to be not inac-
curate if we bring to mind the many instances of spiritual and psychologi-

cal crisis in the nineteenth century in which affectlessness, the loss of the power to feel, played an important part. *Ennui, noia*—how often we meet with them in nineteenth-century biography; and the *acedia* which was once a disorder of the specifically religious life becomes now a commonplace of secular spirituality. Arnold, when he wrote the "Memorial Verses," could not, of course, have read Mill's autobiography, which so specifically and eloquently confirms Arnold's attribution to Wordsworth of a "healing power" through an ability to make us feel. And yet, although Arnold's statement is accurate so far as it goes, and is supported by Wordsworth's own sense of the overarching intention of his poetic enterprise, it does not go far enough. Wordsworth did, or tried to do, more than make us feel: he undertook to teach us how to *be*.

In *The Prelude,* in Book Two, Wordsworth speaks of a particular emotion which he calls "the sentiment of Being." The "sentiment" has been described in this way: "There is, in sanest hours, a consciousness, a thought that rises, independent, lifted out from all else, calm, like the stars, shining eternal. This is the thought of identity—yours for you, whoever you are, as mine for me. Miracle of miracles, beyond statement, most spiritual and vaguest of earth's dreams, yet hardest basic fact, and only entrance to all facts." This, of course, is not Wordsworth, it is Walt Whitman, but I quote Whitman's statement in exposition of Wordsworth's "sentiment of Being" because it is in some respects rather more boldly explicit, although not necessarily better, than anything that Wordsworth himself wrote about the sentiment, and because Whitman goes on to speak of his "hardest basic fact" as a political fact, as the basis, and the criterion, of democracy.

Through all his poetic life Wordsworth was preoccupied by the idea, by the sentiment, by the problem, of being. All experience, all emotions lead to it. He was haunted by the mysterious fact that he existed. He could discover in himself different intensities and qualities of being—"Tintern Abbey" is the attempt to distinguish these intensities and qualities. Being is sometimes animal; sometimes it is an "appetite and a passion"; sometimes it is almost a suspension of the movement of the breath and blood. The *Lyrical Ballads* have many intentions, but one of the chief of them is the investigation of the problems of being. "We are Seven," which is always under the imputation of bathos, is established in its true nature when we read it as an ontological poem; its subject is the question, What does it mean when we say a person *is*? "The Idiot Boy," which I believe to be a great and not a foolish poem, is a kind of comic assertion of the actuality—and, indeed, the peculiar intensity—of being in a person who is outside the range of anything but our merely mechanical understanding. Johnny on the little horse, flourishing his branch of holly under the moon, is a creature of rapture, who, if he is not quite "human," is certainly elemental, magical, perhaps a little divine—"It was Johnny, Johnny everywhere." As much as anyone, and more than many —more than most—he *is*, and feels that he is.

From even the little I have said, it will be seen that as soon as the "sentiment of Being" is named, or represented, there arises a question of its degree of actuality or of its survival. "The glad animal movements" of the boy, the "appetite" and the "passion" of the young man's response to Nature easily confirm the sense of being. So do those experiences which are represented as a "sleep" or "slumber," when the bodily senses are in abeyance. But as the man grows older the stimuli to the experience of the sentiment of being grow fewer or grow less intense—it is this fact rather than any question of poetic creation (such as troubled Coleridge) that makes the matter of the Immortality Ode. Wordsworth, as it were, puts the awareness of being to the test in situations where its presence may perhaps most easily be questioned—in very old people. Other kinds of people also serve for the test, such as idiots, the insane, children, the dead, but I emphasize the very old because Wordsworth gave particular attention to them, and because we can all be aware from our own experience what a strain very old people put upon our powers of attributing to them personal being, "identity." Wordsworth's usual way is to represent the old man as being below the human condition, apparently scarcely able to communicate, and then suddenly, startlingly, in what we have learned to call an "epiphany," to show forth the intensity of his human existence. The old man in "Animal Tranquillity and Decay" is described as being so old and so nearly inanimate that the birds regard him as little as if he were a stone or a tree; for this, indeed, he is admired, and the poem says that his unfelt peace is so perfect that it is envied by the very young. He is questioned about his destination on the road—

> I asked him whither he was bound, and what
> The object of his journey; he replied,
> "Sir! I am going many miles to take
> A last leave of my son, a mariner,
> Who from a sea-fight has been brought to Falmouth,
> And there is dying in an hospital."

The revelation of the actuality of his being, of his humanness, quite dazzles us.[6]

The social and political implication of Wordsworth's preoccupation with ontology is obvious enough. It is not, however, quite what Wordsworth sometimes says it is. The direct political lesson that the poet draws from the Old Cumberland Beggar is interesting, but it is beside his real,

---

[6] The concluding lines of the poem as originally printed in *Lyrical Ballads*, where the poem bears the title "Old Man Travelling," were deleted by Wordsworth in subsequent editions, which is a misfortune.

his essential, point. "Deem not this man useless," he says in his apostrophe to the political theorists who have it in mind to put the Beggar into a workhouse, and he represents the usefulness of the Beggar as consisting in his serving as the object of a habitual charity and thus as a kind of communal institution, a communal bond. But this demonstrated utility of the Beggar is really secondary to the fact that he *is*—he is a person, he takes a pleasure, even though a minimal one, in his being, and therefore he may not in conscience be dealt with as a mere social unit. So with all the dramatis personae of the *Lyrical Ballads*—the intention of the poet is to require us to acknowledge their being and thus to bring them within the range of conscience, and of something more immediate than conscience, natural sympathy. It is an attractive thing about Wordsworth, and it should be a reassuring thing, that his acute sense of the being of others derives from, and serves to affirm and heighten, his acute sense of his own being.

I have spoken of Wordsworth's preoccupation with being as if it were unique, and as if it accounted for, or led to what accounts for, the contemporary alienation from his work and his personality. In some ways his preoccupation *is* unique, and certain aspects of it do lead to the present alienation from him. Yet from what I have said about him, it must be clear that between Wordsworth and the great figures of our literature there is a very close affinity indeed, if only in the one regard of the preoccupation with being. There is scarcely a great writer of our own day who has not addressed himself to the ontological crisis, who has not conceived of life as a struggle to be—not to live, but to be. They do so, to be sure, under a necessity rather different from Wordsworth's, and this necessity makes it seem appropriate that, with Byron, they assert "man's fiery might." (Blake suggests more aptly than Byron the quality of the militancy of most modern writers, but I stay with the terms of the opposition as Arnold gives them to us.) They feel the necessity to affirm the personal qualities that are associated with a former time, presumably a freer and more personally privileged time—they wish, as a character in one of Yeats's plays says, "to bring back the old disturbed exalted life, the old splendor." Their image of freedom and personal privilege is often associated with violence, sometimes of a kind that does not always command the ready assent we are habituated to give to violence when it appears in moral or spiritual contexts. A tenant's sliced-off ear, which is an object of at least momentary pleasure to Yeats, a kick given by an employer to his employee, which wins the approval of Lawrence—these are all too accurately representative of the nature of the political fantasies that Yeats and Lawrence built upon the perception of the loss of freedom and privilege, the loss of the sense of being. Yet we know that this violence stands against an extreme fate of which we are all conscious. We really know in our time what the death of the word can be—for that knowledge we have only to read an account of contemporary Russian literature. We really know what the death of the spirit means—we have seen it overtake whole peoples. Nor do we need to go beyond our own daily lives to become aware, if we dare to, of how we have conspired, in our very virtues, to bring about the devaluation of whatever is bold and assertive and free, replacing it by the bland, the covert, the manipulative. If we wish to understand the violence, the impulse toward charismatic power, of so much of our literature, we have but to consider that we must endure not only the threat to being which comes from without but also the seduction to non-being which establishes itself within. We need, in Coleridge's words, something to "startle this dull pain, and make it move and live." Violence is a means of self-definition; the bad conscience, Nietzsche says, assures us of our existence.

Wordsworth, then, is not separated from us by his preoccupation with being, for it is our preoccupation. Yet he is separated from us. His conception of being seems different from ours.

In Book Five of *The Prelude* Wordsworth gives us a satiric picture of the boy educated according to the "progressive" ideas of his day, and on the whole we follow him readily enough in the objections he makes to these ideas—this can be said even though it often happens that readers, misled by their preconceptions of Wordsworth, take his sarcasm seriously and suppose that he is actually praising "this model of a child." And we follow him when he speaks of the presumptuousness of pedagogical theorists, denouncing them as, in effect, engineers of the spirit: he flatters at least one element of our ambivalence toward the psychological expert. We are responsive to his notion of what a boy should be: "not . . . too good," "not unresentful where self-justified." Possibly we are not in perfect agreement with him on all points—perhaps we will feel that he has dealt rather too harshly with the alert political and social consciousness of the progressive child, or that he goes too far in thinking that a child's imagination should be fed on fanciful books; perhaps, too, the qualities of the boys he really admires would not be precisely the qualities we would specify—"Fierce, moody, patient, venturous, modest, shy." But on the whole his discussion of pedagogics appeals to the enlightened muddled concern with "adjustment" and "aggression" which occupies the P.T.A. segment of our minds, and if we have our reservation about details we can at least, as I say, follow Wordsworth through most of his argument. But I think we cease to follow him when, in the course of the argument, he rises to one of his great poetical moments. This is the passage "There was a Boy. . . ." It was perhaps rather finer when it stood alone as a poem in itself in *Lyrical Ballads,* but it is still very fine in its place in *The Prelude,* where it follows the description of the model child. The Boy is described as having had a trick of imitating the hooting of owls, and at night he would call across Windermere, trying to get the owls to answer; and often they did answer, but sometimes they did not, and then the silence would be strange and significant.

> . . . In that silence, while he hung
> Listening, a gentle shock of mild surprise
> Has carried far into his heart the voice
> Of mountain torrents; or the visible scene
> Would enter unawares into his mind,
> With all its solemn imagery, its rocks,
> Its woods, and that uncertain heaven, received
> Into the bosom of the steady lake.
> [*The Prelude* (1850), V, 381–88]

We may be ready enough to acknowledge the "beauty" of the poem, but the chances are that we will be rather baffled by its intention. We perceive that the Boy is obviously intended to represent something very good and right, meant to be an example of very full being. But what baffles us, what makes us wonder what the poem has to do with education and the development of personality, is that the Boy exercises no will, or at least, when his playful will is frustrated, is at once content with the pleasures that follow upon the suspended will. And as likely as not we will be impelled to refer the poem to that "mysticism" which is supposed to be an element of Wordsworth's mind. Now Wordsworth's mind does have an element of mysticism— it is that "normal mysticism" which, according to a recent writer on the Rabbis, marked the Rabbinical mind.[7] Wordsworth's mysticism, if we wish to call it that, consists of two elements, his conception of the world as being semantic, and his capacity for intense pleasure. When we speak of him as a mystic in any other sense, we are pretty sure to be expressing our incomprehension of the intensity with which he experienced his own being, and our incomprehension of the relation which his sentiment of being bore to his will. Thus, we have no trouble understanding him when, in Book Six of *The Prelude*, in the remarkable episode of the crossing of the Alps, he speaks of the glory of the will.

---

[7] Max Kadushin, *The Rabbinical Mind* (New York: 1951). This impressive work of scholarship has received far less general notice than it deserves. I read it after I had written this essay—read it not only with admiration for its intellectual achievement but also with a peculiar personal pleasure, because its author, in his seminary days, had been one of the long-suffering men who tried to teach me Hebrew, with what success I have indicated; yet he did teach me—it was no small thing for a boy of twelve to be in relation with a serious scholar. Dr. Kadushin has been kind enough to tell me that what I have said about the Rabbis is not wrong. In revising my essay I have not tried to amend my primitive account by what is to be learned from Dr. Kadushin's presentation of the Rabbis in all their great complexity of thought. But the phrase, "normal mysticism," seemed too apt not to quote.

> . . . Whether we be young or old,
> Our destiny, our being's heart and home,
> Is with infinitude, and only there;
> With hope it is, hope that can never die,
> Effort, and expectation, and desire,
> And something evermore about to be.

The note on which the will is affirmed is high, Miltonic—it echoes the accents of Satan's speech in the Council of Hell; and the passage resumes its movement with a line the martial tenor of which we happily respond to: "Under such banners militant, the soul. . . ." But we are checked by what ensues:

> Under such banners militant, the soul
> Seeks for no trophies, struggles for no spoils
> That may attest her prowess, blest in thoughts
> That are their own perfection and reward,
> Strong in herself and in beatitude. . . .
>   [*The Prelude* (1850), VI, 603–13]

The soul's energy is directed to the delight of the soul in itself.

Wordsworth is describing the action of what, at a later time, a man of very different mind, Hegel, was to call a new human faculty, the faculty of *Gemüt*. The word, I gather, is not entirely susceptible of translation —"heart," with the implication of responsiveness, and of high-heartedness and large-heartedness, is an approximation. Hegel defines his faculty of *Gemüt* as expressing itself as a desire, a will, which has "no particular aims, such as riches, honors, and the like; in fact, it does not concern itself with any worldly condition of wealth, prestige, etc., but with the entire condition of the soul—a general sense of enjoyment."

Much that I have said about the tendency of our culture would seem to deny the truth of Hegel's statement that *Gemüt* is one of the characteristics of our time, and much more evidence might be adduced to confirm the impression that nothing could be less characteristic of our time than the faculty of *Gemüt*, that we scarcely conceive of it, let alone exercise it. Yet at the same time I think it is true to say that it plays in our culture a covert but very important part.

Of our negative response to *Gemüt*, to the "sentiment of Being," Mr. Eliot provides an instance—again, for it is Mr. Eliot's high gift to be as pertinent when we think him wrong as when we think him right. In *The Cocktail Party* there is a description of the two virtuous ways of life, that of "the common routine" and that of the spiritual heroism of the saint and martyr. The two ways, Mr. Eliot tells us, are of equal value; the way of the saint is not better than that of the householder. Yet when it comes to describing the life of the common routine, Mr. Eliot says of those who elect it that they

> Learn to avoid excessive expectation,
> Become tolerant of themselves and others,
> Giving and taking in the usual actions
> What there is to give and take. They do not repine;
> And are contented with the morning that separates
> And with the evening that brings together
> For casual talk before the fire
> Two people who know that they do not understand each other,
> Breeding children whom they do not understand
> And who will never understand them.

Well, few of us will want to say much for the life of the common routine, and no doubt, under the aspect of modern life with its terrible fatigues, and in the consciousness of its gross threats, the sort of thing that Mr. Eliot says here will be pretty nearly all that any of us will want to say. Yet if we think of the description of the common routine as being not merely the expression of one possible mood among many—and it is not merely that: it is what it says it is, the description of a "way"—we must find it very strange. There is in it no reference to the pain which is an essential and not an accidental part of the life of the common routine. There is no reference to the principles, the ethical discipline, by which the ordinary life is governed—all is habit. There is no reference to the possibility of either joy or glory—I use the Wordsworthian words by intention. The possibility of *Gemüt* does not appear. Mr. Eliot does not say that his couples are in Limbo, that they are in a condition of not-being, which would of course be a true thing to say of many house-holding couples: he is describing the virtuous way of life that is alternative to the way of the saint. This failure to conceive the actuality of the life of common routine is typical of modern literature since, say, Tolstoi. I do not say this in order to suggest that domestic life, the common routine, in itself makes an especially appropriate subject for literature —I don't think it does—but in order to suggest a limitation of our conception of the spiritual life. Mr. Eliot's representation of the two "ways" exemplifies how we are drawn to the violence of extremity. We imagine, with nothing in between, the dull not-being of life, the intense not-being of death; but we do not imagine being—we do not imagine that it can be a joy. We are in love, at least in our literature, with the fantasy of death. Death and suffering, when we read, are our only means of conceiving the actuality of life.

Perhaps this is not new and we but intensify what is indigenous in our culture. Perhaps this is in the nature of life as Western culture has long been fated to see it. Perhaps it is inescapable for us that the word "tragic" should be used as an ultimate recommendation of a sense of life. Yet we, when we use the word, do not really mean it in its old, complex, mysterious sense—we mean something like "violent" or "conclusive": we mean death. And just here lies a paradox and our point. For it is precisely what Wordsworth implies by his passionate insistence on being, even at a very low level of consciousness, pride, and assertiveness, as well as at the highest level of quasi-mystic intensity, that validates a conception of tragedy, and a conception of heroism. The saintly martyrdom which Mr. Eliot represents in his play is of course not intended to be taken as tragic: the idea of martyrdom precludes the idea of tragedy. But if we ask why the martyrdom seems as factitious as it does, must we not answer that this is because it is presented in a system of feeling which sets very little store by—which, indeed, denies the possibility of—the "beatitude" which Wordsworth thought was the birthright of every human soul? And this seems to be borne out by the emphasis which Mr. Eliot puts on the peculiar horror of the mode of the martyr's death, as if only by an extremity of pain could we be made to realize that a *being* was actually involved, that a life has been sacrificed—or, indeed, has been lived.

Wordsworth's incapacity for tragedy has often been remarked on, and accurately enough. Yet we cannot conclude that Wordsworth's relation to tragedy is wholly negative. The possibility of tragic art depends primarily upon the worth we ascribe not to dying but to living, and to living in "the common routine." The power of the Homeric tragedy, for example, derives from the pathos, which the poet is at pains to bring before us repeatedly, of young men dying, of not seeing ever again the trees of their native farmsteads, of their parents never again admiring and indulging them, of the cessation of their being in the common routine. The tragic hero, Achilles, becomes a tragic hero exactly because he has made choice to give up the life of the common routine, which all his comrades desire, in favor of a briefer but more intense quality of being of transcendent glory. The pathos of his particular situation becomes the great thing it is because of the respondent pathos of Hector and Priam, which is the pathos of the family and the common routine, which we understand less and less and find ourselves more and more uncomfortable with. And I think it can be shown that every tragic literature owes its power to the high esteem in which it holds the common routine, and the sentiment of being which arises from it, the elemental *given* of biology. And that is what Wordsworth had in mind when, in the "Preface" of 1800, defending the idea that poetry should give "immediate pleasure," he said that this idea was "a homage paid to the native and naked dignity of man, to the grand elementary principle of pleasure, by which he knows, and feels, and lives, and moves."

Yet if we are aware of the tendency of our literature I have exemplified by the passage from Mr. Eliot's play, we must at the same time be aware of the equally strong counter-tendency. In speaking of our alienation from Wordsworth, it has not been my intention to make a separation between Wordsworth and the literature of our time. The separation cannot be made. Wordsworth and the great writers of our time stand, as I have said, on the common ground of the concern with being and its problems —Wordsworth, indeed, may be said to have discovered and first explored the ground upon which our literature has established itself. Our hyper-aesthesia, our preference for the apocalyptic subject and the charismatic style, do indeed constitute a taste which alienates many readers from Wordsworth, and no doubt the more if we believe, as some do, that it is a taste wholly appropriate to the actualities of our historical situation. Yet we can without too much difficulty become aware of how much of the Wordsworthian "mildness," which so readily irritates us, and how much of the Wordsworthian quietism (as I have called it), which dismays us, are in the grain of our literature, expressed through the very intensities which seem to deny them. Thus, to bring Wordsworth and James Joyce into conjunction might at first seem a joke or a paradox, or an excess of historicism, at best a mere device of criticism. We will at once be conscious of the calculated hauteur of Joyce's implied personality, the elaborations of his irony, the uncompromising challenge of his style and his manner, and by the association of contrast we will remember that horrendous moment in *The Prelude* when Wordsworth says, "My drift I fear / Is scarcely obvious." How can we fail to think only of the abysses of personality, theory, and culture that separate the two men? And yet when we have become acclimated to Joyce, when the charismatic legend becomes with familiarity not so fierce and the vatic paraphernalia of the style and method less intimidating, do we not find that we are involved in a conception of life that reiterates, in however different a tonality, the Wordsworthian vision? [8] One of the striking things about *Ulysses* (to speak only of that work) is that the idea of evil plays so small a part in it. One hears a good deal about the essential Christian orthodoxy of Joyce, and perhaps this is an accurate opinion, but his orthodoxy, if he has it, takes no account of the evil which is so commonly affirmed by the literary expressions of orthodoxy; the conception of sin has but a tangential relevance to the book. The element of sexuality which plays so large a part in the story does not raise considerations of sin and evil; it is dealt with in the way of poetic naturalism. The character of Leopold Bloom, who figures in the life of Joyce's Poet much as the old men in Wordsworth

---

[8] 1971: At this date the conjunction of Wordsworth and Joyce will probably not seem at all bizarre, especially in view of what we now know of Joyce's admiration for Wordsworth. In a letter of 1905 to his brother Stanislaus, Joyce said, "I think Wordsworth of all English men of letters best deserves your word 'genius.'" (*Letters of James Joyce,* ed. Richard Ellmann [London, 1957–66], II, 91.)

figure in his life—met by chance and giving help of some transcendent yet essentially human kind—is conceived in Wordsworthian terms: in terms, that is, of his humbleness of spirit. If we speak of Wordsworth in reference to the Rabbis and their non-militancy, their indifference to the idea of evil, their acceptance of cosmic contradiction, are we not to say that Bloom is a Rabbinical character? It is exactly his non-militancy that makes him the object of general contempt and, on one occasion, of rage. It is just this that has captivated his author, as the contrast with the armed pride, the jealousy and desire for prestige, the bitter militancy of Stephen Dedalus. Leopold Bloom is deprived of every shred of dignity except the dignity of that innocence which for Joyce, as for Wordsworth, goes with the "sentiment of Being."

Again and again in our literature, at its most apocalyptic and intense, we find the impulse to create figures who are intended to suggest that life is justified in its elemental biological simplicity, and, in the manner of Wordsworth, these figures are conceived of as being of humble status and humble heart: Lawrence's simpler people or primitive people whose pride is only that of plants or animals; Dreiser's Jennie Gerhardt and Mrs. Griffiths, who stand as oases in the wide waste of their creator's dull representation of energy; Hemingway's waiters with their curious silent dignity; Faulkner's Negroes, of whom it is said, as so often it is said in effect of Wordsworth's people, *they endured;* and Faulkner's idiot boys, of whom it is to be said, *they are*—the list could be extended to suggest how great is the affinity of our literature with Wordsworth. And these figures express an intention which is to be discerned through all our literature—the intention to imagine, and to reach, a condition of the soul in which the will is freed from "particular aims," in which it is "strong in itself and in beatitude." At least as early as Balzac our literature has shown the will seeking its own negation—or, rather, seeking its own affirmation by its rejection of the aims which the world sets before it and by turning its energies upon itself in self-realization. Of this particular affirmation of the will Wordsworth is the proponent and the poet.

The Contemporaneity of the *Lyrical Ballads*

by *Robert Mayo*

A fruitful but unfrequented approach to the *Lyrical Ballads* is through the poetry of the magazines. The volume unquestionably belongs to 1798, and seen in relation to the popular verse of that day, its contemporaneous features are very striking. We have been asked to consider too exclusively the revolutionary aspects of the *Lyrical Ballads*. Revolutionary they unquestionably were, but not in every respect. Except that they were much better than other poems published in 1798, the *Ballads* were not such a "complete change" as some writers would have us believe.[1] Even their eccentricity has been exaggerated. Actually, there is a conventional side to the *Lyrical Ballads*, although it is usually overlooked. It is by way of the general taste for poetry in the 1790's that this essay will approach the poems, and it will attempt to show that they not only conformed in numerous ways to the modes of 1798, and reflected popular tastes and attitudes, but enjoyed a certain popularity in the magazines themselves.

The general interest in poetry during the last decades of the eighteenth century, also, is a phenomenon which is largely ignored, although it is relevant in a number of ways to the new poetry of Southey, Coleridge, Wordsworth, Byron, and Scott. Something is known of the popularity of

"The Contemporaneity of the *Lyrical Ballads*" by Robert Mayo. From *PMLA*, 69 (1954). Copyright © 1954 by The Modern Language Association of America. Reprinted by permission of PMLA and the author. A middle section of the essay has been omitted.

[1] "The volume [of 1798] undoubtedly was a puzzle, for it marked a complete change from anything that had appeared before" (Elsie Smith, *An Estimate of William Wordsworth by His Contemporaries*, Oxford, 1932, p. 33). The phrase is T. J. Wise's: ". . . the *Ballads* marked a complete change from the style and character of poetical composition then regarded as classic" (*A Bibliography of the Writings in Prose and Verse of William Wordsworth*, London, 1916, p. 31). But the opinion has been widely expressed. Cf. Oliver Elton: "They [the *Ballads*] are mostly reflective narratives, of a great variety of forms. . . . There had been nothing of the sort before; the very faults were new" (*A Survey of English Literature, 1780–1830*, 4th imp., London, 1933, II, 64). Also Littledale: "The Volume of *Lyrical Ballads* made its appeal in 1798 to a small and unprepared public; it had to create the taste by which it was enjoyed" (*Wordsworth and Coleridge, Lyrical Ballads, 1798*, ed. H. Littledale, London: Oxford University Press, 1931, p. vii).

such writers as Helen Maria Williams, Anna Seward, Erasmus Darwin, W. L. Bowles, "Peter Pindar," Charlotte Smith, Henry James Pye, Mary Robinson, and Mrs. West; but except for Bowles they are usually dealt with summarily as a deservedly forgotten generation. For most historians they are the "modern writers" whose "gaudiness and inane phraseology" were repudiated by the Advertisement and the Preface of the *Lyrical Ballads*. But critical as Wordsworth was of his contemporaries, he cannot be completely dissociated from them. He belonged to their generation, and he addressed himself to their audience. Moreover, he was not insensitive to popular favor. He repeatedly asserted in 1798–99 that he had published the *Lyrical Ballads* to make money; *The Ancient Mariner*, with its "old words" and "strangeness," had hurt the sale of the volume, and in the second edition he "would put in its place some little things which would be more likely to suit the common taste." [2] This is a fairly appropriate description of some of the contents of the second edition.

The student who wishes to consider the coinage of "the common taste" will find in the magazines of the late eighteenth century the richest and most accessible repository. There poetry enjoyed a more honored place than any other form of imaginative writing, and poetry departments were an inevitable feature of such serials as the *Gentleman's Magazine*, the *Monthly Magazine*, the *Scot's Magazine*, the *European Magazine*, and the *Lady's Magazine*—to name only a few of the more popular. Together these five magazines alone published about five hundred poems a year; and their total monthly circulation in 1798 must have exceeded 25,000. At the same time a great number of lesser miscellanies in London, Edinburgh, Glasgow, Dublin, and the provincial towns, sought to satisfy in the same way the general taste for verse. It was, in more than one sense, a period of poetic inflation. Seemingly, anything was acceptable for publication, provided it was not too long, and did not offend the proprieties. The average poetry department was a hodgepodge, which by and large provides a very effective measure of popular taste. Its effectiveness is owing to several factors: the great abundance and immediacy of the poetry printed; the flexible combination of both new and reprinted verse; and the prevailing reader-writer situation, in which amateurs wrote the kind of "original" verse in which they were interested. As a result of the accepted interpretation of the Parliamentary Act of 1710, magazines lay outside the usual restrictions of the copyright laws, and the poetry departments of most miscellanies like the *Lady's Magazine* and the *Universal Magazine* are therefore likely to contain a large number of reprinted poems, collected from new books of verse, reviews of such volumes, newspapers, poetical miscellanies, and other magazines. Such

[2] *The Early Letters of William and Dorothy Wordsworth, 1787–1805*, ed. Ernest de Selincourt (Oxford, 1935), pp. 225–227.

poems were read by—or at least exposed to—thousands of readers, and their influence should be measured accordingly. Pieces like Bürger's *Lenore* and M. G. Lewis' *Alonzo the Brave* enjoyed a tremendous popularity in the magazine world, being caught up and carried from miscellany to miscellany until their total circulation must have reached many thousands. "Because of the trash which infests the magazines," Wordsworth proposed that *The Philanthropist* (The "Monthly Miscellany" which he projected in 1794) offer *reprinted* poetry exclusively, "from new poetical publications of merit, and such *old* ones as are not generally known." [3] The *Lyrical Ballads*, we shall find, were promptly raided in this manner by half a dozen magazines, so that the general acquaintance with *Goody Blake, We are Seven*, and other poems in the volume cannot be gauged by the number of copies of the original publication in circulation.

At the same time that they helped themselves from outside sources, the magazines also printed quantities of what was termed "original poetry"—that is, new poems written by the editor or his acquaintances, by readers, or by professionals. Some of the more substantial miscellanies like the *Gentleman's Magazine*, the *European Magazine*, and the *Monthly Magazine*, published "original poetry" almost exclusively, and were willing to pay for it. *The Ancient Mariner*, for example, was first planned by the two poets as a joint contribution to the new *Monthly Magazine*, for which it was hoped that five pounds might be obtained. But many miscellanies were unwilling to remunerate writers, and sought rather to obtain contributions gratis from their army of readers. The number of amateur scribblers in the 1790's is legion, and they are mostly anonymous. They are also inveterate plagiarists, so that the first appearance of any poem in the magazines, no matter how it is signed, is always a matter of conjecture. The distinction between "original," adapted, and reprinted verses is never sure. The only certainty is that there is a confused and eddying flood of popular poetry flowing through the magazines from the middle of one century to the next—some old, some new, some written by hacks, much more written by amateurs, who endlessly copied the accepted masterpieces of the past and rang changes on the approved models of the day. The vast proportion of this verse literature is hopelessly mediocre, and deservedly forgotten, except that it provides the best available chart for the shifting currents of popular taste. Through it we can partly understand the ground swell of popular favor which helped to raise the *Lyrical Ballads* to eminence in spite of hostile criticism from the Edinburgh reviewer and others.

The student who approaches the *Lyrical Ballads* by way of the magazines may be struck first by differences rather than by resemblances. To

[3] Ibid., p. 122.

most of the verse of the poetry departments the *Ballads* seem to have
little relation, except to represent a kind of recoil. It is easy to see what
the poets were reacting against in the Advertisement. The "common
taste" of the miscellanies not only approved the "gaudy" and "inane";
it was in most respects extremely conservative, if not antique. There is
in much of the magazine verse of the 1790's a literary lag of at least half
a century. In his attacks on Pope, Gray, Prior, and Dr. Johnson in the
1802 Appendix Wordsworth was not exactly beating dead horses. These
poets, together with Gay, Parnell, Thomson, Akenside, and Thomas
Warton, were still the accepted masters for many verse-writers, amateur
and professional alike; and most of the hackneyed elegies, odes, occasional poems, and so on which flooded the poetry departments of the
miscellanies can only be described as the backwash of the Augustan era.

The insipidity of magazine poetry, however, is deceptive. It is not
uniformly antique, and it is far from being homogeneous. Not all of the
verses in the magazines are imitations of Gray's *Elegy*, Pope's *Pastorals*,
and *The Pleasures of Melancholy*. A persistent minority—original and
reprinted alike—are occupied with new subjects of poetry and written
in the new modes of the late eighteenth century. The *Monthly Magazine*
in particular, after 1796, was the resort of many of the new poets, but
actually their writings, and imitations of them, are likely to be encountered anywhere. With the poems of this minority the *Lyrical Ballads* have
a great deal in common, and although the resemblances are often superficial, they are numerous enough to show that Wordsworth and Coleridge were not out of touch with contemporary modes. A great deal of
effort has been admirably expended in the last twenty years in developing the background of the poets' thought, and in showing the organic
relation of the ideas and attitudes expressed in the *Lyrical Ballads* to the
larger movements of eighteenth-century thought and taste. It remains
still to suggest the many ways in which they also conform to the literary
fashions of the 1790's. These we may attempt to describe roughly with
respect first to "content," and second, to "form," although such a separation, of course, is quite artificial.

There are twenty-three poems in the first edition, and viewed in the
light of what we now know of their authorship and composition, the
volume no doubt seems, as Legouis says, "a somewhat random and in-
congruous assemblage." [4] But the incongruities were certainly less likely
to "puzzle and disconcert" contemporaries than they do modern histo-

[4] Emile Legouis, "Some Remarks on the Composition of the *Lyrical Ballads* of 1798,"
Wordsworth and Coleridge: Studies in Honor of George McLean Harper (Princeton,
1939), pp. 3, 7. Cf. also C. H. Herford: "So singular a medley, touching, sometimes on
adjoining pages, the grotesque and the exquisite, the pathetic and the sublime, was
likely to divide or bewilder criticism when it came to be seriously judged at all"
(*Wordsworth*, London: Routledge, 1930, p. 100).

rians. None of the writers of the notices for the 1798 edition, at least, was sufficiently struck with this feature of the volume to remark upon it. They all presumed, without any visible effort, that the poems were of single authorship, and by and large seemed to feel that the collection was not greatly out of line with contemporary practice. It was a period of feverish poetical activity and mawkish experimentalism, and a good deal of the lack of unity which Legouis and others have found in the *Lyrical Ballads* is obviously the heterogeneity of the literary fashion. In fact, compared with Southey's *Poems* of 1797, the *Ballads* are anything but extraordinary in unevenness of style and miscellaneousness of contents. Southey's volume moves with amateurish abruptness from one manner and one subject to another, whereas the movement of the *Lyrical Ballads*, on the surface at least, is fairly simple. Once the Ancient Mariner has gone his way, the other verses in the volume follow a more or less familiar course for 1798. In general, the drift is in several directions only—towards "nature" and "simplicity," and towards humanitarianism and sentimental morality. Without discriminating too precisely between these categories, the reader of that day would tend to construe most of the contents of the *Lyrical Ballads* in terms of these modes of popular poetry, with which he was already familiar.

He would, for example, if the poetry departments of the magazines are any index, regard as perfectly normal a miscellany of ballads on pastoral subjects (treated both sentimentally and jocularly), moral and philosophic poems inspired by physical nature, and lyrical pieces in a variety of kinds describing rural scenes, the pleasures of the seasons, flora and fauna, and a simple life in the out-of-doors. Subjects drawn from "nature," including both landscape and rural life, as many writers have pointed out, were commonplace in the minor verse of the last years of the eighteenth century. Viewed in relation to this considerable body of writing, poems like *Lines Written in Early Spring, Lines Left upon a Seat in a Yew-tree, Lines Written near Richmond,* and *The Nightingale* are obviously not experimental in subject; nor in *form* either, as a matter of fact. Considered as a species of poetry, the "nature" poems of the *Lyrical Ballads* were anything but surprising in 1798.[5] Novelty, of course,

---

[5] A representative list of "Wordsworthian" titles from the magazines of 1788–98 is as follows: *The Delights of a Still Evening, Stanzas on a Withered Leaf, A Thought on the Vicissitudes of the Seasons, On the Singing of a Red-Breast Late in Autumn, Inscription for a Rural Arbour, Sonnet to the River Arun, Inscription for a Coppice near Elsfield, Sonnet Written during a Morning's Walk, To a Tuft of Violets, On the Month of May, On the Return to the Country, An Autumn Thought, The Lake of Wyndemere, Description of a Morning in May, Contemplation by Moonlight, To the Daisy, To the Primrose, Ode to the Cuckoo.* The exact citations will not be given, since there are literally hundreds of such poems. Underneath many of the "nature" poems of the magazines is the familiar conviction that nature is beautiful and full of joy; that man is corrupted by civilization; that God may be found in nature; and

is a very complex and ephemeral quality in any poem or collection of
poems, extremely difficult to isolate. It depends upon a thousand particulars, now vanished, which were once an unmistakable part of the literary
climate. But the more one reads the popular poetry of the last quarter
of the eighteenth century, the more he is likely to feel that the really
surprising feature of these poems in the *Lyrical Ballads* (as well as of
many of the others)—apart from sheer literary excellence—is their intense fulfillment of an already stale convention, and not their discovery
of an interest in rivers, valleys, groves, lakes, and mountains, flowers and
budding trees, the changing seasons, sunsets, the freshness of the morning, and the songs of birds. This fact is a commonplace. Yet it is astonishing how often responsible Wordsworthians go astray in this respect, and
tend to view Wordsworth and Coleridge as reacting with a kind of totality
against contemporary fashions in verse. The question is not whether the
Ballads were altogether conventional, which no one would attempt to
affirm, but whether they were completely out of touch with popular
taste. This was certainly the nineteenth-century conception of Wordsworth, who was viewed as a kind of prophet writing in the wilderness;
and it is evidently still the view of some present-day critics and historians,
who, struck by the phenomenal literary quality of the *Ballads,* tend to
confuse one kind of change with another.[6] They have perhaps been misled by the ambiguities of the Advertisement of 1798, which seems to claim
more than it actually does.[7] . . .

---

that the study of nature not only brings pleasure, therefore, but generates moral
goodness. The nature poetry of the *Christian's Magazine* (1760–67), for example, has
numerous "Wordsworthian" features.

[6] Cf. Catherine M. Maclean: "[Wordsworth] created new interests. But some of these
have now become so much part and parcel of most people's mentality that they have
ceased to interest. These too have become hackneyed. Appreciation of the externals of
Nature is now a commonplace" (*Dorothy and William Wordsworth,* Cambridge, 1927,
p. 118). J. R. Sutherland: "[Wordsworth] himself 'created the taste by which he is to
be enjoyed.' But I am not sure that he has not induced some of his disciples to lose
their sense of proportion about Nature, and he is largely responsible, along with his
fellow romantics, for that dreariest of all cults, the cult of scenery" ("Wordsworth
and Pope," *Proc. Brit. Acad.,* xxx [1944], 49). Derek Patmore: "Readers still under the
influence of the eighteenth-century tradition and its stiff formality were not ready for
Wordsworth with his cult of Nature and his poems about the humble of this world"
("Wordsworth and His Contemporaries," *Tribute to Wordsworth,* London, 1950, p.
229). George Mallaby: "It is . . . a plain fact that in the world of literature Wordsworth ignored the fashion of the age and marched boldly forward along his own
chosen path amongst the jeers of the idle and ignorant scoffers, until he had succeeded
in creating the taste by which he desired to be judged. It is evident enough that the
objects of his poetry . . . and the style . . . do not belong to the eighteenth century . . ." (*Wordsworth, a Tribute,* Oxford, 1950, pp. 27–28).

[7] How much is embraced by the "experiments" of the *Lyrical Ballads?* Is it the
language alone? Or the *style* in a larger sense? Or does it involve also the *materials*
of poetry—"human passions, human characters, and human incidents"? In Hazlitt's

It is well to observe, in terminating this study, that those commentators who have emphasized the "originality" of the *Lyrical Ballads* to the exclusion of their many signs of contemporaneity, or who see the volume as a daring "manifesto" in total defiance of the general taste, overlook Coleridge's explicit statements to the contrary in the *Biographia Literaria.* Writing in 1815–16, at a time removed yet close enough to the event itself, he denied categorically that the *Lyrical Ballads* were "the original occasion of this fiction of a new school of poetry," or even that he and Southey had been the initiators of a tendency which extended back at least to Bowles and Cowper, among modern poets "the first who reconciled the heart with the head." In fact, he appears to support the literary orthodoxy of the *Ballads* in both subject and manner by insisting upon their overwhelming acceptability to the reading public of their time, saying that in his studied opinion at least two-thirds of the poems would have pleased the average reader, and that "the omission of less than a hundred lines [from the 437 pages of the 1800 edition] would have precluded nine-tenths of the criticism on this work"—supposing, of course, "that the reader has taken it up, *as he would have done any other collection of poems* [italics ours] purporting to derive their subjects or interests from the incidents of domestic or ordinary life, intermingled with higher strains of meditation which the poet utters in his own person and character." It was not the subjects or the manner which offended in the volume, according to Coleridge, but "the critical remarks" which were "prefixed and annexed" to it—remarks which were in part erroneous, which were greatly misunderstood, and which invited by their "supposed heresy" attacks from readers who otherwise would have accepted without question the greater part of the work itself.

Viewed casually, in other words, the *Lyrical Ballads* would tend to merge with familiar features of the literary landscape; read carefully, they would give suddenly a tremendous impression of clarity, freshness, and depth. Wordsworth's true genius was "the original gift of spreading the tone, the atmosphere, and with it the depth and height of the ideal world around forms, incidents, and situations, of which, for the common view, custom had bedimmed all the lustre, had dried up the sparkle and the dewdrops." Coleridge is probably speaking here of the "forms, incidents, and situations" of *real* life, rather than of literature; but not necessarily so. It could be both. Certainly the poetry of the magazines was lusterless and stale. The "modifying colors" of Wordsworth's "imagination" could play over the "forms, incidents, and situations" reflected in contemporary verse, as well as those in the life behind it, and the record

---

account (in "My first Acquaintance with Poets") the *Lyrical Ballads* are explicitly described as an experiment in language alone; and this is the burden of the *Biographia* as well.

shows that they unquestionably did. Wordsworth's forte was not producing novelties, but operating in a new dimension where "original" combinations of "fixities and definites" were largely irrelevant. To claim more for his poetry, as some have done, would be for Coleridge to claim less. It would be to throw emphasis upon the *subjects* of his poetry, rather than its *substance*. It would be to confuse the "drapery" of poetic genius with its "soul." It would be to confound the superior powers of imagination with the inferior powers of the fancy.

"The Thorn": Wordsworth's Dramatic Monologue

by Stephen Maxfield Parrish

In Dorothy Wordsworth's Alfoxden journal the entry for March 19, 1798, opens: "Wm. and Basil [Montagu] and I walked to the hill-tops, a very cold bleak day. We were met on our return by a severe hailstorm." The scenes of this walk were familiar, but during the storm Wordsworth's eye was caught and his poetic imagination fired by a solitary, aged tree. Dorothy marked the event by noting laconically as she closed the day's entry: "William wrote some lines describing a stunted thorn." Forty-five years later William corroborated her account of the genesis of one of his "lyrical ballads." "The Thorn," he told Isabella Fenwick, "arose out of my observing, on the ridge of Quantock Hill, on a stormy day, a thorn which I had often passed in calm and bright weather without noticing it. I said to myself, 'Cannot I by some invention do as much to make this Thorn permanently an impressive object as the storm has made it to my eyes at this moment?'"

The lines in which Wordsworth tried to make impressive his vision of a tree in a hailstorm have excited a good deal of critical attention. De Selincourt summed up majority opinion when he called them "the extreme example of W.'s experiment 'to ascertain how far the language of conversation in the middle and lower classes of society is adapted to the purposes of poetic pleasure'" (*Poetical Works*, II, 513). The poem was experimental, but the nature of the experiment has, I believe, been misunderstood, and the poem almost universally misread. Of the dozens of critics who have commented on "The Thorn," hardly one appears to have discerned who the central character is and what the poem is about. The readings fall, roughly, into two traditions. One holds that the narrator mars the poem: "The Thorn" would have been more satisfying had Wordsworth spoken it in his own voice. The other overlooks the narra-

"'The Thorn': Wordsworth's Dramatic Monologue" by Stephen Maxfield Parrish. First printed in *ELH*, 24, no. 2 (1957), 153–63. Copyright © 1957 by The Johns Hopkins Press. The essay has been revised by the author, and is printed by his permission and that of *ELH*.

tor, focusing on the story he tells, the tragedy of Martha Ray: "The Thorn" is a haunting and powerful study in social morality. In the one view, "The Thorn" is a bad poem because of the narrator, in the other, a good poem in spite of the narrator.

It would be hard to decide which view is the more misleading, for what neither recognizes is that the narrator is not only the central figure but, in a sense, the subject of the poem. As its author conceived it, "The Thorn" is not a poem about an abandoned mother and her murdered infant, as nearly all critics have supposed, nor a poem about the maternal passion. It would be more accurate to call it a poem, first, about a tree, and second, about a man. It was intended to be a psychological study, a poem about the way the mind works. The mind whose workings are revealed is that of the narrator, and the poem is, in effect, a dramatic monologue.[1]

That Wordsworth's design should have been lost sight of seems astonishing, for he took unusual pains to make it clear. In the "Advertisement" to the first edition of *Lyrical Ballads* he singled out five poems for comment. Besides touching on the sources of three and on the style of another, he had remarked meaningfully: "The poem of the Thorn, as the reader will soon discover, is not supposed to be spoken in the author's own person: the character of the loquacious narrator will sufficiently shew itself in the course of the story." In 1800, after the narrator's character had totally failed to show itself, Wordsworth attached a lengthy note telling precisely what he had intended to do in "The Thorn." He began by confessing that "this Poem ought to have been preceded by an introductory Poem," implying that he would have sketched there the history of "The Thorn's" narrator, then went on to supply the information that poem might have contained. He asked the reader to visualize "a man, a Captain of a small trading vessel, for example, who being past the middle age of life, had retired . . . to some village or country town of which he was not a native." Why a man of this sort? Because, the poet explained, reaching his point deliberately and then summing it up: "Such men, having little to do, become credulous and talkative from indolence; and from the same cause, and other predisposing causes . . . they are prone to superstition. On which account it appeared to me proper to select a character like this to exhibit some of the general laws by which superstition acts upon the mind."

Could any statement of poetic intent be plainer? As Wordsworth conceived it, "The Thorn" is a portrayal of the superstitious imagination. More literally than any other poem, it carries out the principal object of

---

[1] That is, loosely, a poem in which the events related are meaningful not in themselves but as they reveal the character of the person who relates them. Actually, "The Thorn" is a dialogue, but the second voice enters only to ask questions in language that echoes the narrator's, giving the effect (probably intentional) of a ballad refrain.

Lyrical Ballads: to trace in situations of common life "the primary laws of our nature," chiefly "as regards the manner in which we associate ideas in a state of excitement." For the manner in which the narrator associates ideas is precisely what "The Thorn" is about. The ideas themselves— that is, the "events" of the poem—are unimportant except as they reflect the working of the narrator's imagination. In fact, the point of the poem may very well be that its central "event" has no existence outside of the narrator's imagination—that there is no Martha Ray sitting in a scarlet cloak behind a crag on the mountain top, that the narrator has neither seen her nor heard her, that what he has seen is a gnarled old tree in a blinding storm, that what he has heard (besides the creaking of the branches, or the whistling of the mountain wind) is village superstition about a woman wronged years ago.

This reading of "The Thorn," differing sharply from any traditional reading, alters the poem radically. It becomes not a poem about a woman but a poem about a man (and a tree); not a tale of horror but a psychological study; not a ballad but a dramatic monologue. Based as the reading is on Wordsworth's statements of intent, the question it may seem to raise is whether the poem Wordsworth meant to write resembles the poem he did write. To take the question seriously is to show a singular skepticism about Wordsworth's understanding of his own craft (his careful statements of intent were written after the poem, not before). Yet once raised it must be answered. If we look closely at the poem Wordsworth did write in 1798, we shall find, I think, that it does correspond to the poem he later told us he had meant to write. The design of "The Thorn" is revealed in the order in which the narrator associates ideas—the order, that is, in which the poem's "events" pass through his mind. The poem begins, as it began in Wordsworth's mind, with the tree.

> There is a thorn; it looks so old,
> In truth you'd find it hard to say,
> How it could ever have been young,
> It looks so old and grey.

As the narrator's imagination begins to work (Stanza 2), he sees the old tree, "hung with heavy tufts of moss," engaged in a drama of nature:

> Up from the earth these mosses creep,
> And this poor thorn they clasp it round
> So close, you'd say that they were bent
> With plain and manifest intent,
> To drag it to the ground. . . .

After this brief flight the narrator drops to prosaic detail, describing the thorn's location, the "little muddy pond," and the hill of moss "like an infant's grave in size." Not until Stanza 6 does he mention "a woman in a scarlet cloak," and when his listener asks why the unhappy creature sits by the thorn crying her doleful cry, the flat answer is (Stanza 9):

> I cannot tell; I wish I could;
> For the true reason no one knows. . . .

But two stanzas later it turns out that the narrator can tell what everyone does know—and the story of Martha Ray begins slowly to unfold. His imagination warming, the old mariner relates what he has learned about the incidents that took place "some two and twenty" years ago (long before he came to the village): Martha's abandonment, her pregnancy, and her madness. But again he breaks off abruptly (Stanza 15):

> No more I know, I wish I did,
> And I would tell it all to you;
> For what became of this poor child
> There's none that ever knew:
> And if a child was born or no,
> There's no one that could ever tell;
> And if 'twas born alive or dead,
> There's no one knows, as I have said. . . .

Again, the professions of ignorance prove not to be serious, for we learn at once that Martha was seen that summer on the mountain, and that cries were later heard there, some "plainly living voices," others, it was believed, "voices of the dead" (Stanza 16). Here the narrator exhibits a nice skepticism.

> I cannot think, whate'er they say,
> They had to do with Martha Ray.

To this point, the pattern of the poem has been consistent: as the narrator's loquacity ebbs and flows he retails, piece by piece, village recollection and superstition about Martha Ray. With Stanza 17, however (some two-thirds of the way through the poem), he suddenly offers first-hand testimony. He claims actually to have seen the woman by the tree. His testimony is highly important because he had already suggested that no one else has seen her there. Inviting his listener (Stanza 9) to view the spot, he had cautioned him to make sure first that Martha was in her hut ("Pass by her door—'tis seldom shut"), adding meaningfully:

> I never heard of such as dare
> Approach the spot when she is there.

He would not, we gather, now venture to approach it himself; he had stumbled on it unknowingly (Stanza 17),

> When to this country first I came
> Ere I had heard of Martha's name. . . .

On that occasion, the narrator and the poet now take impressive pains to point out (Stanzas 17 and 18), the visibility was wretched:

> A storm came on, and I could see
> No object higher than my knee.
> 'Twas mist and rain, and storm and rain,
> No screen, no fence could I discover,
> And then the wind! in faith, it was
> A wind full ten times over.
> I looked around, I thought I saw
> A jutting crag, and off I ran,
> Head-foremost, through the driving rain. . . .

But instead of a crag he saw, he thinks, "A woman seated on the ground." After a glimpse of her face through the rain he "turned about," then, above the wind, heard her cry, "O misery! O misery!"

Encouraged, perhaps, by the sound of his own testimony, and with his imagination now glowing hot, the narrator lets fall (Stanzas 20 to 22) the terrible superstitions he has been holding back: some say that Martha hanged her child, some that she drowned it, but all agree that it lies buried in the little mound; some say that the moss is red with blood, some that the infant's face can be seen on the pond, and some that the ground shook when the little tomb was threatened. After these revelations the narrator subsides abruptly, returning in the final stanza to the tree with which he had begun and the testimony he has offered:

> I cannot tell how this may be,
> But plain it is, the thorn is bound
> With heavy tufts of moss, that strive
> To drag it to the ground.
> And this I know, full many a time,
> When she was on the mountain high,
> By day, and in the silent night,
> When all the stars shone clear and bright,
> That I have heard her cry,
> "O misery! O misery!
> "O woe is me! oh misery!"

From this review of its "events" the design of the poem should be clear. Stimulated by his memory of a tree, the narrator begins to relate village gossip about a woman. Some of it is factual, some not. Martha Ray and her lover did evidently exist twenty years ago, and the tree, the pond, the mound, and a "hut" nearby with a woman in it evidently exist now.

On the other hand (Wordsworth was not, it is agreed, a poet of the
supernatural), the ghostly voices from the mountain head, the shaking
grass and the stirring moss, the "shadow of a babe" on the pond, are
superstitions, products of the villagers' imaginations. But as the narrator
retails these superstitions, his own imagination is roused to activity, and
he proceeds to show how superstition acts upon his mind. By the end
of the poem he clings to two ideas: that the moss on the tree is struggling
to drag it down, and that near the spot he has heard the woman's cry.
Both ideas are colored with imagination—"by which word I mean the
faculty," said Wordsworth in his note, "which produces impressive effects
out of simple elements." They may, moreover, be closely related, the first
showing how the narrator first saw the tree, the second suggesting how
he saw it later, under the influence of village superstition—and that is
perhaps why they fall together in the last lines of a poem designed to
make a tree "impressive."

For consider the second idea in its context. After indicating that no
one else could have seen the woman under the thorn, the narrator claims
(but only after working deep into his story) to have glimpsed her once
himself, at the height of a blinding storm. Wordsworth left ambiguities
in the poem, but to leave one here—to suggest that Martha Ray was
really on view by the tree in storms some twenty years after—would have
been to throw away his best opportunity both of making the tree "impressive" and of exhibiting the "laws by which superstition acts upon
the mind." For Martha's presence in the poem surely illustrates one law:
that when a credulous old seaman catches sight in a storm of a sug-
gestively-shaped tree hung with moss and later crams his head with
village gossip, then his imagination can turn the tree into a woman,
the brightly-colored moss into her scarlet cloak, and the creaking of the
branches into her plaintive cry, "O misery! O misery!"

The same effect was evidently created on March 19, 1798, by the
imagination of a poet who had already crammed his head with German
or Scottish ballads and tragedies of real life. One feature of the poem
that has been called "inexplicable" might, on this assumption, be quite
simply explained: this is the naming of Martha Ray after the grand-
mother of little Basil Montagu. When we remember that the boy went
along on the walk past Quantock Hill we may conceivably have a revelation of the way the tree looked to Wordsworth during the hailstorm. By
giving the creature in the poem the name of the creature who flashed
before his eyes, Wordsworth may have been obeying a law of association,
even one of the "laws by which superstition acts upon the mind."

For the growth of the poem in the mind of its author almost certainly
parallels the growth of the story on the mind of its narrator. In this connection, the sources of "The Thorn" have been as widely misunderstood
as its subject. Most critics have attached heavy importance to parallel

recitals of the poem's "events." But these are superficial analogies, and they throw little light on the genesis of "The Thorn." Far more important than any literary parallels are the scenes in nature that haunted Wordsworth's imagination, often seeming to come alive and take on human shape or significance: the rock in the shape of an old woman seated on Helm Crag, the "Stone-Man" on the top of a hill at Grasmere, the lonely whistling hawthorns and ghostly yews in Somerset and the Lakes, "The single sheep, and the one blasted tree" of the *Prelude* (XI, 379), the single "Tree, of many, one, / A single Field which I have looked upon" of the "Intimations" Ode. The way in which such materials could work on a youthful poet's imagination is told in the *Prelude,* not only in the "spots of time" passages, but more explicitly where Wordsworth speaks of certain habits of his early fancy (VIII, 510–540). For a time, before he outgrew it,

> From touch of this new power
> Nothing was safe: the Elder-tree that grew
> Beside the well-known Charnel-house had then
> A dismal look; the Yew-tree had its Ghost,
> That took its station there for ornament.

No common sight, no common event could escape exaggeration. If a widow were seen to visit her husband's grave once or twice,

> The fact was caught at greedily, and there
> She was a visitant the whole year through,
> Wetting the turf with never-ending tears
> And all the storms of Heaven must beat on her

—just as they beat on Martha Ray, in the old Captain's superstitious imagination.

Whatever the case, it may be helpful here to turn for a moment to *Peter Bell,* composed at about the same time as "The Thorn," a time when Wordsworth was preoccupied with the power of the human imagination.[2] Addressing the "Spirits of the Mind" who seize control of men's faculties, "Disordering colour form and stature" (l. 813), the poet testifies (ll. 826–830):

> Your presence I have often felt
> In darkness and the stormy night;

[2] In the letter to Southey, April 7, 1819, prefaced to *Peter Bell,* Wordsworth touched on a central belief which had governed that poem's composition and probably also "The Thorn's," "a belief that the Imagination not only does not require for its exercise the intervention of supernatural agency, but that, though such agency be excluded, the faculty may be called forth as imperiously, and for kindred results of pleasure, by incidents within the compass of poetic probability, in the humblest departments of daily life." *Poetical Works,* II, 331.

And well I know, if need there be,
Ye can put forth your agency
When earth is calm, and heaven is bright.

A few stanzas later, the vision that Peter sees under the Spirits' influence,
when "Distraction reigns in soul and sense" (l. 968), strikingly resembles
the vision that haunted "The Thorn's" narrator. Peter's vision begins
with a shrub—not a thorn, but a "flowering furze"—and features an
abandoned female wailing a rhythmic lament (ll. 976–980):

> And stretch'd beneath the furze he sees
> The Highland girl—it is no other;
> And hears her crying, as she cried
> The very moment that she died,
> "My mother! oh my mother!"

Wordsworth left fewer ambiguities in *Peter Bell* than in "The Thorn"
(perhaps because while still working on it he had the instructive experience of seeing "The Thorn" misread), but he must have felt that
even in "The Thorn" he was planting ample evidence that the narrator's
vision was the handiwork of "Spirits of the Mind," called up not by
guilt but by superstition.

That evidence is complemented by one fact of the poem's later history:
Wordsworth did not, it soon became clear, consider "The Thorn" to be
essentially a poem about the maternal passion. The title alone might
suggest this fact, but plainer suggestions lie in the way the piece was
classified. In the letter to Coleridge of May, 1809, in which Wordsworth
first spoke of collecting his poems, he designated as a separate class "those
relating to Maternal feeling, connubial or parental," and named as
examples "The Sailor's Mother," "The Emigrant Mother," "The Affliction of Margaret ——," "The Mad Mother," and "The Idiot Boy." In
the collected edition of 1815 all these pieces, together with "The Complaint of a Forsaken Indian Woman," and others, turned up as "Poems
founded on the Affections."

But not "The Thorn." It was never linked with any of these titles. In
1809 Wordsworth placed it in a class of poems "relating to human life."
His account of the class is somewhat diffuse, but a meaningful distinction
does emerge, a distinction between the "affections" and the imagination,
and as might be expected "The Thorn" turned up in 1815 among "Poems
of the Imagination," where it remained in later editions.

If "The Thorn's" classification was fixed by 1815, however, its form
was not. The event that led to its alteration was the appearance of
Biographia Literaria, in which "The Thorn" was given more critical
attention than any other single poem. Coleridge, who had remained
perversely insensitive to his partner's experimental study of the supersti-

tious imagination, used it to point up his dissent from the theories about rustic characters and the language of common life set forth in the preface to *Lyrical Ballads*. Maintaining (Chapter 17) that "it is not possible to imitate truly a dull and garrulous discourser, without repeating the effects of dullness and garrulity," Coleridge suggested that "The Thorn's" best passages were those "which might as well or still better have proceeded from the poet's own imagination, and have been spoken in his own character," while the worst were those "exclusively appropriate to the supposed narrator." His dissent stood even more sharply revealed toward the close of Chaper 17, which ended with a quotation from Wordsworth's "Thorn" note of 1800. Wordsworth had explained: "It was my wish in this poem to show the manner in which such men [as the narrator] cleave to the same ideas; and to follow the turns of passion, always different, yet not palpably different, by which their conversation is swayed." Hence the narrator wanders from one superstitious idea to another, repeats himself, strains for precision on unimportant details (as in the line measuring the pond—"'Tis three feet long, and two feet wide"), alternately pleads ignorance and floods his listener with facts, as he proceeds to make the tree "impressive" (both to his listener and to the reader) by communicating casually yet inexorably and always with passion, his vision of horror. This technique Coleridge pointedly condemned (II, 42–43): "It is indeed very possible to adopt in a poem the unmeaning repetitions, habitual phrases, and other blank counters, which an unfurnished or confused understanding interposes at short intervals, in order to keep hold of his subject, which is still slipping from him, and to give him time for recollection; or in mere aid of vacancy. . . . But what assistance to the poet, or ornament to the poem, these can supply, I am at a loss to conjecture."

These remarks indicate that Coleridge had no sympathy with Wordsworth's immediate aim in "The Thorn"—to show how superstition works upon the mind—and little understanding of Wordsworth's ultimate aim —to make a tree "impressive." It is one thing to say that Wordsworth lacked dramatic skill, or that he chose his narrator unwisely. It is quite another to suggest that he should have dispensed with the narrator and related the "events" of the poem himself. Coleridge appears never to have accepted the idea that the "events" might be a product of the narrator's imagination, that "The Thorn" was not a ballad but a dramatic monologue.

The profound disagreement between the partners in *Lyrical Ballads* which comes into focus in Coleridge's remarks—a disagreement, essentially, about dramatic method—is a highly important one, but it was over by the time the remarks were published. Wordsworth, who had defended "The Thorn" for years, was now ready to abandon the struggle: he revised the poem extensively for the edition of 1820. The revisions had a single end, to elevate the language, making it less dramatic and more "poetic." Ironically, by yielding to the first of Coleridge's somewhat contradictory charges against the poem—that the narrator's language was homely—Wordsworth laid himself more open to the second, which was more substantial—that the dramatic illusion was not sustained. However, the revisions hardly changed the poem. Their importance is that they marked a retreat on Wordsworth's part from a daring and skillful experiment in a new genre. They have also, unfortunately, done their share to keep generations of readers and critics from appreciating the nature of that experiment, or its meaning, or its success.

"The Idiot Boy": Wordsworth's Narrative and Dramatic Voices

by John F. Danby

Wordsworth seems to have had an exceptional ear for tones of voice. "The Waggoner" (1802) is evidence of his ventriloquism. There the narrator's voice is replaced naturally by the Cumberland tones of the Waggoner himself or of an understanding Cumberland neighbour. We are constantly aware of the two levels. Wordsworth obtains his effect by modulating neither into dialect syntax nor vocabulary, but by reproducing the much subtler thing only a native ear could recognize—the vowel harmonies of the northern rhymes and word-sequences:

> The rain rushed down—the road was battered,
> As with the force of billows shattered;
> The horses are dismayed, nor know
> Whether they should stand or go;
> And Benjamin is groping near them,
> Sees nothing, and can scarcely hear them.
> He is astounded,—wonder not,—
> With such a charge in such a spot;
> Astounded in the mountain gap
> With thunder peals, clap after clap,
> Close-treading on the silent flashes—
> And somewhere, as he thinks, by crashes
> Among the rocks; with weight of rain,
> And sullen motions long and slow,
> That to a dreary distance go—
> Till, breaking in upon the dying strain,
> A rending o'er his head begins the fray again.
>
> [ll. 188–304]

" 'The Idiot Boy': Wordsworth's Narrative and Dramatic Voices" (editor's title). From John F. Danby, *The Simple Wordsworth: Studies in the Poems, 1797–1807* (London: Routledge & Kegan Paul, 1960). Copyright © 1960 by John F. Danby. Reprinted by permission of Routledge & Kegan Paul Ltd., Barnes & Noble, and the author. This selection is part of chapter 2.

All poets need to find their voice, or voices. Wordsworth began, as most do, with a voice not his own but belonging to the eighteenth century. *The Borderers* which followed closely on the early period may have opened out the possibilities of dramatic projection. In *Lyrical Ballads,* at any rate, Wordsworth has discovered his vehicle—the voice of the "Statesman," or peasant small-holder, the voice of the retired sea-captain or West-country balladist; a literary personality that had not been used for serious purposes in this way before.

The mixed mode of the dramatic-narrative poem allows for a range of voices, and each voice for an ironic shift in point of view. It is unfortunate that Wordsworth's irony has not been much remarked. If irony, however, can mean perspective and the co-presence of alternatives, the refusal to impose on the reader a predigested life-view, the insistence on the contrary that the reader should enter, himself, as full partner in the final judgement on the facts set before him—then Wordsworth is a superb ironist in *Lyrical Ballads.* In the mixed mode of the poems the poet can take up and lay down his masks. And with each assumption or discard a new, sometimes excitingly dramatic, shift of standpoint is possible. The narrator, the characters involved in the story, the poet himself as the finally responsible assembler—these are the three main levels at which the voices work. By changing the voice one can step from one frame to another and back again. Stepping apparently out of the frame of mere "literature" altogether and into the reader's own reality (his reality of experience and of judgement), confronting the reader with the need to be aware of what he is judging with as well as what he is judging —this is, above all, the Wordsworthian trick in *Lyrical Ballads.* . . .

Apart from Hutchinson and Dowden few people have thought of Wordsworth as a comic poet. Yet it is clear that in *Lyrical Ballads* Wordsworth, in some of his most successful poems, is writing in a humorous vein. Hutchinson's note is fairly dismissive:

> The humour and pathos of *The Idiot Boy* are sadly marred by his clumsy attempts at mirth. Hazlitt, in his pen-portrait of Wordsworth, speaks of a certain "convulsive inclination to laughter about the mouth, a good deal at variance with the solemn, stately expression of the rest of his face." Not less awkward and incongruous, surely, are the heavy pleasantries in which the poet of *Peter Bell* and *The Idiot Boy* seeks an occasional vent for his exuberant cheerfulness. "At rare times in his poetry Wordsworth shows an inclination for frolic: it is the frolic of good spirits in the habitually grave, and he cannot caper lightly and gracefully."

One has to bear in mind, of course, that for the nineteenth-century critic serious poetry could not be both serious and comic at the same time. One has also to bear in mind, in justice to the commentators, that on the whole serious Wordsworthian comedy is rare. There is, however, the testimony of *Lyrical Ballads,* and the undeniable evidence of the introduction to "Peter Bell," which belongs to the same period.

"The Thorn" and "The Idiot Boy" were Wordsworth's own favourites in the *Lyrical Ballads* volume. And Wordsworth may have been right. He was a mature twenty-seven, the volume was a sophisticated experiment as well as a revolutionary manifesto, and the poet had clear ideas as to what he was doing.

From the start of the poem we are aware of the distinctive narrating voice, and of the narrator's power to merge his own voice in that of the actors in the story, as well as of his capacity to re-emerge when necessary and regain his commenting distinctness. The story-teller is near enough in social status to Betty Foy to have ready and sympathetic insight into the working of her mind. At the same time he is not in her shoes. He does not share either her concern or her simple-mindedness. He is, however, in every sense, a good neighbour. The mergence of his voice with his neighbours is all the easier because he has the same village language, and the outlook that goes with it:

> 'Tis eight o'clock—a clear March night,
> The moon is up—the sky is blue,
> The owlet in the moonlight air,
> He shouts from nobody knows where;
> He lengthens out his lonely shout,
> Halloo! halloo! a long halloo!
>
> —Why bustle thus about your door,
> What means this bustle, Betty Foy?
> Why are you in this mighty fret?
> And why on horseback have you set
> Him whom you love, your idiot boy?
>
> Beneath the moon that shines so bright,
> Till she is tired, let Betty Foy
> With girth and stirrup fiddle-faddle;
> But wherefore set upon a saddle
> Him whom she loves, her idiot boy?

The voice expresses surprise, impatience, and some disapproval. The observer is neither an idiot, nor a silly woman: "fiddle-faddle" carries its own comment on the fussy confusion of Betty's muddledness and misplaced pride, and on the womanish clumsiness with "girth and stirrup" —those traditionally masculine implements of management and control.

But, once the silliness might really lead to serious consequences, the observer can easily slip into Betty's and Susan's situation:

> Poor Susan moans, poor Susan groans,
> "As sure as there's a moon in heaven,"
> Cries Betty, "he'll be back again;
> They'll both be here, 'tis almost ten,
> They'll both be here before eleven!"

He can even assume the point of view of the pony, which is included in the same comprehensive sentence, and awarded in the poem a wisdom and dignity of its own:

> But then he is a horse that thinks!
> But when he thinks his pace is slack;
> Now, though he knows poor Johnny well,
> Yet for his life he cannot tell
> What he has got upon his back.

The tone is beautifully mock-solemn and yet indulgently ready with its sympathy. We are encouraged to take the other's point of view, but not allowed to forget the observer's. It is not a dismissive fun, nor the detachment of aloofness. The superiority is also a magnanimity. We are called on for tenderness rather than condescension: but not to surrender our own identity. Wordsworth's peculiar achievement is an irony of detachment and loving-kindness.

It is Wordsworth himself, of course, who is the narrator, and he makes us aware of his masks. Dropping the rôle of merged narrator he steps in front of the curtain when Betty's anxiety has reached its climax. The timing is perfect—and so is the surprise: the irony that is now turned on the reader himself:

> Oh reader! now that I might tell
> What Johnny and his horse are doing!
> What they've been doing all this time,
> Oh could I put it into rhyme,
> A most delightful tale pursuing!
>
> Perhaps, and no unlikely thought!
> He with his pony now doth roam
> The cliffs and peaks so high that are,
> To lay his hands upon a star,
> And in his pocket bring it home.
>
> Perhaps he's turned himself about,
> His face unto his horse's tail,
> And still and mute, in wonder lost,

All like a silent horseman-ghost,
He travels on along the vale.

And now, perhaps, he's hunting sheep,
A fierce and dreadful hunter he!
Yon valley, that's so trim and green,
In five months' time, should he be seen,
A desert wilderness will be.

Perhaps, with head and heels on fire,
And like the very soul of evil,
He's galloping away, away,
And so he'll gallop on for aye,
The bane of all that dread the devil.

I to the Muses have been bound,
These fourteen years, by strong indentures;
Oh gentle muses! let me tell
But half of what to him befel,
For sure he met with strange adventures.

Oh gentle Muses! is this kind?
Why will ye thus my suit repel?
Why of your further aid bereave me?
And can ye thus unfriended leave me?
Ye muses! whom I love so well.

The irony turns against the reader. The reader wants marvels? Wordsworth will hold up a screen on which he can project his own. They are
terribly stale literary stock—the sublimely whimsical, the Monk Lewis,
the Quixotic; mad Ajaxes and romantic wild-men. Wordsworth conjures
up the fancies in order to indulge so many reading-public weaknesses,
and, again, detach himself from them. But as he can tolerate the silliness
he can cater for the vacuity. The equable rebuke, however, or warning,
is implicit in his manner all the time. The simpleton-narrator uses his
folly as a stalking horse. This is the point in the poem (a point occurring,
too, in "Simon Lee" and "The Thorn") of the defecation of the "literary."
Betty finds Johnny safe. On their return home Susan is better. When
Johnny is asked how he spent his time, his reply is the idiotic verse which
set Wordsworth off writing the poem:

"The cocks did crow to-whoo, to-whoo,
And the sun did shine so cold."
—Thus answered Johnny in his glory,
And that was all his travel's story.

"The Idiot Boy" is a comedy, though admittedly a Wordsworthian comedy. The story has mock-epic features: a life-and-death issue; the last chance of success depending on the last person likely to succeed; mental conflict between mother-love and good-neighbourliness; the anguished search and rescue of the rescuer; finally, the happy issue out of everyone's afflictions, Susan's included. At times Wordsworth's management of stanza and rhyme can remind us of the professional humourist:

> Long Susan lay deep lost in thought,
> And many dreadful fears beset her,
> Both for her messenger and nurse;
> And as her mind grew worse and worse,
> Her body it grew better.

That is at least as good as Tom Hood, but instead of the merely local pun on a word there is a kind of story-pun: Betty having gone off after Johnny, Susan catches a cumulative anxiety for them both. There is also the sane psychology as well as the joke, and the moral implied: Susan is cured of her psychological bed-riddenness by an honest and maybe unwonted care for others. Generosity rallies to the aid of generosity. The fun never falls outside Wordsworth's major convictions concerning what being human entails.

Wordsworth is capable also however of a comic vision that points more to his eighteenth-century origin than to his mid-Victorian destination. There is, for example, the encounter with the Doctor:

> And now she's at the doctor's door,
> She lifts the knocker, rap, rap, rap;
> The doctor at the casement shews
> His glimmering eyes that peep and doze;
> And one hand rubs his old night-cap.
>
> "Oh Doctor! Doctor! where's my Johnny?"
> "I'm here, what is't you want with me?"
> "Oh Sir! you know I'm Betty Foy,
> "And I have lost my poor dear boy,
> "You know him—him you often see;
>
> "He's not so wise as some folk be."
> "The devil take his wisdom!" said
> The Doctor, looking somewhat grim,
> "What, woman! should I know of him?"
> And, grumbling, he went back to bed.

There is nothing here of the clumsy frolic Dowden objected to. The social observation is swift and accurate. The rattling comic tempo is perfectly maintained. Everything happens in character, and the best joke is one that Wordsworth doesn't labour:

> "Oh Doctor! Doctor! where's my Johnny?"
> "I'm here, what is't you want with me?"

Wordsworth displays great tact in not underlining his jokes. It is obvious, for example, that Betty should have carried Johnny's message to the Doctor: that she forgot is part of the comedy. Wordsworth, however, at this point, is willing to let the joke look after itself. He is more concerned to preserve the proportion between joke and seriousness that his poem requires. With all the comedy we are reminded that Betty is genuinely upset, and that Wordsworth has a sincere regard for her capacity to care.

It is most important to remember the seriousness that embraces the comic in Wordsworth's achievement. Wordsworth's irony, we have said, is an irony of detachment and loving-kindness. His comedy, too, requires us to overcome the taboo on tenderness. From Jonson onwards literary laughter had had to be punitive and corrective. Wordsworth asks us to understand (which implies detachment) and to forgive (which implies engagement). He neither scorns nor sentimentalizes the actors in his story. And, in fact, none of the emotions woven into the plot are mean or reprehensible. Susan is a neighbour really in distress. Betty Foy is a mother and a neighbour really attempting something noble whichever way the situation throws her. Her fiddle-faddle and infatuation may be both silly and risky, but neither is contemptible. Her anguished anxiety also is only laughable if our laughter has the Wordsworthian correlative: if we would be as ready to relieve it as to point out its (eventually to be made apparent) unnecessariness.

There is an essential poignancy and idiocy in emotion itself. Only the final upshot can decide which aspect will come uppermost. The great comedy of "The Idiot Boy," quite apart from its surface jokes, has to do with this: it is a comedy of the passions. Far from being another Man of Feeling Wordsworth, in this poem, is the satirist of feeling. Betty's access of concern for Susan makes her send Johnny off on the errand. Fatuously she sees her idiot son as public hero. When he does not return, fear for his safety brings her back to the facts, and dispels neighbourly concern—and so on. And, as we have already hinted, the pattern is repeated in Susan, too. Her mysterious illness vanishes as she frets more and more about the others. Finally she is cured of imaginary illness by real emotional distress. Passions spin the plot—but arbitrarily. The idiocy of passion can precipitate its puppets into irrational misery or unpredictable joy. It all depends, but the dependence is not on the actors in the story as prudent agents. Man, as mere man of feeling, sits on a crazy seesaw.

The Idiot Boy himself, of course, gives still another dimension. The Idiot is not on the see-saw of passion. This means, from one point of view, he will escape its particular kinds of silliness. Wordsworth is fully aware of the Divine Fool archetype he is using. In his letter to Wilson (1802) he wrote

> *I have often applied to idiots, in my own mind, that sublime expression of Scripture that Their Life is Hidden with God.* They are worshipped, probably from a feeling of this sort, in several parts of the East. . . . I have, indeed, often looked upon the conduct of parents, in the lower ranks of society, toward idiots as a great triumph of the human heart. *It is there that we see the strength, disinterestedness, and grandeur of love;* nor have I ever been able to contemplate an object that calls out so many excellent and virtuous sentiments without finding it hallowed thereby, and having something in one which bears down before it like a deluge every feeble sensation of disgust and aversion.

The primitive force of the symbol exerts itself throughout the poem. Johnny has a dual rôle. He cannot be responsible for his actions, and it is his failure to fetch the doctor that is more effective than his mother's concern for her neighbour. That is the comic side. The divine is suggested not only through "the strength, the disinterestedness, and the grandeur of love" he evokes in Betty and Susan (though not in the doctor), but also in the invulnerability of the joy that goes with him, an inaccessible but real emotion, the incomprehensible but mysteriously meaningful dialogue in which he takes part:

> Burr, burr—now Johnny's lips they burr,
> As loud as any mill, or near it,
> Meek as a lamb the pony moves,
> And Johnny makes the noise he loves,
> And Betty listens, glad to hear it.

> Away she hies to Susan Gale:
> And Johnny's in a merry tune,
> The owlets hoot, the owlets curr,
> And Johnny's lips they burr, burr, burr,
> And on he goes beneath the moon.

It would be easy to exaggerate this side of the Idiot in the poem. He is there, certainly, however, as an indication of the possibility of other dimensions, worlds unrealized that may be realizable. But Wordsworth does not make him more than a token of the possibilities. More important for the Wordsworthian seriousness of the tale is the Wordsworthian background into which Johnny is merged: the pony "meek as

a lamb," the moon, the river and waterfall, the whole natural universe
that comes to life at the moments of greatest human stress or distraction:

> She listens, but she cannot hear
> The foot of horse, the voice of man;
> The streams with softest sound are flowing,
> The grass you almost hear it growing,
> You hear it now if e'er you can.
>
> The owlets through the long blue night
> Are shouting to each other still:
> Fond lovers, yet not quite hob nob,
> They lengthen out the tremulous sob,
> That echoes far from hill to hill.

It is the background which incarnates all the values the human world
does not; energy and calm, permanence and process, spontaneity and
order, ranging from the stars in the sky to the nearby birds:

> By this the stars were almost gone,
> The moon was setting on the hill,
> So pale you hardly looked at her:
> The little birds began to stir,
> Though yet their tongues were still.

Johnny is shut out from the various harmony of this order as inevitably
as he is excluded from the confusions of the human order. Where the
Idiot is concerned, Wordsworth is a realist:

> Of moon or stars he takes no heed:
> Of such we in romances read.

That is why we are left with Johnny's mad remark at the end:

> "The cocks did crow to-whoo, to-whoo,
> And the sun did shine so cold."

The Idiot has an insulated joy; Betty and Susan the confined, pitiful
vulnerability of conflicting compassions; the Doctor sullenly slams the
window on both. Nowhere in the human sphere is there the massive and
potent integration of force, serenity, and tenderness, we find in the world
of the waterfall, moon, and owls. The comedy, then, has its sombre side.

The especially poignant thing about the happy ending is its chance-
givenness. Wordsworth will need, ultimately a third position beyond the
dilemma which both "The Thorn" and "The Idiot Boy" leave him with.
For Martha Ray and the Idiot Boy are the two horns of a dilemma. In
spite of their surface differences in mood and in conclusion, the two

94*John F. Danby*

poems agree that feeling, as feeling, is a kind of unhingement. The alienation of the normal which we see in "The Idiot Boy" might be an even more pessimistic vision than that of "The Thorn": for Martha's tragedy can be regarded, mitigably, as exceptional and personal. Betty's and Susan's, and the Doctor's, on the other hand is the alienation of the everyday and general. From this, complete idiocy is the only escape, unless an ultimate marriage of human mind and natural order might somehow and somewhere be possible.

The Myth of Memory and Natural Man

by Harold Bloom

I. Tintern Abbey

Tintern Abbey (July 1798) is a miniature of the long poem Words-worth never quite wrote, the philosophical and autobiographical epic of which The Prelude, the Recluse fragment, and The Excursion would have been only parts. As such, Tintern Abbey is a history in little of Wordsworth's imagination. The procedure and kind of the poem are both determined by Coleridge's influence, for The Eolian Harp (1795) and Frost at Midnight (February 1798) are its immediate ancestors, with the eighteenth-century sublime ode in the farther background. Yet we speak justly of the form of Tintern Abbey as being Wordsworth's, for he turns this kind of poem to its destined theme, the nature of a poet's imagination and that imagination's relation to external Nature. Coleridge begins the theme in his "conversation poems," but allows himself to be distracted from it by theological misgivings and self-abnegation. Tintern Abbey, and not The Eolian Harp, is the father of Shelley's Mont Blanc and Keats's Sleep and Poetry.

In the renewed presence of a remembered scene, Wordsworth comes to a full understanding of his poetic self. This revelation, though it touches on infinity, is extraordinarily simple. All that Wordsworth learns by it is a principle of reciprocity between the external world and his own mind, but the story of that reciprocity becomes the central story of Wordsworth's best poetry. The poet loves Nature for its own sake alone, and the presences of Nature give beauty to the poet's mind, again only for that mind's sake. Even the initiative is mutual; neither Nature nor poet gives in hope of recompense, but out of this mutual generosity an identity is established between one giver's love and the other's beauty. The process of reciprocity is like a conversation that never stops, and cannot therefore be summed up discursively or analyzed into static elements. The most im-

"The Myth of Memory and Natural Man" (editor's title). From Harold Bloom, The Visionary Company: A Reading of English Romantic Poetry (Ithaca, N.Y.: Cornell University Press, 1971). Copyright © 1961 by Harold Bloom; copyright © 1971 by Cornell University. Reprinted by permission of the publisher and the author. This selection consists of two parts from chapter 2, "William Wordsworth."

mediate consequence of this process is a certain "wide quietness," as Keats was to call it in his *Ode to Psyche*. As the dialogue of love and beauty ensues, love does not try to find an object, nor beauty an expression in direct emotion, but a likeness between man and Nature is suggested. The suggestion is made through an intensification of the dominant aspect of the given landscape, its seclusion, which implies also a deepening of the mood of seclusion in the poet's mind:

> —Once again
> Do I behold these steep and lofty cliffs,
> That on a wild secluded scene impress
> Thoughts of more deep seclusion; and connect
> The landscape with the quiet of the sky.

The further connection is with the quiet of Wordsworth's mind, for the thoughts of more deep seclusion are impressed simultaneously on the landscape and on its human perceiver.

We murder to dissect, Wordsworth wrote in another context, and to dissect the renewed relationship between the poet and this particular landscape ought not to be our concern. Wordsworth wants to understand the interplay between Mind and Nature without asking *how* such dialogue can be, and this deliberate refusal to seek explanation is itself part of the meaning of *Tintern Abbey*. The poet has reached a point where the thing seen

> yields to a clarity and we observe,

> And observing is completing and we are content,
> In a world that shrinks to an immediate whole,

> That we do not need to understand, complete
> Without secret arrangements of it in the mind.

This is Wallace Stevens, in *Description without Place*, a poem that tries to suggest that to seem is to be, so that seeming, as well as everything we say of the past, is description without place, "a cast of the imagination." Until *Peele Castle*, natural seeming and reality are one for Wordsworth, and so his theory of poetry is a theory of description also. The language of description is employed by him both for the external world and for himself; if he will not analyze Nature, still less will he care to analyze man. The peculiar *nakedness* of Wordsworth's poetry, its strong sense of being alone with the visible universe, with no myth or figure to mediate between ego and phenomena, is to a surprisingly large extent not so much a result of history as it is of Wordsworth's personal faith in the reality of the body of Nature.

Away from the landscape he now rejoins, the poet had not forgotten it, but indeed had owed to memories of it sensations sweet, felt in hours

of urban weariness, and therapeutic of the lonely ills he has experienced.
Such tranquil restoration is only one gift of memory. Another is of more
sublime aspect:

> that blessed mood,
> In which the burthen of the mystery,
> In which the heavy and the weary weight
> Of all this unintelligible world,
> Is lightened:—that serene and blessed mood,
> In which the affections gently lead us on,—
> Until, the breath of this corporeal frame
> And even the motion of our human blood
> Almost suspended, we are laid asleep
> In body, and become a living soul:
> While with an eye made quiet by the power
> Of harmony, and the deep power of joy,
> We see into the life of things.

This is not mysticism but, rather, a state of aesthetic contemplation.
All contemplation of objects except the aesthetic is essentially practical,
and so directed toward personal ends. The poet's genius frees contemplation from the drive of the will, and consequently the poet is able to see
with a quiet eye. To see into the life of things is to see things for themselves and not their potential use. The poet attains to this state through
memories of Nature's presence, which give a quietness that is a blessed
mood, one in which the object world becomes near and familiar, and ceases
to be a burden. The best analogue is the difference we feel in the
presence of a stranger or a good friend. From this serenity the affections
lead us on to the highest kind of naturalistic contemplation, when we
cease to *have* our bodies, but *are* our bodies, and so are "laid asleep / In
body, and become a living soul."

Having made this declaration, Wordsworth gives his first intimation of
doubt as to the efficacy of Nature's presences:

> And now, with gleams of half-extinguished thought,
> With many recognitions dim and faint,
> And somewhat of a sad perplexity,
> The picture of the mind revives again.

The "sad perplexity" concerns the future and the enigma of the imagination when transposed from past to future time. In this moment of
renewed covenant with a remembered and beloved landscape, is there
indeed life and food for future years?

> And so I dare to hope,
> Though changed, no doubt, from what I was when first
> I came among these hills.

The process of change is what troubles Wordsworth. He speaks of three stages of development already accomplished, and fears the onset of a fourth. The "glad animal movements" of his boyish days preceded any awareness of nature. Then came the time when his perception of natural objects brought an immediate joy, so that he speaks of the simultaneity of vision and emotion as

> An appetite; a feeling and a love,
> That had no need of a remoter charm,
> By thought supplied, nor any interest
> Unborrowed from the eye.

That time is past, and Wordsworth has lost its "aching joys" and "dizzy raptures." He has entered into a third time, and other gifts have recompensed him for such loss. In this mature stage he *looks* on Nature, and *hears* in it

> The still, sad music of humanity,
> Nor harsh nor grating, though of ample power
> To chasten and subdue.

The dialectic of the senses here is vital in Wordsworth. The young child has an organic sense that combines seeing and hearing. The older child, awakening to the phenomenal world, sees a gleam in it that the mature man cannot see again. But the man gains an intimation of immortality, of his renewed continuity with the young child, by hearing a still, sad music *as* he sees a soberer coloring in Nature. Here in *Tintern Abbey*, eight years before the completion of the Great Ode, Wordsworth anticipates the totality of its myth. As he listens to the sad music ("still" because it pipes to the spirit, not to the sensual ear of man) he hears evidence not only of man's mortality but of man's inseparable bond with Nature. But perception and response are no longer simultaneous, and it is an act of meditation that must bring the riven halves together. This meditation does not start in the mind, but is first felt as a presence that disturbs the mind with the joy of elevated thoughts:

> a sense sublime
> Of something far more deeply interfused,
> Whose dwelling is the light of setting suns,
> And the round ocean and the living air,
> And the blue sky, and in the mind of man:
> A motion and a spirit, that impels
> All thinking things, all objects of all thought
> And rolls through all things.

This is parallel to Coleridge's *The Eolian Harp*:

> O! the one Life within us and abroad,
> Which meets all motion and becomes its soul,
> A light in sound, a sound-like power in light,
> Rhythm in all thought, and joyance every where.

As a consecration or sacramental vision this becomes the main burden of Wordsworth's song, until in *Peele Castle* it is exposed as only a dream, and the great light pervading it is deprecated as "the light that never was, on sea or land." When Wordsworth still believed in that light, as in this crucial passage from *Tintern Abbey*, he was able to see and hear a primal unity manifested simultaneously in all subjects and all objects. Again, it is a laziness of our imaginations that tempts us to call this vision mystical, for the mystical is finally incommunicable and Wordsworth desires to be a man talking to men about matters of common experience. The emphasis in *Tintern Abbey* is on things seen and things remembered, on the light of sense, not on the invisible world. The presence of outer Nature disturbs the mind, sets it into motion, until it realizes that Nature and itself are not utterly distinct, that they are mixed together, interfused. They are more interfused than the reciprocal relation between the outer presence and the mind's inner elevation in response would seem to indicate, for in speaking of that relation the poet still uses the vocabulary of definiteness and fixity. But the imagination dissolves such separateness. Within both Nature and Wordsworth is something that moves and breathes, and that blends subject and object as it animates them. *Therefore* the poet, though he has lost the aching joy that is Nature's direct gift, still loves Nature as he can apprehend it by eye and ear:

> —both what they half create,
> And what perceive; well pleased to recognise
> In nature and the language of the sense
> The anchor of my purest thoughts, the nurse,
> The guide, the guardian of my heart, and soul
> Of all my moral being.

But why "half create"? Though the boundaries between man and Nature have wavered, Wordsworth wishes to avoid the suggestion of a total absorption of Nature into man. Man is almost totally absorbed in Nature in his childhood, and again in extreme old age, as in *The Old Cumberland Beggar* and the Leech Gatherer of *Resolution and Independence*. But for the mature man, outward Nature must be recognized as external. That is his freedom and his grief. His consolation is that he half creates as well as perceives "outward" Nature, for what is outward comes to him only through the gates of his own perception, and whatever cannot come to him is not relevant to his condition. Eyes and ears, the gates of perception, are not passive but selective. He cannot create the phenomena that present themselves to him; they are given. But his choice among them is a kind of creation, and his choice is guided by memory. Memory is the mother of poetry for Wordsworth because the poem's half of the act of creation cannot proceed without the catalyst of recollecting the poet's response to an earlier version of the outward presence of Nature. Nature's half of the act is mysterious, except that Wordsworth insists that it cannot proceed without the initiating expression of man's love for what is outside himself.

This mature love for Nature leads to love for other men, to hearing the still, sad music of *humanity*. The soul of a man's moral being, its inwardness, *is* Nature once the earlier relation between man and Nature, where no meditation was necessary between perception of natural beauty and the deep joy of the perceiver's response, is in the past. The meditation of the later stage, the time of mature imagination, brings vision and joy together again by linking both with the heart's generosity toward our fellow men.

This is the teaching that preserves Wordsworth's "genial spirits" from decay, but the teacher himself is uncertain of the efficacy of his doctrine in the fourth stage that is to come, when natural decay may dull his responsiveness to the presences of beauty. He turns therefore to his sister Dorothy as an incarnation of his earlier self, as one who still feels the dizzy joys of natural communion that he himself can only recollect. The curious element in this ritualistic substitution is that the poet is only twenty-eight, and his sister just a year younger. Wordsworth's troubled forebodings were nevertheless justified; his imagination aged very quickly, and Dorothy's remained young and perpetually receptive to the beauty of the natural world:

> and in thy voice I catch
> The language of my former heart, and read
> My former pleasures in the shooting lights
> Of thy wild eyes. Oh! yet a little while
> May I behold in thee what I was once,
> My dear, dear Sister!

There is an urgency in the tone of this which deepens almost to a desperation:

> and this prayer I make,
> Knowing that Nature never did betray
> The heart that loved her.

The prayer thus heralded is never quite expressed in the remainder of the poem. Its burden is more life, survival, imaginative immortality. More directly, it is a desire to be free of the fear that enters so early into the poet's life and his poem. When he bounded like a roe over the mountains, and followed wherever Nature led, he was

> more like a man
> Flying from something that he dreads than one
> Who sought the thing he loved.

He sped as if to out-distance time, and sought an immediacy he was doomed to lose. Only Nature has the privilege of leading us from joy to joy; we have to wait upon her, brood on past joys, and have faith that she will not abandon hearts that have loved her. Wordsworth uses the strong word "betray" with its sexual implications, which are certainly present in the opening lines of the poem, where the poet's renewed passion is a lover's return. The lover returns, not to the wild ecstasy he had known, but to the sober pleasure of a marriage with Nature.

The most beautiful lines in *Tintern Abbey* invoke the possibility of perpetual renewal for Dorothy:

> Therefore let the moon
> Shine on thee in thy solitary walk;
> And let the misty mountain-winds be free
> To blow against thee.

As in *Michael* and *The Prelude*, the freedom of mountain mist and wind, sudden in their comings and goings, is a natural type of the wild freedom of ecstatic human imagination, the deep joy of that time when Nature for us is all in all.

Wordsworth looks forward to Dorothy's return to the beloved landscape, and prophesies the healing power memories of it will have for her. The fear of mortality, which has been haunting the poem, finally becomes overt:

> Nor, perchance—
> If I should be where I no more can hear
> Thy voice, nor catch from thy wild eyes these gleams
> Of past existence—wilt thou then forget
> That on the banks of this delightful stream
> We stood together.

In her wild eyes he sees the gleam that he can no longer see in Nature, but that once he did see, so that he almost literally reads his former pleasures in the eyes of another. His survival will be in those eyes, even as his earlier self has already survived there. He will live in her memory, and his faith will have its historical record:

> and that I, so long
> A worshipper of Nature, hither came

> Unwearied in that service: rather say
> With warmer love—oh! with far deeper zeal
> Of holier love.

This is the vocabulary of religious devotion, displaced into a naturalistic mode. Certainly he protests too much; we feel a desperation in his insistence, another presage of waning faith, or faith affirmed more vehemently even as it ebbs. We begin to understand the prayer he intends but does not make explicit. It is "Do not forget, or the life in me, the creative joy, will die." The closing lines, with their immense music, are not complete:

> Nor wilt thou then forget
> That after many wanderings, many years
> Of absence, these steep woods and lofty cliffs,
> And this green pastoral landscape, were to me
> More dear, both for themselves and for thy sake!

He leaves out "for my sake," but the poem has made clear that his salvation, as man and poet, is dependent upon the renovation he celebrates. The parallels of *Tintern Abbey* exist in many kinds of experience, including sexual and religious, but we do best to hold to the poem's own central story, its account of aesthetic contemplation and its personal myth of memory as salvation.

The misgivings and the ultimate fear of mortality are part of the poem because of Wordsworth's insistence upon autobiographical honesty. They help to make *Tintern Abbey* the major testament it is, for through them the poem convinces us it has earned the heights upon which it moves. The consoling story of a natural growth that tests the soul, teaches it generosity, and accepts its love becomes finally what Wallace Stevens in *The Rock* calls "a cure of the ground and of ourselves, in the predicate that there is nothing else." This predicate of nakedness is a sublime act of honesty, and prepares us for the Wordsworth who is the first poet ever to present our human condition in its naturalistic truth, vulnerable and dignified, and irreducible, not to be explained away in any terms, theological or analytical, but to be accepted as what it is. The mind, knowing only itself and Nature, but remembering a time when Nature gave it direct joy, and having remoter memories of an earlier time when it knew itself only in union with Nature, is able to turn back through memory for a faith that at last gives courage and a love for others. Blake did not believe in the goodness of the natural heart, and Coleridge could neither believe in nor deny it, but Wordsworth brings its possibility as truth alive into our hearts, as he did into the heart of Keats. There are greater Romantic poems than *Tintern Abbey,* but they surpass it as vision or rhetoric, not as consolation. No poem, unless it be *The Old Cumberland Beggar,* humanizes us more.

II. The Old Cumberland Beggar

The Old Cumberland Beggar (1797) is Wordsworth's finest vision of the irreducible natural man, the human stripped to the nakedness of primordial condition and exposed as still powerful in dignity, still infinite in value. The Beggar reminds us of the beggars, solitaries, wanderers throughout Wordsworth's poetry, particularly in *The Prelude* and *Resolution and Independence.* He differs from them in that he is not the agency of a revelation; he is not responsible for a sudden release of Wordsworth's imagination. He is not even of visionary utility; he is something finer, beyond use, a vision of reality in himself. I am not suggesting that *The Old Cumberland Beggar* is the best of Wordsworth's poems outside *The Prelude*; it is not in the sublime mode, as are *Tintern Abbey,* the Great Ode, *Resolution and Independence.* But it is the most Wordsworthian of poems, and profoundly moving.

Nothing could be simpler than the poem's opening: "I saw an aged Beggar in my walk." The Old Man (the capitalization is the poet's) has put down his staff, and takes his scraps and fragments out of a flour bag, one by one. He scans them, fixedly and seriously. The plain beginning yields to a music of love, the beauty of the real:

> In the sun,
> Upon the second step of that small pile,
> Surrounded by those wild unpeopled hills,
> He sat, and ate his food in solitude:
> And ever, scattered from his palsied hand,
> That, still attempting to prevent the waste,
> Was baffled still, the crumbs in little showers
> Fell on the ground; and the small mountain birds,
> Not venturing yet to peck their destined meal,
> Approached within the length of half his staff.

It is difficult to describe *how* this is beautiful, but we can make a start by observing that it is beautiful both because it is so matter of fact, and because the fact is itself a transfiguration. The Old Man is in his own state, and he is radically innocent. The "wild unpeopled hills" complement his own solitude; he is a phenomenon of their kind. And he is no more sentimentalized than they are. His lot is not even miserable; he is too absorbed into Nature for that, as absorbed as he can be and still retain human identity.

He is even past further aging. The poet has known him since his child-

hood, and even then "he was so old, he seems not older now." The Old
Man is so helpless in appearance that everyone—sauntering horseman or
toll-gate keeper or post boy—makes way for him, taking special care to
keep him from harm. For he cannot be diverted, but moves on like a
natural process. "He travels on, a solitary Man," Wordsworth says, and
then repeats it, making a refrain for that incessant movement whose only
meaning is that it remains human though at the edge of our condition:

> He travels on, a solitary Man;
> His age has no companion. On the ground
> His eyes are turned, and, as he moves along,
> They move along the ground; and, evermore,
> Instead of common and habitual sight
> Of fields with rural works, of hill and dale,
> And the blue sky, one little span of earth
> Is all his prospect.

He is bent double, like the Leech Gatherer, and his vision of one little
span of earth recalls the wandering old man of Chaucer's *Pardoner's Tale*.
But Chaucer's solitary longed for death, and on the ground he called his
mother's gate he knocked often with his staff, crying, "Dear mother, let
me in." Wordsworth's Old Man sees only the ground, but he is tenaciously
alive, and is beyond desire, even that of death. He sees, and yet hardly
sees. He moves constantly, but is so still in look and motion that he can
hardly be seen to move. He is all process, hardly character, and yet almost
stasis.

It is so extreme a picture that we can be tempted to ask, "Is this life?
Where is its use?" The temptation dehumanizes us, Wordsworth would
have it, and the two questions are radically dissimilar, but his answer to
the first is vehemently affirmative and to the second an absolute moral
passion. There is

> a spirit and pulse of good,
> A life and soul, to every mode of being
> Inseparably linked.

The Old Man performs many functions. The most important is that
of a binding agent for the memories of good impulses in all around him.
Wherever he goes,

> The mild necessity of use compels
> To acts of love.

These acts of love, added one to another, at last insensibly dispose
their performers to virtue and true goodness. We need to be careful in our
reaction to this. Wordsworth is not preaching the vicious and mad doc-

trine that beggary is good because it makes charity possible. That would properly invoke Blake's blistering reply in *The Human Abstract*:

> Pity would be no more
> If we did not make somebody Poor;
> And Mercy no more could be
> If all were as happy as we.

Wordsworth has no reaction to the Old Man which we can categorize. He does not think of him in social or economic terms, but only as a human life, which necessarily has affected other lives, and always for the better. In particular, the Old Man has given occasions for kindness to the very poorest, who give to him from their scant store, and are the kinder for it. Again, you must read this in its own context. Wordsworth's best poetry has nothing directly to do with social justice, as Blake's or Shelley's frequently does. The old beggar is a free man, at home in the heart of the solitudes he wanders, and he does not intend the humanizing good he passively causes. Nor is his social aspect at the poem's vital center; only his freedom is:

> —Then let him pass, a blessing on his head!
> And, long as he can wander, let him breathe
> The freshness of the valleys; let his blood
> Struggle with frosty air and winter snows;
> And let the chartered wind that sweeps the heath
> Beat his grey locks against his withered face.

Pity for him is inappropriate; he is pathetic only if shut up. He is a "figure of capable imagination," in Stevens' phrase, a Man perfectly complete in Nature, reciprocating its gifts by being himself, a being at one with it:

> Let him be free of mountain solitudes;
> And have around him, whether heard or not,
> The pleasant melody of woodland birds.

Mountain solitudes and sudden winds are what suit him, whether he reacts to them or not. The failure of his senses does not cut him off from Nature; it does not matter whether he can hear the birds, but it is fitting that he have them around him. He has become utterly passive toward Nature. Let it be free, then, to come in upon him:

> if his eyes have now
> Been doomed so long to settle upon earth
> That not without some effort they behold
> The countenance of the horizontal sun,
> Rising or setting, let the light at least
> Find a free entrance to their languid orbs.

The Old Man is approaching that identity with Nature that the infant at first knows, when an organic continuity seems to exist between Nature and consciousness. Being so naturalized, he must die in the eye of Nature, that he may be absorbed again:

> And let him, *where* and *when* he will, sit down
> Beneath the trees, or on a grassy bank
> Of highway side, and with the little birds
> Share his chance-gathered meal; and, finally,
> As in the eye of Nature he has lived,
> So in the eye of Nature let him die!

The poem abounds in a temper of spirit that Wordsworth shares with Tolstoy, a reverence for the simplicities of *caritas*, the Christian love that is so allied to and yet is not pity. But Tolstoy might have shown the Old Cumberland Beggar as a sufferer; in Wordsworth he bears the mark of "animal tranquillity and decay," the title given by Wordsworth to a fragment closely connected to the longer poem. In the fragment the Old Man travels on and moves not with pain, but with thought:

> He is insensibly subdued
> To settled quiet . . .
> He is by nature led
> To peace so perfect that the young behold
> With envy, what the Old Man hardly feels.

We know today, better than his contemporaries could, what led Wordsworth to the subject of human decay, to depictions of idiocy, desertion, beggars, homeless wanderers. He sought images of alienated life, as we might judge them, which he could see and present as images of natural communion. The natural man, free of consciousness in any of our senses, yet demonstrates a mode of consciousness which both intends Nature for its object and at length blends into that object. The hiding places of man's power are in his past, in childhood. Only memory can take him there, but even memory fades, and at length fades away. The poet of naturalism, separated by organic growth from his own past, looks around him and sees the moving emblems of a childlike consciousness in the mad, the outcast, and the dreadfully old. From them he takes his most desperate consolation, intimations of a mortality that almost ceases to afflict.

Wordsworth and the Tears of Adam

by Neil Hertz

This essay on literary influence grew out of my bewilderment with one of the better-documented relationships in English poetry, that of Wordsworth to Milton. How was one to understand this case of influence? It was not just a theoretical problem but a puzzle, line by line, to the practical critic. Anyone who has tried to draw the lines of force between two poets, one in the more distant, one in the more recent past, will know what I mean: a reader quickly finds himself perplexed, conscious not only of the movement of the texts relative to each other, but of the shifting, contingent quality of his own relation to either poet's work. Of course this may be the case with any interpretive effort, but the study of influence has a way of bringing the point home with particular force. For what one finds, again and again, is that one's most interesting perceptions seem suspiciously anachronistic—as if it were really Wordsworth who was influencing Milton—or subjective—as if it were merely one's own interpretive acts that had become a source of fascination, a distracting influence from still another direction.

Yet it may be that both a sense of anachronism and of a certain kind of subjectivity are not only unavoidable in such studies, but often signs that one is on the right track; for they may mean that the reader is moving into that order of time in which works of literature have their existence and in which the significant encounters between writers take place. In the pages that follow, since I would like to show what can be gained by ignoring chronology, I shall begin by looking at a poem of Wordsworth's, then, with that in mind, turn to look backwards towards a passage in *Paradise Lost,* then finally move forward again to consider "The Ruined Cottage." Fortunately, we are dealing with two writers who would find this approach congenial. Their works have traditionally raised questions about the nature of poetic subjectivity, and they are poets for whom anachronism held no terrors, to whom phrases like "the child is father of the man" or "Adam the goodliest man of men since born his sons" were both meaningful and peculiarly satisfying. As such,

"Wordsworth and the Tears of Adam" by Neil Hertz. From *Studies in Romanticism,* 7 (1967). Copyright © 1967 by Boston University. Reprinted, with revisions by the author, by his permission and that of *Studies in Romanticism.*

it will not only be in their relation to one another, but in the encounters that take place within their individual works, that Milton and Wordsworth can help us to understand the encounter of poet with poet.

I

Here, first, is a text in many ways typical of Wordsworth: the experience it records is a characteristic one, and Wordsworth rightly considered his rendering of it an example of his best blank verse. But there are two things that are unusual about it which make it, from my point of view, particularly interesting. We most frequently find Wordsworth, in his major poems, writing in the first person and engaged in the imaginative retrieval of events in the more or less distant past. He is, we know, the poet of the egotistical sublime, and he is the poet who, in his own words, was "unused to make a present joy the matter of a song." But here we shall find him offering a third-person account of an experience which we know from his note to have been his own, and which he turned into poetry almost immediately after it had occurred. What is surprising is how little these differences seem to matter: the poem remains perfectly illustrative of Wordsworth's recurrent concerns. To understand how this can be so is to learn something about the quality of Wordsworthian subjectivity and of Wordsworth's interest in the past. The poem is "A Night-Piece" (1798):

> —The sky is overcast
> With a continuous cloud of texture close,
> Heavy and wan, all whitened by the Moon,
> Which through that veil is indistinctly seen,
> A dull, contracted circle, yielding light
> So feebly spread, that not a shadow falls,
> Chequering the ground—from rock, plant, tree, or tower.
> At length a pleasant instantaneous gleam
> Startles the pensive traveller while he treads
> His lonesome path, with unobserving eye
> Bent earthwards; he looks up—the clouds are split
> Asunder,—and above his head he sees
> The clear Moon, and the glory of the heavens.
> There, in a black-blue vault she sails along,
> Followed by multitudes of stars, that, small
> And sharp, and bright, along the dark abyss
> Drive as she drives: how fast they wheel away,
> Yet vanish not! the wind is in the tree,
> But they are silent;—still they roll along
> Immeasurably distant; and the vault,

Built round by those white clouds, enormous clouds,
Still deepens its unfathomable depth.
At length the Vision closes; and the mind,
Not undisturbed by the *delight* it feels,
Which slowly settles into peaceful calm,
Is left to muse upon the solemn scene.[1]

The poem traces the movement of a mind imaginatively engaged with the external world, a movement that could be charted in a number of ways. For example, we might notice how the moon is gradually realized as a powerful presence. At first totally denaturalized ("a dull, contracted circle"), then "the clear Moon," she finally emerges, fully personified, in line 14. When that happens, the visible world is transformed: it no longer makes up a field for empirical observation. Instead it is reconstituted, under the presiding light of the moon, as a "Vision," a "solemn scene" which bears musing on, because it is now emblematic.[2]

Inseparable from this process is another, involving the transformation of the voice we hear telling the story. The speaker of the opening lines is calmly and rather distantly observing the scene: his language, in its neutral, faintly scientific accuracy ("continuous cloud," "texture," "contracted circle"), corresponds in want of feeling to the "dull" quality of the scene itself. Whoever this spectator may be, he is certainly *ab extra*: the "pensive traveller" only appears in the ninth line, and his "unobserving eye / Bent earthwards" is presumably not the eye that so carefully registered details of cloud and moonlight earlier. But as the moon is revealed, and the power and significance of the scene take possession of the traveller, the narrative voice is itself changed, moving from the (still uninvolved) notation of emotional response ("a pleasant . . . gleam / Startles the pensive traveller") to conventional hyperbole ("the glory of the heavens"), then to a more excited participation: "how fast they wheel away / Yet vanish not!"

In that exclamation, the speaker's response is indistinguishable from the traveller's. Both seem to have been brought alive by this silent and powerful manifestation. We can speak of their state as one of heightened subjectivity, but here we must note that characteristically in Wordsworth such heightening creates not a more highly individualized subject, but a more impersonal and generalized one. So it is here: speaker and traveller no longer occupy distinct points of view, and it is because of this coalescence that the poem can end as it does, now no longer referring

---

[1] Quotations in this paper are from *The Poetical Works of William Wordsworth*, ed. E. de Selincourt (Oxford, 1940–49); and *The Poetical Works of John Milton*, ed. Helen Darbishire (Oxford Univ. Press, 1958).

[2] On the transformation of the scene, see David Ferry, *The Limits of Mortality* (Middletown, Conn., 1959), pp. 30–31; and James Kissane, "'A Night-Piece': Wordsworth's Emblem of the Mind," *MLN*, LXXI (1956), 183–186.

either to a pensive traveller or an anonymous observer or even to a poet
recollecting emotion in tranquillity, but inclusively to "the mind." Indeed, one measure of the poem's success is that the encompassing gesture
implicit in saying "the mind" embraces the reader as well, for he too, as
the last lines settle into a calm regularity of cadence, is made to participate
in the mind that muses on the solemn scene.

Wordsworth's note to the poem[3] confirms what we may have suspected
anyway, that the observer, the pensive traveller and the writer of the
poem were really one and the same; they are simply aspects of Wordsworth's self following one upon the other in time. But the poem
Wordsworth chose to write does not take that continuity for granted:
rather, he seems in this case to have gone out of his way, by writing in
the third person, to insist on the disjunctive nature of the self. The note
suggests why this maneuver may have seemed necessary to him. If the
poem was, in fact, composed extempore, the entire experience—the visual
revelation and its verbal repetition—would have had about it a specious
feeling of personal continuity. The man who works into blank verse the
exclamation "How fast they wheel away . . . !" at, say, 9:35 p.m. is very
obviously—too obviously, for Wordsworth's purposes—the same man
who, at 9:30, had initially exclaimed those words. No great effort of the
imagination would seem necessary in order to recapture sensations so
recently experienced. By writing in the third person, Wordsworth deliberately introduces into this apparently seamless experience a gap, a
vacancy between aspects of the self that makes his account of this "present
joy" identical in structure to the more familiar poetry of childhood remembered. Here are some lines from the Second Book of *The Prelude*
(1805):

> A tranquillizing spirit presses now
> On my corporeal frame: so wide appears
> The vacancy between me and those days,
> Which yet have such self-presence in my mind
> That, sometimes, when I think of them, I seem
> Two consciousnesses, conscious of myself
> And of some other Being. (ll. 27–33)

These are the circumstances in which Wordsworth's finest poetry is
written, and what "A Night-Piece" makes clear is how necessary it was
for him to experience this doubling of consciousness. It was a state of
mind that would come more or less naturally when he was musing on the
almost-forgotten past, but here we find him obliged to induce it quite

---

[3] "Composed on the road between Nether Stowey and Alfoxden, extempore. I dis-
tinctly recollect the very moment when I was struck, as described,—'He looks up at
the clouds, etc.'" *The Poetical Works*, II, 503.

deliberately, by manipulating the dramatic structure of his account. The result is to split the self into a poet existing in the present and "some other Being" who acts as a mediating figure—often a childhood self, but in this case the mature man seen as "pensive traveller." But this mediator is also involved in another powerfully resonant relation, usually with a natural object—as the pensive traveller is, here, with the moon—and it is precisely this relational moment that Wordsworth seeks to bring into connection with his present poetic activity. What he thus succeeds in creating is a chain of successive and analogous relations: the moon is to the pensive traveller as the pensive traveller is to the poet as the poet is to the reader; or, to schematize the more frequently encountered sequence, Nature : child :: child : poet :: poet : reader. The intention of Wordsworth's major poetry is never essentially the recreation of the past. When his imagination turns backward towards the original experience, it is in search of that "other Being"—neither poet nor reader—who will, when paired with the poet, occupy the central position in the chain of relations I have just described.

I want to linger on this metaphor of a chain because I believe it will make it easier to bring into connection a number of aspects of Wordsworth's thought. For one thing, it suggests why a critic's interest in Wordsworthian rhetoric (that is, the relation of reader to poet) is inseparable from an interest in Wordsworthian memory (the relation of poet to child) and in Wordsworthian metaphysics (the relation of child to Nature). Secondly, it can give us an insight into the peculiar quality of time encountered in Wordsworth's poetry, and into the connection between that time and the kind of human consciousness—autonomous, subjective, and impersonal—that comes into existence at certain moments in his poetry, moments like the one we have observed towards the end of "A Night-Piece." There we noticed that the center of subjectivity, "the mind," was inclusively that of the traveller, the poet, and the reader. Yet Wordsworth was insisting that there was a gap between poet and traveller of the same sort that exists between poet and reader, and that that gap may be bridged but is not thereby removed. As a result, the poem testifies to a remarkable generosity, a willingness on Wordsworth's part to confer autonomy on prior moments in his own existence and on the consciousness of his reader as well. But the order of time in which this autonomous subjectivity is constituted, in which the chain of relations is created, is not ordinary historical time. If we ask when the exclamation "How fast they wheel away!" takes place, we cannot locate it exclusively at the moment of the traveller's original experience, nor can we place it at the moment at which the poet repeats the words, nor yet at the moment the reader encounters them. The chain exists in a mode of present time—call it the narrative present—which is a creation of the language of the poem, of the telling of the story, and in which traveller and poet and reader mutually participate. Finally, the metaphor of a chain will be helpful when we turn to examine another relation, that of poet to poet, of Wordsworth to Milton, for it suggests that there might be a way of thinking about literary influence that honors the autonomy of both poets involved.

II

We can begin by raising the question of Milton's subjectivity, that is, of the quality of his presence in his work. That question no longer engages our attention as it once did that of the Romantics, probably because the whole issue was so badly confused during the nineteen-thirties. Then too much of the wrong sort of attention was paid to the ways Milton's personality made itself heard in *Paradise Lost,* usually on the part of critics who found him personally offensive and who were bothered by any signs of his intrusion. Attacks on his personality generally were accompanied by attacks on his idiosyncrasies as a stylist or as a thinker; so, in reply, recent students of *Paradise Lost* have taken pains to show that particular aspects of Milton's poetry are neither as strange nor as peculiar to him as they were once held to be. These later studies have generally been convincing, and working together they have produced a more sophisticated sense of Milton's location in history. But one consequence of this emphasis has been a relative lack of interest in what Coleridge spoke of as the "subjectivity of the poet, as of Milton, who is himself before himself in every thing he writes." [4] The lines of Wordsworth's we have just considered can suggest the variety of ways in which a poet can be "before himself" as he writes, as well as the impersonal quality of the highest reach of poetic subjectivity; as such they can serve as a guide to a still-disputed and interesting section of *Paradise Lost.*

In the Eleventh Book, the Archangel Michael, sent to expel Adam from the Garden, first offers him a prophetic account of history, that is, of the long-range consequences of his fall. The prophecy takes the form of a series of visions, each of which provokes a response from Adam—usually one of grief or dismay, for the scenes Adam is shown are almost universally grim. Each of Adam's responses, in turn, elicits an explanation from Michael, and the tone of these explanations in general matches the visions, and sometimes even surpasses them, in grimness. Commenting on a group of sinners who appear to be enjoying

[4] In *Table Talk,* May 12, 1830; reprinted in *Coleridge on the Seventeenth Century,* ed. Roberta Florence Brinkley (Durham, N.C., 1955), p. 587.

themselves, Michael is made to say, with the air of a man clearly enjoying *him*self, that they

> now swim in joy,
> (Erelong to swim at large) and laugh; for which
> The World erelong a world of tears must weepe. (xi, 625–627)

Critics have fastened on lines such as these as proof that there was something immoderately sour about Milton's view of history, imputing the edge in Michael's tone either to the personal bitterness the poet may be imagined to have felt after the Restoration or, in less flatly *ad hominem* terms, to the rigors of his later theology. "In this portion of the poem," one writer complains, "Milton's imagination seems to take wing only in delineating scenes of destruction." [5]

I have seen no defense of the Eleventh Book that directly confronts these *ad hominem* complaints. Instead, admirers of this section of the poem argue their case in more objective terms, locating Milton's imaginative investment either in his reworking a vein of Christian historiography that goes back to St. Paul, or in his careful plotting of the drama of Adam's education. [6] Both these interpretations are valid, although, like much educational dialogue, the exchanges of Adam and Michael constitute a rather lumbering "drama." But there is another dramatic movement discernible in Book xi, one which involves Milton more directly in the fabric of his poem, and one which our Wordsworthian model puts us in a position to appreciate.

Late in the Book, Milton's own voice interrupts the dialogue of Adam and the Angel; the poet breaks off his account of Noah's Flood in order to address his sympathy directly to Adam:

> How didst thou grieve then, *Adam,* to behold
> The end of all thy Ofspring, end so sad,
> Depopulation; thee another Floud,
> Of tears and sorrow a Floud thee also drownd,
> And sunk thee as thy Sons; till gently reard
> By th' Angel, on thy feet thou stoodst at last,
> Though comfortless, as when a Father mourns
> His Children, all in view destroyd at once. (xi, 754–761)

---

[5] Louis L. Martz, *The Paradise Within* (New Haven, 1964), p. 153.

[6] A brief summary of critical opinion on Books xi and xii followed by a perceptive and informed account of their significance can be found in Barbara Keifer Lewalski, "Structure and the Symbolism of Vision in Michael's Prophecy, *Paradise Lost,* Books xi–xii," *PQ,* xlii (1963), 25–35. See also George Williamson, "The Education of Adam," and Lawrence A. Sasek, "The Drama of Paradise Lost, Books xi and xii," both articles available in Arthur E. Barker's anthology, *Milton: Modern Essays in Criticism* (New York, 1965).

This far along in the poem, we have become accustomed to the constant and often subtle pressure Milton exercises to shape his reader's response to the story he is telling; and we are also accustomed to his sometimes turning away from his readers entirely, in prayer or invocation. What is rare—I count only three instances throughout the poem[7]—is for the poet to thus address himself to a character. Even more surprising is the quality of this address: the tenderness implicit in the repeated use of *thee* and *thou* and *thy,* and the powerful sense of loss these lines communicate. Tenderness, we know, has not been the dominant note of Book XI, nor have we been led to expect Milton to grieve at the thought of sinners being swept away. Yet here it seems as if the act of imagining the Flood, far from providing a source of grim pleasure to Milton, has liberated in him a flow of compassion: "thee another Floud, / Of tears and sorrow a Floud thee also drown'd."

"In the Paradise Lost," wrote Coleridge, "the sublimest parts are the revelations of Milton's own mind, producing itself and evolving its own greatness." [8] He was thinking of the Invocation to Light in Book III when he wrote this, but signs of the same evolution may be observed in the Eleventh Book: it is possible to read this section as a dramatic development of the poet's consciousness, analogous to the movement of mind recorded in Wordsworth's "Night-Piece," and tending toward the address to Adam. To read the passage in this way is to accept the imputations of *ad hominem* critics, to agree that Milton's personal resentment (along with other less damaging sentiments) may be heard in the voice of the Archangel; but it is also to carry the tonal analysis one step further, and to insist that the accents of personal resentment that we may catch in Michael's speech are no longer audible when Milton himself addresses Adam. Paradoxically, that moment when Milton speaks out in his own voice is among the least personal in the poem. It is worth considering how this might have come about, and what its implications are for a reading of the rest of *Paradise Lost.*

A good place to begin is with one of the lessons that Michael's account of history seems intended to teach: where there are multitudes, there is sin. Adam's fall has put God's command to increase and multiply in a new and ironic light. The sequence of visions Adam is shown brings home the lesson, as each new scene is enlarged in scope and more confusingly populous. Counterpointing this association of sin with human multitudes is an increasing stress on the unique and isolated figure of the righteous man. This is less obvious in the opening vision

[7] The other moments occur when Milton addresses Adam and Eve at IV, 773 ("Sleep on, / Blest pair . . ."), and Eve at IX, 404 ("O much deceived, much failing, hapless *Eve* . . .").
[8] In *The Literary Remains of Samuel Taylor Coleridge* (London, 1836–39), I, 172 f.; reprinted in Brinkley, p. 578.

of Cain and Abel, although Michael makes the point when he comments that "th'unjust the just hath slain" (XI, 455); but in the later visions of Enoch ("The onely righteous in a World perverse" [XI, 701]) and of Noah ("The one just Man alive" [XI, 818]) this Old Testament motif that had so long and so deeply engaged Milton's imagination is made quite explicit.

If we set out—as *ad hominem* critics do—to ground this dialectic in the actualities of Milton's life, it is easy enough to see how, in the 1660s, the figures of the citizen as the One Just Man or the poet as the severe but truth-telling Archangel would have been appealing images to Milton, stirring in him the bitter satisfactions of self-righteousness. Something of this sort is undoubtedly going on in Book XI; but it soon becomes clear that the demands of Milton's imagination are not fully met by these mediators, and that his mind is moving beyond them toward a confrontation with what Wordsworth would call "some other Being," a figure who will mediate to him a truer sense of his poetic identity. That figure is Adam, not Adam seen as an archetype of innocence, but Adam after the Fall, surviving but mortal, and listening in tears to the sad tale of loss.

The turning point is the story of the Flood, which begins with an account of Noah testifying against the ways of the multitude and preaching "Conversion and Repentance":

> But all in vain: which when he saw, he ceas'd
> Contending, and remov'd his Tents farr off;
> Then from the Mountain hewing Timber tall,
> Began to build a Vessel of huge bulk.   (XI, 726–729)

This is the One Just Man in his finest hour, aloof but irreproachably so. But now the mood of the poem changes as Milton turns for his text from the account in *Genesis* to the stranger poetry of Deucalion's flood in Ovid:

> Meanwhile the Southwind rose, and with black-wings
> Wide hovering, all the Clouds together drove
> From under Heav'n; the Hills to their supplie
> Vapour, and Exhalation dusk and moist,
> Sent up amain; and now the thick'nd Skie
> Like a dark Ceeling stood; down rushd the Rain
> Impetuous, and continu'd till the Earth
> No more was seen; the floating Vessel swum
> Uplifted; and secure with beaked prow
> Rode tilting o'er the Waves, all dwellings else
> Flood overwhelm'd, and them with all thir pomp
> Deep under water rould; Sea coverd Sea,

> Sea without shour; and in thir Palaces
> Where luxurie late reignd, Sea-monsters whelpd
> And stabl'd.   (XI, 738–752)

This is certainly Ovid moralized; the grotesque underwater details illustrate the wages of sin, for Milton is still concerned with "*thir* pomp," "*thir* Palaces / Where luxurie late reignd." But the metamorphic power of these images and cadences, the sense of sea-change familiar to readers of "Lycidas," reaches out beyond the sinful multitudes—those others— to involve the consciousness of the righteous poet as well. As the scene is radically diminished in scope, the pathos of loss is suddenly the dominant feeling, mingled with a sense of how fragile is the vessel in which righteousness survives: "of Mankind, so numerous late, / All left, in one small bottom swum imbarkt" (XI, 752–753). With this the transformation of the poet's voice is completed, and he can turn, in sympathy and in the recognition of kinship, to Adam.

But what are the grounds of this kinship? Adam's response to the vision turns out to be characteristically generous but, as usual, exaggerated, for it is based on a misapprehension. Moved by the scope of the disaster and ignorant of its outcome, he naturally assumes that all mankind did indeed perish, including Noah and his family, whom he imagines finally dying of "Famine and anguish . . . Wandring that watrie Desert" (XI, 778–779). Later, when Michael enlightens him and goes on to describe the receding of the waters and the renewal of the Covenant, Adam joyfully brings his feelings into line with his new understanding of the event:

> Farr less I now lament for one whole World
> Of wicked Sons destroyd, then I rejoyce
> For one Man found so perfet and so just.   (XI, 874–876)

Adam's self-correction has about it some of the same harsh zest with which Milton, in a more famous passage in the poem—the description of Mulciber's fall—suddenly reins in his own erring imagination. The comparison is worth considering, for just as there Milton had allowed his verse to affectionately linger over the story as the Greeks told it before pulling himself up short to insist on its falsity, so in directly addressing himself to Adam, in taking Adam's interpretation of the scene so readily for granted, he has lent himself to this error. To break into the texture of the poem at this point is to imaginatively assume the burden of Adam's ignorance and of his innocence of Christian doctrine. It is as if Milton had been moved by the compelling poetry of the Flood to momentarily suspend his sense of the certainties of his faith—moved back beyond doctrine, beyond the hope of redemption, to an encounter with Adam in the heart of loss.

This interpretation needn't obscure the Christian intention of *Paradise Lost* or the presence of a redemptive pattern as a structural element in the last two books. The poetry of the Flood takes its place in that pattern, of course, for Michael's prophecy is intended to serve as an object lesson for Adam in Pauline faith, in "the substance of things unseen." So the lines that unfold the dimensions of Adam's loss may be read as part of his education, a negative experience designed to detach his hopes from the wrong objects so that they may fix themselves on the promised end. We have seen what Adam learns from the first account of the Flood: it is to "renounce a World of wicked Sons," to temper his hopes that blood lineage can provide an alternative to the permanence he has forfeited at the Fall. Later, there is another passage intended to teach him a related lesson, to purge him of any false hopes about the permanence of his dwelling place. It comes from Michael's speech after the vision of the Flood, and it is unusual in one respect: for it has not been Michael's practice, when commenting on the visions he produces, to get so caught up in their detail. Yet here he begins by interpreting the Flood and ends by vividly retelling the story. He has come to the point where Noah is commanded to "save himself and houshold from amidst / A World devote to universal rack":

> No sooner hee with them of Man and Beast
> Select for life shall in the Ark be lodg'd,
> And shelterd round, but all the Cataracts
> Of Heav'n set op'n on the Earth shall powre
> Raine day and night, all fountains of the Deep
> Broke up, shall heave the Ocean to usurp
> Beyond all bounds, till inundation rise
> Above the highest Hills: then shall this Mount
> Of Paradise by might of Waves be moovd
> Out of his place, pusht by the horned floud,
> With all his verdure spoild, and Trees adrift
> Down the great River to the op'ning Gulf,
> And there take root an Iland salt and bare,
> The haunt of Seales and Orcs, and Sea-mews' clang:
> To teach thee that God attributes to place
> No sanctitie, if none be thither brought
> By Men who there frequent, or therein dwell.   (xi, 822–838)

The moral is clear and relevant, but it is not at all adequate to the full suggestiveness of this poetry. Nor can we really account for the length of this reprise or for its appearance at this point in the poem by reflecting on Michael's motives as a prophet or as a teacher. It is certainly Milton whose imagination is caught up in the story, and to understand the fascination that the Flood held for him, I think that, instead of looking further along in the poem for signs of the redemptive pattern, we should turn back to the poet's address to Adam.

I have suggested that Milton, in addressing Adam, has achieved the same quality of impersonality that can be heard in Wordsworth's voice in the climactic lines of "A Night-Piece": there are still other analogies between the two texts which I would like to pursue. Consider what it means for Milton to break into his narrative and speak to a character: it involves an odd—and, for the surprised reader, a very exciting—leap of the imagination in time. For if we ask when this address takes place, we must say it occurs neither in Adam's ordinary time—sometime between the Fall and the Expulsion—nor in Milton's—sometime in the 1660s. Chronology becomes misleading and we must locate this point of imaginative contact in another order of time. This is the same situation we found ourselves in when we were considering "A Night-Piece," and asking when the exclamation "How fast they wheel away . . . !" occurs. In the case of Wordsworth's poetry, I have called that order of time the narrative present, and noted that it was a creation of the language of the poem, brought into being by the telling of a story, and hence available for the participation of the reader or the hearer of the tale. And that too may be said of this moment in *Paradise Lost*. For what moves Adam to tears is not an event in his immediate experience but the image of one that has not yet taken place, as it is summoned up for him, in a prospective vision, by the angelic narrator; and what moves Milton to compassion is not his witnessing the Flood itself, but his imaginative participation in Adam's subjective response to it. For an instant, Adam and Milton meet, not as eye-witnesses to a disaster, but as members of Michael's audience, and much of the poignancy of their encounter is due to this. Like Milton's own audience they are, in effect, listening to a story, one which will be perpetuated by successive retellings—Michael to Adam, Moses to the children of Israel, and so on. In fact, what Milton's audience is listening to is simultaneously both the earliest and the most recent telling of the tale; for Adam was the first to hear it, and its latest rehearsal is here and now, as a story within the story of *Paradise Lost*.

This, of course, is true of the entire prophecy in Books XI and XII. But within that structure the story of the Flood is unique, not only because of its length or the generally high quality of its verse, but because so many elements in that section of the poem are brought into tight and resonant interrelation. The lines describing the drowning of the sinful are also the occasion of a symbolic drowning or transformation of the poet's voice, a movement from a self-righteous identification with the One Just Man, through a moment of self-loss, toward a compassionate identification with Adam fallen, who is now recognizable as a fellow-survivor, someone who has himself experienced, as he weeps for his descendants, a death-by-water. Finally these multiplied and interinvolved instances of loss are related to the most formal element in the encounter of Milton and Adam, the fact that it takes place through the mediation of a prospective vision or story. For listening to a story, regardless of its theme, is also an experience of self-loss, of the suspension of one's commitments in ordinary time in favor of an alternative sequence of events in narrative time. Yet here formal and thematic elements are inseparable: Milton's moving out of self-righteousness is concurrent with his moving through the poetry of the Flood into the story, into the time in which he can confront Adam. When that encounter takes place, a chain of relations is established similar to that created in Wordsworth's poem, for not only Adam and Milton, but Milton's reader as well has been brought into the narrative continuum: if we are moved by what we hear in these lines, then we find ourselves in a relation to the voice of their poet that is not identical with but analogous to the relation he is in to Adam, and that Adam bears to Michael's vision of his drowning sons.

What I would like to suggest is that this perpetuation of the story of the Flood provides Milton with an emblem of continuity which is as compelling to his imagination as is the perpetuation of faith in the redemptive process. For it is through the rehearsal of the story that the encounter with Adam is brought about, and the poet led to an insight into the nature of loss and the nature of human subjectivity and the relation between the two. It is the firm—although fleeting—possession of that insight which underwrites the new note of generosity that can be heard in Milton's voice, a compassion that embraces, in Adam, mankind at large, the sinful and the righteous alike. For Milton to have arrived at that height of address is a sign that he has, in one sense, gone as far as he can go: the transformed voice no longer sounds in need of redemption. Perhaps this can help to explain the rather perfunctory treatment which the Redemption receives in Book xii, as well as the relative inertness of the verse there when compared with these passages on the Flood.

There are other points in *Paradise Lost* where an analysis of the play of personal and impersonal accents in the poet's voice would produce very different conclusions: in the great invocations, for example, the means by which the voice arrives at its authority are quite consciously and traditionally Christian. But the poetry of the Flood both participates in the central Christian intention of the poem and enacts other Miltonic intentions which are, at best, tangential to Christian thought. This situation is not unique in Milton's poetry. The last eight lines of "Lycidas," for example, come as a surprise, after the totally convincing language of Christian apotheosis, by introducing a new speaker, one who detaches himself from the body of the poem and contemplates it at a distance. His doing so is not at all felt to be ironically destructive of the religious concerns of the poem, yet this movement of the imagination does not seem to have grown out of those concerns, nor does the cool, impersonal but highly subjective voice to be heard in those last lines seem to draw its authority from Milton's faith. If it is possible to discriminate such distinct intentions in "Lycidas" or in *Paradise Lost* it is chiefly because the achievement of poets like Wordsworth has set the body of Miltonic poetry in a new light. I would like now to turn to a final Wordsworthian text, a poem which is at once an indication of his achievement and an illustration of what is most Miltonic about his imagination.

III

"The Ruined Cottage" was more or less completed in 1798, not long after Wordsworth composed "A Night-Piece," but it was not immediately published. It was put aside for a few years, taken up and revised during the winter of 1801–02, then finally printed as the first book of *The Excursion* in 1814. There it serves as an introduction to the character Wordsworth calls "the Wanderer," who functions as the poet's hero and spokesman throughout that long work. In its final form, "The Ruined Cottage" begins with the poet moving "across a bare wide Common," toward a prearranged meeting with the Wanderer, a rendezvous set in a shady grove surrounding an abandoned and dilapidated cottage. Wordsworth comes in sight of the grove, but postpones his account of their meeting until he has described at length how the Wanderer had come to be as he is, an exemplary Wordsworthian man, aged, wisely passive, profoundly and serenely in touch with Nature. The description of the Wanderer's childhood could have been composed for the opening books of *The Prelude,* but Wordsworth avoids insisting on his likeness to the older man. Rather he admiringly sets the Wanderer off at a distance, in a realm of calm self-possession that the poet himself has yet to attain. This distancing provides Wordsworth with a principle of dramatic structure for the rest of the poem, which falls quite naturally into two roughly equal sections. The first describes the Wanderer's education, a model of the gentle and molding power of Nature; the second half of the poem obliquely echoes this process, for it is concerned with what is really an incident in the poet's education, although this time it is not Nature but the Wanderer's words that exercise the benign influence. Like Adam listening to Michael, Wordsworth is gradually led toward the truth, and toward the appropriate response to the truth, as he listens to the Wanderer tell a sad story, the history of the last occupants of the now-ruined cottage.

Characteristically the Wanderer insists that what he is telling is only "a common tale, / An ordinary sorrow of man's life" (ll. 636–637), but the accents in which he begins his story mark his intention as prophetic:

Thus did he speak. "I see around me here
Things which you cannot see: we die, my Friend,
Nor we alone, but that which each man loved
And prized in his peculiar nook of earth
Dies with him, or is changed; and very soon
Even of the good is no memorial left.　　　(ll. 469–474)

And that is the burden of the story which follows. A family disinte-
grates; the wife, Margaret, abandoned by her husband, gradually loses
hope of his return, allows one of her children to leave her for a distant
farm, the other to fall ill and die. She herself finally dies, and her
cottage and its garden are now to be seen caught in the slow process
of wasting back into the landscape. Like Milton's story of the Flood,
the story of Margaret may be taken as an object lesson: the dead child,
the overgrown garden, the ruined cottage speak of the same losses that
Adam is made to feel as he learns that the Flood will sweep away his
descendants and his dwelling-place; and the play of Wordsworth's curios-
ity and grief against the wiser but not entirely impassive understanding
of the Wanderer recapitulates the dialogue of Adam and the Archangel.
There is even a Wordsworthian analogue of the redemptive process, for
it is suggested that Nature herself, the Nature that ministered to the
Wanderer as a child, is providentially overseeing this episode in human
history. But it is chiefly in the telling of the tale, in the rehearsal in
words of the truth of loss, that the poem asserts a saving continuity; the
pathos of Margaret's history is given additional depth and poignancy because it comes to us as a story within a story, and, just as in *Paradise Lost,*
a chain of mediations is established that brings the reader into the continuum, into the repetitive process by which reality is turned into truth.[9]

These structural and thematic resemblances would, in themselves, make
us suspect that Wordsworth had meditated on Milton's story of the
Flood. But they also can tell us more than that, for they point beyond
the similarities of these particular texts towards a clue to Milton's influence on Wordsworth and, possibly to the general nature of literary
influence. In this particular case, influence is best understood not by
picking up the echoes of specific bits of Milton's language or the re-
appearance of Miltonic themes, but by noticing the interrelation of theme
and structure, of the theme of loss and the structure of narrative. The
loss of human continuities is the burden of ordinary historical time; the
creation of another order of time, in which that loss is confronted and

---

[9] I am indebted to Geoffrey Hartman's discussion of "The Ruined Cottage" in
Wordsworth's Poetry 1787–1814 (New Haven, 1964), pp. 135–140, 302–306, and to his
remark *à propos* of "Michael" that "the poet is Michael's true heir" (p. 266). I should
also record the degree to which Hartman's article "Milton's Counterplot," *ELH*, xxv
(1958), 1–12, has encouraged me to read *Paradise Lost* xi as I do.

acknowledged, is the achievement of narrative. Taken singly, both the poetry of the Flood and "The Ruined Cottage" embody these truths; taken together, they exemplify the kind of continuity with which each is concerned. For the encounter of poet with poet is analogous to that of Michael with Adam, or of Milton with Adam, or of Wordsworth with the Wanderer.

I would like to close with one more quotation, this time not from the poetry but from Dorothy Wordsworth's *Journal*. It is intended to illustrate once again the nature of the influence we have been considering, by bringing the relation of poet to poet more closely in line with that of reader to poet. In the early months of 1802, Wordsworth was at work revising "The Ruined Cottage," which by that time he had taken to calling "The Pedlar." Here is part of Dorothy's entry for Tuesday, February 2nd:

> The sun shone but it was cold. After dinner William worked at *The Pedlar*. After tea I read aloud from the eleventh book of *Paradise Lost*. We were much impressed, and also melted into tears.[10]

For a moment, the two orders of time we have been considering—historical time and the narrative present—meet here as Wordsworth listens to *Paradise Lost*: the tears he wept that afternoon are the same tears that Adam weeps in Milton's poem.

[10] *Journals of Dorothy Wordsworth*, ed. E. de Selincourt (New York, 1941), I, 106.

The Ruined Cottage as Tragic Narrative

by Jonathan Wordsworth

The Ruined Cottage and *Michael* are both about the refusal to admit despair, but there is the important difference that positive hope is possible in the one and not the other. Michael's refusal shows itself in an acceptance of the hopelessness of his position, and an unrelenting continuation of the life he has always lived. Margaret, by contrast, increasingly lacks the will to keep up the routine of life, but never ceases to hope that Robert will return. It is in the moment of apparently total despair that one becomes aware of the greatness of Margaret's hope:

> Margaret stood near, her infant in her arms,
> And, seeing that my eye was on the tree,
> She said, "I fear it will be dead and gone
> Ere Robert come again."
>
> Towards the house
> Together we returned, and she inquired
> If I had any hope. But for her Babe,
> And for her little friendless Boy, she said,
> She had no wish to live—that she must die
> Of sorrow. Yet I saw the idle loom
> Still in its place. His sunday garments hung
> Upon the self-same nail, his very staff
> Stood undisturbed behind the door.   (ll. 423–34)

As before, there is the balancing of appearance and reality, but the positions are reversed. Where Margaret's state had been shown on the evidence of her garden to be worse than it seemed, now she herself appears utterly despairing, but the house belies her words. She may say that she is living only for the child, but her husband's things are still

where he would expect to find them. The point is reinforced by the speed
with which Wordsworth moves on to

> And when
> I passed this way beaten by Autumn winds,
> She told me that her little babe was dead
> And she was left alone.   (ll. 434–7)

The brief reference to autumn winds is the only reminder of the elaborate
transitions used to separate the Pedlar's earlier visits. The manuscript in
fact reads straight on with no more than a comma to divide the two
ideas, and mark the six months' gap:

> his very staff
> Stood undisturbed behind the door, and when
> I passed this way. . . .

The child for whom alone she wished to live is dead, and she lives on,
still hoping for Robert's return:

> That very time,
> I yet remember, through the miry lane
> She walked with me a mile, when the bare trees
> Trickled with foggy damps, and in such sort
> That any heart had ached to hear her, begged
> That wheresoe'er I went I still would ask
> For him whom she had lost.   (ll. 437–43)

The pace of the narrative has quickened. It is not only that there is no
longer time for the leisurely building up towards successive climaxes:
the garden-descriptions which formed the lulls between moments of dialogue are actually incompatible with the hope that Wordsworth now
wishes to stress. The garden at the beginning of the poem is gloomy—
"Within that cheerless spot . . ."—and as long as Margaret's story is
considered in purely human terms, its return to wildness can only record
the progress towards gloom.

   The Ruined Cottage as a whole is remarkable for the extent to which
Wordsworth has visualized the movements and positions of his characters. Again and again a brief reference to the setting intensifies one's
response:

> Margaret looked at me
> A little while, then turned her head away
> Speechless, and *sitting down upon a chair*
> Wept bitterly.   (ll. 247–50)

> "I perceive
> You look at me, and you have cause. . . ."   (ll. 347–8)

The last part of Margaret's story particularly depends on this technique. Up to this point Wordsworth has recorded the stages of her decline, but now his precise time-sequence is abandoned, and he talks instead of "*the* warm summer," "*the* long winter." [1] Five tedious years are evoked in a series of moving individual scenes: Margaret on her bench, her eye

> busy in the distance, shaping things
> Which made her heart beat quick.   (ll. 456–7)

Margaret spinning hemp, but stopping to ask soldiers and crippled sailors about Robert; Margaret standing to open the gate for horsemen so that she may ask "the same sad question"—if she dares; Margaret, "Last human tenant" of walls already ruined. She dies, still hoping, of sickness brought on by the decay of her cottage. On a conscious level she has "no wish to live," and though kept alive by torturing hope she cannot keep up the routine of survival, symbolized in Robert's closing up of chinks "At the first nippings of October frost." There is no question of despair, but hope is no longer the resilient optimism which enabled her to take up Robert's tools at the end of the Pedlar's first visit:

> And so she lived
> Through the long winter, reckless and alone,
> Till this reft house, by frost, and thaw, and rain,
> Was sapped; and when she slept, the nightly damps
> Did chill her breast, and in the stormy day
> Her tattered clothes were ruffled by the wind
> Even at the side of her own fire. Yet still
> She loved this wretched spot, nor would for worlds
> Have parted hence; and still that length of road,
> And this rude bench, one torturing hope endeared,
> Fast rooted at her heart. And here, my friend,
> In sickness she remained; and here she died,
> Last human tenant of these ruined walls.   (ll. 480–92)

It has been suggested that *The Ruined Cottage* ceases to be tragic when an optimistic conclusion is added. Lindenberger, for instance, compares it to Tate's version of *King Lear*:

> The additional lines, especially the image of the spear-grass and mist, are lovely in themselves and provide a cool, elegiac close to the stark tale narrated earlier; but we must also recognize that they (plus other additions to the pedlar's role) have created a new poem altogether and, above all, a poem of an entirely different genre, as different from the poem which

---

[1] There is bound to be awkwardness in referring to the narrative sequence of a poem where the end was written before the middle.

Coleridge first read in 1797 as the *King Lear* of Nahum Tate is from Shakespeare's tragedy.[2]

But it would be more to the point to say that Wordsworth first ended his *Lear*,

> "Why should a Dog, a Horse, a Rat have life,
> And thou no breath at all?"

then made it tolerable—though not retrospectively less terrible—by making Lear's heart "burst smilingly" ("She sleeps in the calm earth, and peace is here"), and settling the business of a return to normality (the Pedlar and Poet's exit to a rustic inn).

The whole question of Wordsworth's attitude to suffering at this period has recently been brought up by Cleanth Brooks, who cites as examples first *The Old Cumberland Beggar* and then *The Ruined Cottage*. But the two cases are radically different. Of the Cumberland Beggar's usefulness he writes:

> carrying out this function costs the old man something. The beggar serves, but he suffers in the process. How justify, for example, letting an old man walk the roads in all weathers? Here Wordsworth has been shockingly candid. In the very act of breathing a blessing on the beggar's head, the poet rather goes out of his way to express a wish that the beggar's blood should "Struggle with frosty air and winter snows," and adds:
>
> > let the chartered wind that sweeps the heath
> > Beat his gray locks against his withered face.[3]

In Wordsworthian terms the beggar does not suffer. His life may or may not seem attractive to modern readers, but the wind that sweeps the heath is "chartered" because it too is breathing a blessing on the old man's head. Wordsworth no more wishes suffering on him than he wishes it on his sister—"let the misty mountain-winds be free / To blow against thee . . ."—at the end of *Tintern Abbey*.[4]

The Ruined Cottage is very different. Margaret *does* suffer, and her suffering is presented as almost without relief. She too lives "in the eye

---

[2] *On Wordsworth's "Prelude,"* pp. 228–9. Cf. Edward E. Bostetter: "In affixing such a conclusion, Wordsworth has in effect repudiated the story as he has told it, denied the truth of his artistic experience." *The Romantic Ventriloquists* (Seattle, 1963), p. 65.

[3] "Wordsworth and Human Suffering: Notes on Two Early Poems," *From Sensibility to Romanticism, Essays Presented to Frederick A. Pottle,* ed. Frederick W. Hilles and Harold Bloom (New York, 1965), p. 377.

[4] Bostetter, *op. cit.,* p. 55, concedes Wordsworth's good intentions, but is indignant that "The beggar himself is not consulted or thought of as a man." Wordsworth is not interested as he should be in the social injustice of beggary, and his blessing on the old man is "a chilling prayer," "an illuminating example of selfish projection." But, like Brooks, he is surely upset by a suffering that is no part of the poem.

of Nature," but it is no comfort to her. Brooks puts the relevant questions:

> Is Wordsworth saying here that, seen in the full perspective of nature, seen as a portion of nature's beautiful and unwearied immortality, Margaret with her sorrows is simply one detail of an all-encompassing and harmonious pattern? One can, for example, look at the rabbit torn by the owl in something like this fashion, and the rabbit's agony, no longer isolated and dwelt upon in itself, may cease to trouble us when understood as a necessary part of a total pattern, rich and various and finally harmonious, in which even the rabbit's pain becomes not a meaningless horror since it partakes of the beauty of the whole.

Or does *The Ruined Cottage* anticipate

> what might be called the reconciliation of suffering in the aesthetic vision. . . . Man is so various, so wonderful, capable of so much triumph and agony, suffering and joy, malice and goodness, that if one can take his stance far enough away from the individual case to allow him to see life in its wholeness, with all its rich variety—if one can do that, he can accept not only suffering but active wickedness as an inevitable and necessary part of the human drama, and can even rejoice in it as a testimony to the depths of man's feeling and his power to experience and endure.[5]

The first position Brooks is unwilling to accept—"One shrinks from concluding that such an interpretation as this is Wordsworth's own; and I do not mean to do so"—but, attractive or otherwise, it must be largely right. To some extent the second point of view is implied in all tragic writing, and it is the basis of one's attitude during the main part of *The Ruined Cottage*; but the consolation offered at the end of the poem is clearly that Margaret is now part of a total pattern. It is not just that she is no longer "stretched" on the rack of this tough world: where Lear in conventional terms was "better" dead, she is positively *happier*.

Several things contribute to make this position tolerable. Perkins has written:

> as the narrator looks raptly at the grass, in the close of this story, the pathetic history of Margaret's life appears to him only as an "idle dream." The reader is supposed to quit the poem not with vibrant feelings of grief or protest, but with "meditative sympathies." . . .[6]

Perhaps this may be so. By the same token we are supposed to leave *The Mayor of Casterbridge* wondering with Elizabeth-Jane

> at the persistence of the unforeseen, when the one to whom such unbroken tranquillity had been accorded in the adult stage was she whose

---

[5] *Op. cit.* pp. 385–6.
[6] David Perkins, *Wordsworth and the Poetry of Sincerity* (Cambridge, Mass., 1964), p. 116.

youth had seemed to teach that happiness was but the occasional episode in a general drama of pain.[7]

But we don't. If it was Wordsworth's intention to show Margaret's life as in retrospect an "idle dream" he was fortunately very undogmatic about it. It is presented as the Pedlar's view—and one takes comfort from the fact that Margaret's pain *can* be so generalized—but the Poet, who has throughout been identified with the reader, does not specifically accept it. His acceptance is implied in the "slant and mellow radiance" which replaces the "thirsty heat" of the opening lines, just as peace is implied in the changing roles of the speargrass, but in neither case is a message forced on one. Nor are Brooks' analogies entirely justified. Margaret is not the rabbit harmoniously torn by the owl. In death she becomes, or can be seen as being, part of a total pattern; but her suffering is not retrospectively explained or condoned. Wordsworth does not suggest that the rabbit's pain is needful or meaningful. He offers a comforting personal view of death, or rather of the state of being dead. It is the mood which Dorothy Wordsworth describes in her *Journal* of April 1802:

> We then went to John's grove, sate a while at first. Afterwards William lay, and I lay, in the trench under the fence—he with his eyes shut, and listening to the waterfalls and the Birds. . . . William heard me breathing and rustling now and then, but we both lay still, and unseen by one another; he thought that it would be as sweet thus to lie so in the grave, to hear the *peaceful* sounds of the earth, and just to know that our dear friends were near.
>
> (*Journals*, p. 152—Dorothy's italics)

Margaret "sleeps" in the calm earth. The word is undeniably euphemism, and perhaps self-deception too on the part of the poet; but it is not felt to be either. The valid comparison in this case is *Lycidas*. Presumably few readers would take literally the thought of saints singing to Edward King, and drying his eyes for him—

> There entertain him all the Saints above,
> In solemn troops, and sweet societies,
> That sing, and singing in their glory move,
> And wipe the tears forever from his eyes.

—and yet the beauty of the lines is not diminished. One can if one chooses reduce them to the prose statement, "Edward King is in heaven"

[7] Cf. Edgar's fatuous final comment in *King Lear*:
> The oldest hath borne most, we that are young,
> Shall never see so much, nor live so long.

The tendency of tragic writers to stand back at the end and generalize in fact makes very little difference to the total effect of their work.

and say that one doubts it, or that it is no sufficient consolation for his friends; but to do so has no more relevance than Dr. Johnson's famous literal-minded remark: "We know that they never drove a field, and that they had no flocks to batten . . . ." The lines work within the context of the poem. And similarly in *The Ruined Cottage* one is *imaginatively* convinced that Margaret is at peace because she is part of a world whose beauty is the outward sign of its beneficence. It is an idea that has, as Wordsworth put it, "sufficient foundation in humanity." [8] That it is "untrue" has no importance unless it is felt to be so, and the power of the poetry ensures that it is not:

> She sleeps in the calm earth, and peace is here.
> I well remember that those very plumes,
> Those weeds, and the high spear-grass on that wall,
> By mist and silent rain-drops silvered o'er,
> As once I passed, did to my mind convey
> So still an image of tranquility,
> So calm and still, and looked so beautiful
> Amid the uneasy thoughts that filled my mind,
> That what we feel of sorrow and despair
> From ruin and from change, and all the grief
> The passing shews of being leave behind,
> Appeared an idle dream that could not live
> Where meditation was. I turned away
> And walked along my road in happiness.   (ll. 512–25)

The consolation that Wordsworth asks his readers to accept is not in fact on a very different level from the rest of the poem. The "retreat from 'uneasy thoughts,'" as Perkins points out, is achieved largely by "converting the events of Margaret's life into abstractions" ("sorrow and despair / From ruin and from change . . .").[9] These generalize, but they do not falsify, the story that has been told. Nor is Margaret herself depersonalized in a way that does violence to the earlier descriptions. Previously she has been seen as the rose that is pulled down, the appletree whose tender stem is nibbled round by truant sheep: now she becomes by implication the speargrass "silvered o'er" with mist and—in a curiously peaceful, evocative phrase—"*silent* raindrops." The full force of "passing *shews* of being" is certainly hard to accept, but the Pedlar's words are offered as personal experience, the description of a single occasion and a particular mood: "As *once* I passed did to my mind con-

---

[8] "I took hold of the notion of pre-existence as having sufficient foundation in humanity for authorising me to make for my purpose the best use of it I could as a Poet." (Note on the *Intimations Ode, Poetical Works,* ed. de Selincourt, IV, 464.)

[9] [*The Poetry of Sincerity,* p. 116—Ed.]

vey . . . ." Their effect is to distance Margaret's suffering, making bear-
able a story which in its original conclusion was too painful, too abrupt.
    But the poem does not end here. There is the last section, in which
Lycidas becomes not a parallel, but a positive influence:

> Thus sang the uncouth swain to th'oaks and rills,
> While the still morn went out with sandals gray;
> He touched the tender stops of various quills,
> With eager thought warbling his Doric lay:
> And now the sun had stretched out all the hills,
> And now was dropped into the western bay;
> At last he rose, and twitched his mantle blue:
> Tomorrow to fresh woods, and pastures new.   (ll. 186–993)

> He ceased. By this the sun declining shot
> A slant and mellow radiance, which began
> To fall upon us where beneath the trees
> We sate on that low bench. And now we felt,
> Admonished thus, the sweet hour coming on:
> A linnet warbled from those lofty elms,
> A thrush sang loud, and other melodies
> At distance heard, peopled the milder air.
> The old man rose and hoisted up his load,
> Together casting then a farewell look
> Upon those silent walls, we left the shade;
> And, ere the stars were visible, attained
> A rustic inn, our evening resting-place.   (ll. 526–38)

"The old man rose and hoisted up his load" sounds like parody when
placed too close to "At last he rose, and twitched his mantle blue," but
the correspondence between the two passages goes beyond mere verbal
echo. Wordsworth was reminded of *Lycidas* by the need to round his
poem off, and by genuine likeness of situation. His ending too says in
effect, "Tomorrow to fresh woods, and pastures new." In *Lycidas*, however, the final passage stands outside the dramatic framework of the
poem—it is the only place where the writer speaks in his own voice—
whereas the last lines of *The Ruined Cottage* are a culmination of what
has gone before. At the beginning of the poem the Poet and Pedlar enter
separately, with their separate attitudes: at the end they go off together,
their differences resolved through their shared response to the story that
is told. At the beginning of the poem the Poet toils through the sun
"with thirsty heat oppressed," the Pedlar sleeps contentedly his face
dappled by shadows from the "breezy elms above": at the end both
equally are *admonished* by the "slant and mellow radiance." The word
is important. In the central stanza of *The Leech Gatherer* the old man is

said to be "like a man from some far region sent" to give the poet "human strength *by apt admonishment*," but in *The Ruined Cottage* strength comes from being in harmony with one's surroundings, not from quasi-supernatural interventions. At the end of the poem the Poet and Pedlar are at peace with the world into which Margaret has been absorbed. The pattern is complete.

There seem to be two forms of tragedy—or at least two extremes—the fight against odds (*The Agamemnon, Beowulf*, perhaps *The Mayor of Casterbridge*) and the tragedy of waste (*Othello, Lear, Clarissa, Tess of the D'Urbervilles*). The first is moving because despite human dignity happiness is known to be impossible, the second precisely because one feels that happiness *was* possible, though in fact prevented by circumstance. In a curious way *The Ruined Cottage* unites the two. Margaret's story opens with her death, is told among the ruins where she died. She herself doesn't know that Robert will not return, but the reader does. Her suffering from the first is known to be pointless, her courage futile; and this constant awareness creates much that is beautiful in the poem. But fated tragedy is the lesser form, and Margaret's hope is moving not merely in its emptiness. In it one sees the power of her love. *The Ruined Cottage* shows a relationship pointlessly destroyed, a relationship which one is convinced could have made for great happiness. Angel Clare sleepwalks with Tess in his arms because he cannot accept her awake, Desdemona dies trying to shield Othello—

> *Emilia*
> Oh who hath done this deed?
>
> *Desdemona*
> No body: I my selfe, farewell:
> Commend me to my kinde Lord:

—Lovelace rides impotently by the house where Clarissa is dying; Margaret's love is less dramatic, but the force which makes her go on living, go on hoping as she grows weaker and more and more intellectually certain that Robert will not return, is no less tragic.

In the last resort literary criticism is personal: one has to fall back on "This moves me," "This doesn't." [10] Coleridge said that he had never read *The Brothers* with "an unclouded eye," but described *The Ruined Cottage* as "the finest poem in our language, comparing it with any of the same or similar *length*." Myself I find *The Brothers* deeply moving, *Michael* much more so, while *The Ruined Cottage* moves me as I am

---

[10] "I may be wrong, but I speak as I felt, and the most profitable criticism is the record of sensations. . . ." Wordsworth to J. H. Reynolds, November 1816 ([*Letters: The Middle Years*], p. 759). For a more fashionable view, see W. K. Wimsatt Jr., "The Affective Fallacy," *The Verbal Icon* (Lexington, 1954).

moved by only one other poem, the medieval Scottish *Testament of Cresseid,* by two plays (*Lear* and *Othello*), and by a handful of novels. F. R. Leavis has stated categorically that it is Wordsworth's finest poem; but it is difficult to find standards of comparison. Perhaps one has to fall back on saying that in its idiom it is as great as are *The Prelude* and the *Ode* in theirs. It shows in Wordsworth a humanity, an insight into emotions not his own, that is wholly convincing—places him, perhaps unexpectedly, among the very few great English tragic writers.

Intentional Structure of the Romantic Image

by Paul de Man

In the history of Western literature, the importance of the image as a dimension of poetic language does not remain constant. One could conceive of an organization of this history in terms of the relative prominence and the changing structure of metaphor. French poetry of the sixteenth century is obviously richer and more varied in images than that of the seventeenth, and medieval poetry of the fifteenth century has a different kind of imagery than that of the thirteenth. The most recent change remote enough to be part of history takes place towards the end of the eighteenth century and coincides with the advent of romanticism. In a statement of which equivalences can be found in all European literatures, Wordsworth reproaches Pope for having abandoned the imaginative use of figural diction in favor of a merely decorative allegorization. Meanwhile the term *imagination* steadily grows in importance and complexity, in the critical as well as in the poetic texts of the period. This evolution in poetic terminology—of which parallel instances could easily be found in France and in Germany—corresponds to a profound change in the texture of poetic diction. The change often takes the form of a return to a greater concreteness, a proliferation of natural objects that restores to the language the material substantially which had been partially lost. At the same time, in accordance with a dialectic that is more paradoxical than may appear at first sight, the structure of the language becomes increasingly metaphorical and the image—be it under the name of symbol or even of myth—comes to be considered as the most prominent dimension of the style. This tendency is still prevalent today, among poets as well as among critics. We find it quite natural that theoretical studies such as, for example, those of Gaston Bachelard in France, of Northrop Frye in America, or of William Empson in England should take the metaphor as their starting point for an investigation of literature in general—an approach that would have been inconceivable for Boileau, for Pope, and even still for Diderot.

An abundant imagery coinciding with an equally abundant quantity of natural objects, the theme of imagination linked closely to the theme of nature, such is the fundamental ambiguity that characterizes the poetics of romanticism. The tension between the two polarities never ceases to be problematic. We shall try to illustrate the structure of this latent tension as it appears in some selected poetic passages.

In a famous poem, Hölderlin speaks of a time at which "the gods" will again be an actual presence to man:

> . . . nun aber nennt er sein Liebstes
> Nun, nun müssen dafür Worte, wie Blumen entstehn.
> ("Brot und Wein," stanza 5)

Taken by itself, this passage is not necessarily a statement about the image: Hölderlin merely speaks of words *("Worte")*, not of images *("Bilder")*. But the lines themselves contain the image of the flower in the simplest and most explicit of all metaphorical structures, as a straightforward simile introduced by the conjunction *wie*. That the words referred to are not those of ordinary speech is clear from the verb: to originate ("entstehn"). In everyday use words are exchanges and put to a variety of tasks, but they are not supposed to originate anew; on the contrary, one wants them to be as well known, as "common" as possible, to make certain that they will obtain for us what we want to obtain. They are used as established signs to confirm that something is recognized as being the same as before; and re-cognition excludes pure origination. But in poetic language words are not used as signs, not even as names, but in order *to name:* "Donner un sens plus pur aux mots de la tribu" (Mallarmé) or "erfand er für die Dinge eigene Nahmen" (Stefan George): poets know of the act of naming—"nun aber *nennt* er sein Liebstes"— as implying a return to the source, to the pure motion of experience at its beginning.

The word "entstehn" establishes another fundamental distinction. The two terms of the simile are not said to be identical with one another (the word = the flower), nor analogous in their general mode of being (the word is like the flower), but specifically in the way they originate (the word originates like the flower).[1] The similarity between the two terms does not reside in their essence (identity), or in their appearance (anal-

---

[1] The line is ambiguous, depending on whether one gives the verb "entstehn" a single or a double subject. It can mean: words will originate that are like flowers ("Worte, die wie Blumen sind, müssen dafür entstehn"). But the meaning is much richer if one reads it: words will have to originate in the same way that flowers originate ("Worte müssen dafür entstehn wie Blumen entstehn"). Syntax and punctuation allow for both readings.

ogy), but in the manner in which both originate. And Hölderlin is not speaking of any poetic word taken at random, but of an authentic word that fulfills its highest function in naming being as a presence. We could infer, then, that the fundamental intent of the poetic word is to originate in the same manner as what Hölderlin here calls "flowers." The image is essentially a kinetic process: it does not dwell in a static state where the two terms could be separated and reunited by analysis; the first term of the simile (here, "words") has no independent existence, poetically speaking, prior to the metaphorical statement. It originates with the statement, in the manner suggested by the flower-image, and its way of being is determined by the manner in which it originates. The metaphor requires that we begin by forgetting all we have previously known about "words"—"donner un sens plus pur aux mots de la tribu"—and then informing the term with a dynamic existence similar to that which animates the "flowers." The metaphor is not a combination of two entities or experiences more or less deliberately linked together, but one single and particular experience: that of origination.

How do flowers originate? They rise out of the earth without the assistance of imitation or analogy. They do not follow a model other than themselves which they copy or from which they derive the pattern of their growth. By calling them *natural* objects, we mean that their origin is determined by nothing but their own being. Their becoming coincides at all times with the mode of their origination: it is as flowers that their history is what it is, totally defined by their identity. There is no wavering in the status of their existence: existence and essence coincide in them at all times. Unlike words, which originate like something else ("like flowers"), flowers originate like themselves: they are literally what they are, definable without the assistance of metaphor. It would follow then, since the intent of the poetic word is to originate like the flower, that it strives to banish all metaphor, to become entirely literal.

We can understand origin only in terms of difference: the source springs up because of the need to be somewhere or something else than what is now here. The word "entstehn," with its distancing prefix, equates origin with negation and difference. But the natural object, safe in its immediate being, seems to have no beginning and no end. Its permanence is carried by the stability of its being, whereas a beginning implies a negation of permanence, the discontinuity of a death in which an entity relinquishes its specificity and leaves it behind, like an empty shell. Entities engendered by consciousness originate in this fashion, but for natural entities like the flower, the process is entirely different. They originate out of a being which does not differ from them in essence but contains the totality of their individual manifestations within itself. All particular flowers can at all times establish an immediate identity with an original Flower, of which they are as many particular emanations.

The original entity, which has to contain an infinity of manifestations of a common essence, in an infinity of places and at an infinity of moments, is necessarily transcendental. Trying to conceive of the natural object in terms of origin leads to a transcendental concept of the Idea: the quest for the Idea that takes the natural object for its starting-point begins with the incarnated "minute particular" and works its way upwards to a transcendental essence. Beyond the Idea, it searches for Being as the category which contains essences in the same manner that the Idea contains particulars. Because they are natural objects, flowers originate as incarnations of a transcendental principle. "Wie Blumen entstehn" is to become present as a natural emanation of a transcendental principle, as an epiphany.

Strictly speaking, an epiphany cannot be a beginning, since it reveals and unveils what, by definition, could never have ceased to be there. Rather, it is the rediscovery of a permanent presence which has chosen to hide itself from us—unless it is we who have the power to hide from it:

> So ist der Mensch; wenn da ist das Gut und es sorget mitgaben
> Selber ein Gott für ihn, kennet und sieht er es nicht.
>
> ("Brot und Wein," stanza 5)

Since the presence of a transcendental principle, in fact conceived as omnipresence (parousia), can be hidden from man by man's own volition, the epiphany appears in the guise of a beginning rather than a discovery. Hölderlin's phrase: "Wie Blumen entstehn" is in fact a paradox, since origination is inconceivable on the ontological level; the ease with which we nevertheless accept it is indicative of our desire to forget. Our eagerness to accept the statement, the "beauty" of the line, stems from the fact that it combines the poetic seduction of beginnings contained in the word "entstehn" with the ontological stability of the natural object—but this combination is made possible only by a deliberate forgetting of the transcendental nature of the source.

That this forgetting, this ignorance, is also painful becomes apparent from the strategic choice of the word "flower," an object that seems intrinsically desirable. The effect of the line would have been thoroughly modified if Hölderlin had written, for instance, "Steinen" instead of "Blumen," although the relevance of the comparison would have remained intact as long as human language was being compared to a natural thing. The obviously desirable sensory aspects of the flower express the ambivalent aspiration towards a forgotten presence that gave rise to the image, for it is in experiencing the material presence of the particular flower that the desire arises to be reborn in the manner of a natural creation. The image is inspired by a nostalgia for the natural object, expanding to become nostalgia for the origin of this object. Such a nostalgia can only exist when the transcendental presence is forgotten, as in the "dürftiger Zeit" of Hölderlin's poem which we are all too eager to circumscribe as if it were a specific historical "time" and not Time in general. The existence of the poetic image is itself a sign of divine absence, and the conscious use of poetic imagery an admission of this absence.

It is clear that, in Hölderlin's own line, the words do *not* originate like flowers. They need to find the mode of their beginning in another entity; they originate out of nothing, in an attempt to be the first words that will arise as if they were natural objects, and, as such, they remain essentially distinct from natural entities. Hölderlin's statement is a perfect definition of what we call a natural image: the word that designates a desire for an epiphany but necessarily fails to be an epiphany, because it is pure origination. For it is in the essence of language to be capable of origination, but of never achieving the absolute identity with itself that exists in the natural object. Poetic language can do nothing but originate anew over and over again: it is always constitutive, able to posit regardless of presence but, by the same token, unable to give a foundation to what it posits except as an intent of consciousness. The word is always a free presence to the mind, the means by which the permanence of natural entities can be put into question and thus negated, time and again, in the endlessly widening spiral of the dialectic.

An image of this type is indeed the simplest and most fundamental we can conceive of, the metaphorical expression most apt to gain our immediate acquiescence. During the long development that takes place in the nineteenth century, the poetic image remains predominantly of the same kind that in the Hölderlin passage we took for our starting-point—and which, be it said in passing, far from exhausts Hölderlin's own conception of the poetic image. This type of imagery is grounded in the intrinsic ontological primacy of the natural object. Poetic language seems to originate in the desire to draw closer and closer to the ontological status of the object, and its growth and development are determined by this inclination. We saw that this movement is essentially paradoxical and condemned in advance to failure. There can be flowers that "are" and poetic words that "originate," but no poetic words that "originate" as if they "were."

Nineteenth century poetry reexperiences and represents the adventure of this failure in an infinite variety of forms and versions. It selects, for example, a variety of archetypal myths to serve as the dramatic pattern for the narration of this failure; a useful study could be made of the romantic and post-romantic versions of Hellenic myths such as the stories of Narcissus, of Prometheus, of the War of the Titans, of Adonis, Eros and Psyche, Proserpine, and many others; in each case, the tension and duality inherent in the mythological situation would be found to reflect the inherent tension that resides in the metaphorical language itself. At times, romantic thought and romantic poetry seem to come so close to giving in completely to the nostalgia for the object that it becomes difficult to distinguish between object and image, between imagination and perception, between an expressive or constitutive and a mimetic or literal language. This may well be the case in some passages of Wordsworth and Goethe, of Baudelaire and Rimbaud, where the vision almost seems to become a real landscape. Poetics of "unmediated vision," such as those implicit in Bergson and explicit in Bachelard, fuse matter and imagination by amalgamating perception and reverie, sacrificing, in fact, the demands of consciousness to the realities of the object. Critics who speak of a "happy relationship" between matter and consciousness fail to realize that the very fact that the relationship has to be established within the medium of language indicates that it does not exist in actuality.

At other times, the poet's loyalty towards his language appears so strongly that the object nearly vanishes under the impact of his words, in what Mallarmé called "sa presque disparition vibratoire." But even in as extreme a case as Mallarmé's, it would be a mistake to assume that the ontological priority of the object is being challenged. Mallarmé may well be the nineteenth century poet who went further than any other in sacrificing the stability of the object to the demands of a lucid poetic awareness. Even some of his own disciples felt they had to react against him by reasserting the positivity of live and material substances against the annihilating power of his thought. Believing themselves to be in a situation where they had to begin their work at the point where Mallarmé had finished his, they took, like Claudel, the precise counterpart of his attitudes or, like Valéry, reversed systematically the meaning of some of his key-images. Yet Mallarmé himself had always remained convinced of the essential priority of the natural object. The final image of his work, in *Un Coup de Dés*, is that of the poet drowned in the ubiquitous "sea" of natural substances against which his mind can only wage a meaningless battle, "tenter une chance oiseuse." It is true that, in Mallarmé's thought, the value-emphasis of this priority has been reversed and the triumph of nature is being presented as the downfall of poetic defiance. But this does not alter the fundamental situation. The alternating feeling of attraction and repulsion that the romantic poet experiences towards nature becomes in Mallarmé the conscious dialectic of a reflective poetic consciousness. This dialectic, far from challenging the supremacy of the order of nature, in fact reasserts it at all times. "Nous savons, victimes d'une formule absolue, que certes n'est que ce qui est," writes Mallarmé, and this absolute identity is rooted, for him, in "la première en date, la nature. Idée tangible pour intimer quelque réalité aux sens frustes. . . ."

Mallarmé's conception and use of imagery is entirely in agreement with this principle. His key-symbols—sea, winged bird, night, the sun, constellations, and many others—are not primarily literary emblems but are taken, as he says, "au répertoire de la nature"; they receive their meaning and function from the fact that they belong initially to the natural world. In the poetry, they may seem disincarnate to the point of abstraction, generalized to the point of becoming pure ideas, yet they never entirely lose contact with the concrete reality from which they spring. The sea, the bird, and the constellation act and seduce in Mallarmé's poetry, like any earthly sea, bird, or star in nature; even the Platonic "oiseau qu'on n'ouit jamais" still has about it some of the warmth of the nest in which it was born. Mallarmé does not linger over the concrete and material details of his images, but he never ceases to interrogate, by means of a conscious poetic language, the natural world of which they are originally a part—while knowing that he could never reduce any part of this world to his own, conscious mode of being. If this is true of Mallarmé, the most self-conscious and anti-natural poet of the nineteenth century, it seems safe to assert that the priority of the natural object remains unchallenged among the inheritors of romanticism. The detailed study of Mallarmé bears this out; the same is true, with various nuances and reservations, of most Victorian and post-Victorian poets. For most of them, as for Mallarmé, the priority of nature is experienced as a feeling of failure and sterility, but nevertheless asserted. A similar feeling of threatening paralysis prevails among our own contemporaries and seems to grow with the depth of their poetic commitment. It may be that this threat could only be overcome when the status of poetic language or, more restrictively, of the poetic image, is again brought into question.

The direction that such a reconsideration might take can better be anticipated by a reading of the precursors of romanticism than by the study of its inheritors. Assumptions that are irrevocably taken for granted in the course of the nineteenth century still appear, at an earlier date, as one among several alternative roads. This is why an effort to understand the present predicament of the poetic imagination takes us back to writers that belong to the earlier phases of romanticism such as, for example, Rousseau. The affinity of later poets with Rousseau—which can well be considered to be a valid definition of romanticism as a whole—can, in turn, be best understood in terms of their use and underlying conception of imagery. The juxtaposition of three famous passages can serve as an illustration of this point and suggest further developments.

The three passages we have selected each represent a moment of spiritual revelation; the use of semi-religious, "sacred," or outspokenly sublime language in all three makes this unquestionably clear. Rousseau is probably the only one to have some awareness of the literary tradition that stands behind the topos: his reference to Petrarch (*La Nouvelle Héloise*, Part I, XXIII) suggests the all-important link with the Augustinian lesson contained in Petrarch's letter narrating his ascent of Mont Ventoux. A similar experience, in a more Northern Alpine setting, is related in the three passages. The Rousseau text is taken from the letter in *La Nouvelle Héloise* in which Saint-Preux reports on his sojourn in the Valais:

> Ce n'était pas seulement le travail des hommes qui rendait ces pays étranges si bizarrement contrastés; la nature semblait encore prendre plaisir à s'y mettre en opposition avec elle-même, tant on la trouvait différente en un même lieu sous divers aspects. Au levant les fleurs du printemps, au midi les fruits de l'automne, au nord les glaces de l'hiver: elle réunissait toutes les saisons dans le même instant, tous les climats dans le même lieu, des terrains contraires sur le même sol, et formait l'accord inconnu partout ailleurs des productions des plaines et de celles des Alpes. . . . J'arrivai ce jour là sur des montagnes les moins élevées, et, parcourant ensuite leurs inégalités, sur celles des plus hautes qui étaient à ma portée. Après m'être promené dans les nuages, j'atteignis un séjour plus serein, d'ou l'on voit dans la saison le tonerre et l'orage se former au-dessous de soi; image trop vaine de l'âme du sage, dont l'exemple n'exista jamais, ou n'existe qu'aux mêmes lieux d'où l'on en a tiré l'emblême.
>
> Ce fut là que je démêlai sensiblement dans la pureté de l'air où je me trouvais la véritable cause du changement de mon humeur, et du retour de cette paix intérieure que j'avais perdue depuis si longtemps. En effet, c'est une impression générale qu'éprouvent tous les hommes, quoiqu'ils ne l'observent pas tous, que sur les hautes montagnes, où l'air est pur et subtil, on se sent plus de facilité dans la respiration, plus de légèreté dans le corps, plus de sérénité dans l'esprit; les plaisirs y sont moins ardents, les passions plus modérées. Les méditations y prennent je ne sais quel caractère grand et sublime, proportionné aux objets qui nous frappent, je ne sais quelle volupté tranquille qui n'a rien d'âcre et de sensuel. Il semble qu'en s'élévant au-dessus du séjour des hommes on y laisse des sentiments bas et terrestres, et qu'à mesure qu'on approche des régions éthérées, l'âme contracte quelquechose de leur inaltérable pureté. On y est grave sans mélancolie, paisible sans indolence, content d'être et de penser. . . . Imaginez la variété, la grandeur, la beauté de mille étonnants spectacles; le plaisir de ne voir autour de soi que des objets tout nouveaux, des oiseaux étranges, des plantes bizarres et inconnues, d'observer en quelque sorte une autre nature, et de se trouver dans un nouveau monde. Tout cela fait aux yeux un mélange inexprimable, dont le charme augmente encore par la subtilité de l'air qui rend les couleurs plus vives, les traits plus marqués, rapproche tous les points de vue; les distances paraissent moindres que dans les plaines, où l'épaisseur de l'air couvre la terre d'un voile, l'horizon présente aux yeux plus d'objets qu'il semble n'en pouvoir contenir: enfin le spectacle a je ne sais quoi de magique, de surnaturel, qui ravit l'esprit et les sens; on oublie tout, on s'oublie soi-même, on ne sait plus où l'on est. . . .

Wordsworth's text is taken from Book VI of *The Prelude* and describes the poet's impressions in crossing the Alps, after having taken part in one of the celebrations that mark the triumph of the French Revolution. Wordsworth begins by praying for the safeguard of the Convent of the Grande Chartreuse, threatened with destruction at the hands of the insurrection; his prayer is first aimed at God, then "for humbler claim" at nature:

> . . . and for humbler claim
> Of that imaginative impulse sent
> From these majestic floods, yon shining cliffs,
> The untransmuted shapes of many worlds,
> Cerulean ether's pure inhabitants,
> These forests unapproachable by death,
> That shall endure as long as man endures,
> To think, to hope, to worship, and to feel,
> To struggle, to be lost within himself
> In trepidation, from the blank abyss
> To look with bodily eyes, and be consoled.
>
> *(The Prelude,* 1850 ed., VI, 461–471)

Somewhat later in the same section, Wordsworth describes the descent of the Simplon pass:

> . . . The immeasurable height
> Of woods decaying, never to be decayed,
> The stationary blasts of waterfalls,
> And in the narrow rent at every turn
> Winds thwarting winds, bewildered and forlorn,
> The torrents shooting from the clear blue sky,
> The rocks that muttered close upon our ears,
> Black drizzling crags that spake by the way-side
> As if a voice were in them, the sick sight
> And giddy prospect of the raving stream,
> The unfettered clouds and region of the Heavens,
> Tumult and peace, the darkness and the light--
> Were all like workings of one mind, the features
> Of the same face, blossoms upon one tree;
> Characters of the great Apocalypse,
> The types and symbols of Eternity,
> Of first, and last, and midst, and without end.
>
> *(The Prelude,* VI, 624–640)

Hölderlin's poem "Heimkunft" begins by the description of a sunrise in the mountains, observed by the poet on his return from Switzerland to his native Swabia:

> Drin in den Alpen ists noch helle Nacht und die Wolke,
> Freudiges dichtend, sie deckt drinnen das gähnende Tal.

Dahin, dorthin toset und stürzt die scherzende Bergluft,
Schroff durch Tannen herab glänzet und schwindet ein Strahl.
Langsam eilt und kämpft das freudigschauernde Chaos,
Jung an Gestalt, doch stark, feiert es liebenden Streit
Unter den Felsen, es gärt und wankt in den ewigen Schranken,
Denn bacchantischer zieht drinnen der Morgen herauf.
Denn es wächst unendlicher dort das Jahr und die heilgen
Stunden, die Tage, sie sind kühner geordenet, gemischt.
Dennoch merket die Zeit der Gewittervogel und zwischen
Bergen, hoch in der Luft weilt er und rufet den Tag.
. . . .
Ruhig glänzen indes die silbernen Höhen draüber,
Voll mit Rosen ist schon droben der leuchtende Schnee.
Und noch höher hinauf wohnt über dem Lichte der reine
Selige Gott vom Speil heiliger Strahlen erfreut.
Stille wohnt er allein, und hell erscheinet sein Antlitz,
Der ätherische scheint Leben zu geben geneigt. . . .
("Heimkunft," st. I and II)

Each of these texts describes the passage from a certain type of nature, earthly and material, to another nature which could be called mental and celestial, although the "Heaven" referred to is devoid of specific theological connotations. The common characteristic that concerns us most becomes apparent in the mixed, transitional type of landscape from which the three poets start out. The setting of each scene is located somewhere between the inaccessible mountain peaks and the humanized world of the plains; it is a deeply divided and paradoxical nature that, in Rousseau's terms, "seems to take pleasure in self-opposition." Radical contradictions abound in each of the passages. Rousseau deliberately mixes and blurs the order of the seasons and the laws of geography. The more condensed, less narrative diction of Wordsworth transposes similar contradictions into the complexity of a language that unites irreconcilable opposites; he creates a disorder so far-reaching that the respective position of heaven and earth are reversed: ". . . woods decaying, never to be decayed . . . ," ". . . torrents shooting from the sky . . . ," ". . . the stationary blasts of waterfalls. . . ." Hölderlin's text also is particularly rich in oxymorons; every word-combination, every motion expresses a contradiction: "helle Nacht," "langsam eilt," "liebende Streit," "toset und stürzt," "geordnet, gemischt," "freudigschauernd," etc. One feels everywhere the pressure of an inner tension at the core of all earthly objects, powerful enough to bring them to explosion.

The violence of this turmoil is finally appeased by the ascending movement recorded in each of the texts, the movement by means of which the poetic imagination tears itself away, as it were, from a terrestrial nature and moves towards this "other nature" mentioned by Rousseau, associated with the diaphanous, limpid and immaterial quality of a light that dwells nearer to the skies. Gaston Bachelard has described similar images of levitation very well, but he may not have stressed sufficiently that these rêveries of flight not only express a desire to escape from earthbound matter, to be relieved for a moment from the weight of gravity, but that they uncover a fundamentally new kind of relationship between nature and consciousness; it is significant, in this respect, that Bachelard classifies images of repose with earth and not with air, contrary to what happens in the three selected texts. The transparency of air represents the perfect fluidity of a mode of being that has moved beyond the power of earthly things and now dwells, like the God in Hölderlin's "Heimkunft," higher even than light ("über dem Lichte"). Like the clouds described by Wordsworth, the poets become "Cerulean ether's pure inhabitants." Unlike Mallarmé's "azur" or even the constellation at the end of *Un Coup de Dés* which are always seen from the point of view of the earth by a man about to sink away, their language has itself become a celestial entity, an inhabitant of the sky. Instead of being, like the "flower" in Hölderlin's "Brot und Wein," the fruit of the earth, the poetic word has become an offspring of the sky. The ontological priority, housed at first in the earthly and pastoral "flower," has been transposed into an entity that could still, if one wishes, be called "nature," but could no longer be equated with matter, objects, earth, stones, or flowers. The nostalgia for the object has become a nostalgia for an entity that could never, by its very nature, become a particularized presence.

The passages describe the ascent of a consciousness trapped within the contradictions of a half-earthly, half-heavenly nature "qui semblait prendre plaisir à (se) mettre en opposition avec elle-même," towards another level of consciousness, that has recovered "cette paix intérieure . . . perdue depuis si longtemps." (It goes without saying that the sequel of the three works from which the passages have been taken indicate that this tranquillity is far from having been definitively reconquered. Yet the existence of this moment of peace in *La Nouvelle Héloïse*, in *The Prelude*, and in the poem "Heimkunft"—"*Ruhig* glänzen indes die silbernen Höhen darüber . . ."—determines the fate of the respective authors and marks it as being an essentially poetic destiny.) In the course of this movement, in a passage that comes between the two descriptions we have cited, Wordsworth praises the faculty that gives him access to this new insight, and he calls this faculty "Imagination":

> Imagination! lifting up itself
> Before the eye and progress of my Song
> Like an unfather'd vapour; . . .
>   . . . in such strength

Of usurpation, in such visitings
Of awful promise, when the light of sense
Goes out in flashes that have shewn to us
The invisible world, doth Greatness make abode,

. . . .

The mind beneath such banners militant
Thinks not of spoils or trophies, nor of aught
That may attest its prowess, blest in thoughts
That are their own perfection and reward,
Strong in itself, and in the access of joy
Which hides it like the overflowing Nile.
                (*The Prelude*, 1805 ed., VI, 525–548)

But this "imagination" has little in common with the faculty that produces natural images born "as flowers originate." It marks instead a possibility for consciousness to exist entirely by and for itself, independently of all relationship with the outside world, without being moved by an intent aimed at a part of this world. Rousseau stressed that there was nothing sensuous ("rien d'âcre et de sensuel") in Saint-Preux's moment of illumination; Wordsworth, who goes so far as to designate the earth by the astonishing periphrase of "blank abyss," insists that the imagination can only come into full play when "the light of sense goes out" and when thought reaches a point at which it is "its own perfection and reward"—as when Rousseau, in the Fifth *Rêverie,* declares himself "content d'être" and "ne jouissant de rien d'extérieur à soi, de rien sinon de soi-même et de sa propre existence."

We know very little about the kind of images that such an imagination would produce, except that they would have little in common with what we have come to expect from familiar metaphorical figures. The works of the early romantics give us no actual examples, for they are, at most, *underway* towards renewed insights and inhabit the mixed and self-contradictory regions that we encountered in the three passages. Nor has their attempt been rightly interpreted by those who came after them, for literary history has generally labeled "primitivist," "naturalistic," or even pantheistic the first modern writers to have put into question, in the language of poetry, the ontological priority of the sensory object. We are only beginning to understand how this oscillation in the status of the image is linked to the crisis that leaves the poetry of today under a steady threat of extinction, although, on the other hand, it remains the depository of hopes that no other activity of the mind seems able to offer.

The Via Naturaliter Negativa

by Geoffrey H. Hartman

Many readers have felt that Wordsworth's poetry honors and even worships nature. In this they have the support of Blake, a man so sensitive to any trace of "Natural Religion" that he is said to have blamed some verses of Wordsworth's for a bowel complaint which almost killed him.[1] Scholarship, luckily, tempers the affections, and the majority of readers have emphasized the poet's progression from nature worship or even pantheism to a highly qualified form of natural religion, with increasing awareness of the "ennobling interchange" between mind and nature and a late yielding of primacy to the activity of the mind or the idealizing power of imagination. A very small group, finally, has pointed to the deeply paradoxical character of Wordsworth's dealings with nature and suggested that what he calls imagination may be *intrinsically* opposed to nature. This last and rarest position seems to me closest to the truth, yet I do not feel it conflicts totally with more traditional readings stressing the poet's adherence to nature. It can be shown, via several important episodes of *The Prelude*, that Wordsworth thought nature itself led him beyond nature; and, since this movement of transcendence, related to what mystics have called the negative way, is inherent in life and achieved without violent or ascetic discipline, one can think of it as the progress of a soul which is *naturaliter negativa.*

I

The Prelude opens with a success immediately followed by a failure. Released from the "vast city" and anticipating a new freedom, the poet pours out a rush of fifty lines: "poetic numbers came / Spontaneously

"The Via Naturaliter Negativa." From Geoffrey Hartman, *Wordsworth's Poetry, 1787–1814* (New Haven: Yale University Press, 1964). Copyright © 1964 by Yale University. Reprinted by permission of the publisher and the author. This selection is chapter 2, sections 1–3.

[1] See *Blake, Coleridge, Wordsworth, Lamb, etc., Being Selections from the Remains of Henry Crabb Robinson*, ed. E. J. Morley (Manchester, 1932), pp. 5 and 15.

to clothe in priestly robe / A renovated spirit" (I.51–53).[2] Here is the consecration, the promise of poetry as a sacrament, a gift efficacious beyond the moment. Why should a chance inspiration assume such significance? The reason is that Wordsworth was not used to make "A present joy the matter of a song"; yet here, apparently, is evidence that he may soon become self-creative, or need no more than a "gentle breeze" (the untraditional muse of the epic's opening) to produce a tempest of poetry. "Matins and vespers of harmonious verse!" is the hope held out to him, and having punctually performed matins the poet is content to slacken, to be gradually calmed by the clear autumn afternoon.

He meditates beneath a tree on a great poetic work soon to be begun. The sun sets, and city smoke is "ruralised" by distance. He starts to continue his journey, but now it is clearly time for vespers:

> It was a splendid evening, and my soul
> Once more made trial of her strength, nor lacked
> Aeolian visitations.   (I.94–96)

An outside splendor challenges the creative mind. Is the poet strong enough to answer it spontaneously, as if he needed only a suggestion, the first chord?

> but the harp
> Was soon defrauded, and the banded host
> Of harmony dispersed in straggling sounds,
> And lastly utter silence! "Be it so;
> Why think of any thing but present good?"   (I.96–100)

Wordsworth once again sees present good, like present joy, strangely opposed to the quickening of verse. The poetic outburst which he had considered a religious thing ("punctual service high . . . holy services") is now disdained as profane and *servile:*

> So, like a home-bound labourer I pursued
> My way beneath the mellowing sun, that shed
> Mild influence; nor left in me one wish
> Again to bend the Sabbath of that time
> To a servile yoke.   (I.101–05)

His reversal of mood is surprisingly complete. One who, at the impassioned outset of his reflections, had been so sure of the freely creative, autonomous nature of his poetic soul that famous passages on the eman-

---

*. . . Quotations from *The Prelude* . . . are from the 1850 text. . . .

cipated spirit—from *Paradise Lost* and Exodus[3]—swell the current of his verse, while he thinks to possess total freedom of choice,

> now free,
> Free as a bird to settle where I will   (I.8–9)

that same person now writes of himself, with a slight echo of Gray's *Elegy:*

> So, like a home-bound labourer I pursued
> My way.

The meaning of the reversal is not immediately clear. It does not deject the poet; it endows him, on the contrary, with a Chaucerian kind of cheer and leisure:

> What need of many words?
> A pleasant loitering journey, through three days
> Continued, brought me to my hermitage.
> I spare to tell of what ensued, the life
> In common things—the endless store of things.   (I.105–09)

The form of the reversal is that of a return to nature, at least to its rhythm. For the moment no haste remains, no tempest, no impatience of spirit. It is the mood of the hawthorn shade, of a portion of Wordsworth's Cambridge days, when he laughed with Chaucer and heard him, while birds sang, tell tales of love (III.278–81).

In the exultant first lines of *The Prelude,* Wordsworth had foreseen the spirit's power to become self-creative. Though fostered by nature it eventually outgrows its dependence, sings and storms at will (I.33–38). The poet's anticipation of autonomy is probably less a matter of pride than of necessity: he will steal the initiative from nature so as to freely serve or sustain the natural world should its hold on the affections slacken. His poetic power, though admittedly in nature's gift, must perpetuate, like consecration, vital if transitory feelings. Without poetry the supreme moment is nothing.

> Dear Liberty! Yet what would it avail
> But for a gift that consecrates the joy?   (I.31–32)

But he is taught that the desire for immediate consecrations is a wrong form of worship. The world demands a devotion less external and willful, a wise passiveness which the creative will may profane. The tempest "vexing its own creation" is replaced by a "mellowing sun, that shed / Mild influence." Nature keeps the initiative. The mind at its most free is still part of a deep mood of weathers.

Wordsworth's failure to consecrate, through verse, the splendid evening is only the last event in this reversal. It begins with the poet placing

---

[3] Emancipated—but through exile. For the allusions to *Paradise Lost* and Exodus, see *Prelude* I.14 and 16–18.

(so to say) the cart before the horse, Poetry before Nature: "To the open fields I told / A prophecy: poetic numbers came . . ." (I.50 ff.). He never, of course, forgets the double agency of inward and outward which informs every act of poetry. So his heart's frost is said to be broken by both outer and inner winds (I.38 ff.).[4] Such reciprocity is at the heart of all his poems. Yet he continually anticipates a movement of transcendence: Nature proposes but the Poet disposes. Just as the breeze engendered in the mind a self-quickening tempest, so poetry, the voice from that tempest, re-echoing in the mind whence it came, seems to increase there its perfection (I.55 ff.). The origin of the whole moves farther from its starting point in the external world. A *personal* agent replaces that of nature: "I paced on . . . down I sate . . . slackening my thoughts by choice" (I.60 ff.). There is a world of difference between this subtle bravado and the ascendancy of *impersonal* constructions in the final episode: "Be it so; / Why think of any thing but . . . What need of many words? . . . I pursued / My way . . . A pleasant loitering journey . . . brought me to my hermitage."

This change, admittedly, is almost too fine for common language. Syntax becomes a major device but not a consistent one. In the 1850 text, while the poet muses in the green, shady place, certain neoclassical patterns, such as the noble passive combined with synecdoche, create an atmosphere in which personal and impersonal, active and passive, blend strongly:

> Many were the thoughts
> Encouraged and dismissed, till choice was made
> Of a known Vale, whither my feet should turn.   (I.70–72)

Devices still more subtle come into play. In the passage immediately preceding, Wordsworth describes the quiet autumn afternoon:

>   a day
> With silver clouds, and sunshine on the grass,
> And in the sheltered and the sheltering grove
> A perfect stillness.   (I.67–70)

"Sheltered and sheltering"—typical Wordsworthian verbosity? The redundance, however, does suggest that whatever is happening here happens in more than one place; compare "silver clouds, and sunshine on the grass." The locus doubles, redoubles: that twofold agency which seems to center on the poet is active all around to the same incremental effect. The grove, sheltered, shelters in turn, and makes "A perfect stillness." The poet, in a sense, is only a single focus to something universally active.

---

[4] Cf. M. H. Abrams, "The Correspondent Breeze: A Romantic Metaphor," in *English Romantic Poets*, ed. Abrams (Galaxy paperback, New York, 1960), pp. 37–54.

He muses on this intensifying stillness, and within him rises a picture, gazing on which with *growing* love "a higher power / Than Fancy" enters to affirm his musings. The reciprocal and incremental movement, mentioned explicitly in I.31 ff., occurs this time quite unself-consciously, clearly within the setting and through the general influences of Nature.

No wonder, then, that the city, which the poet still strove to shake off in the first lines, appears now not only distant but also "ruralised," taking on the colors of nature, as inclosed by it as the poet's own thought. The last act of the reversal is the episode of the splendid sunset. Wordsworth not only cannot, he *need* not steal the initiative from nature. Her locus is universal, not individual; she acts by expedients deeper than will or thought. Wordsworth's failure intensifies his sense of a principle of generosity in nature. That initial cry of faith, "I cannot miss my way" (I.18), becomes true, but not because of his own power. The song loses its way.

Wordsworth's first experience is symptomatic of his creative difficulties. One impulse vexes the creative spirit into self-dependence, the other exhibits nature as that spirit's highest object. The poet is driven at the same time from and toward the external world. No sooner has he begun to enjoy his Chaucerian leisure than restiveness breaks in. The "pilgrim," despite "the life / In common things—the endless store of things," cannot rest content with his hermitage's sabbath. Higher hopes, "airy phantasies," clamor for life (I.114 ff.). The poet's account of his creative difficulties (I.146–269) documents in full his vacillation between a natural and a more than natural theme, between a Romantic tale and one of "natural heroes," or "a tale from my own heart" and "some philosophic song"—but he adds, swinging back to the more humble, "Of Truth that cherishes our daily life." Is this indeterminacy the end at which nature aims, this curious and never fully clarified restlessness the ultimate confession of his poetry?

It would be hard, in that case, to think of *The Prelude* as describing the "growth of a poet's mind"; for what the first part of Book I records is, primarily, Wordsworth's failure to be a visionary or epic poet in the tradition of Spenser and Milton. No poem of epic length or ambition ever started like his. The epic poet begins confidently by stating his subject, boasts a little about the valor of his attempt, and calls on the Muse to help him. Yet Wordsworth's confident opening is deceptive. He starts indeed with a rush of verses which are in fact a kind of self-quotation, because his subject is poetry or the mind which has separated from nature and here celebrates its coming-of-age by generously returning to it. After this one moment of confidence, all is problematic. The song loses its way, the proud opening is followed by an experience of aphasia, and Wordsworth begins the story of the growth of his mind to prove, at least to himself, that nature had intended him to be a poet.

Was it for this, he asks, for this timidity or indecision, that nature spent all her care (I.269 ff.)? Did not nature, by a process of both accommodation and weaning, foster the spirit's autonomy from childhood on? Yet when the spirit tries to seize the initiative, to quicken of itself like Ezekiel's chariot, either nature humbles it or Wordsworth humbles himself before her. "Thus my days," says Wordsworth sadly, "are past / In contradiction; with no skill to part / Vague longing, haply bred by want of power, / From paramount impulse not to be withstood, / A timorous capacity from prudence, / From circumspection, infinite delay" (I.237–42).

Wordsworth never achieved his philosophic song. *Prelude* and *Excursion* are no more than "ante-chapels" to the "gothic church" of his unfinished work. An unresolved opposition between Imagination and Nature prevents him from becoming a visionary poet. It is a paradox, though not an unfruitful one, that he should scrupulously record nature's workmanship, which prepares the soul for its independence from sense-experience, yet refrain to use that independence out of respect of nature. His greatest verse *still takes its origin* in the memory of given experiences to which he is often pedantically faithful. He adheres, apparently against nature, to natural fact.

II

There are many who feel that Wordsworth could have been as great a poet as Milton but for this return to nature, this shrinking from visionary subjects. Is Wordsworth afraid of his own imagination? Now we have, in *The Prelude,* an exceptional incident in which the poet comes, as it were, face to face with his imagination. This incident has many points in common with the opening event of *The Prelude;* it also, for example, tells the story of a failure of the mind vis-à-vis the external world. I refer to the poet's crossing of the Alps, in which his adventurous spirit is again rebuffed by nature, though by its strong absence rather than presence. His mind, desperately and unself-knowingly in search of a nature adequate to deep childhood impressions, finds instead *itself,* and has to acknowledge that nature is no longer its proper subject or home. Despite this recognition, Wordsworth continues to bend back the energy of his mind and of his poem to nature, but not before we have learned the secret behind his fidelity.

Having finished his third year of studies at Cambridge, Wordsworth goes on a walking tour of France and Switzerland. It is the summer of 1790, the French Revolution has achieved its greatest success and acts as a subtle, though, in the following books, increasingly human background to his concern with nature. Setting out to cross the Alps by way of the Simplon Pass, he and a friend are separated from their companions and try to ascend by themselves. After climbing some time and not overtaking anyone, they meet a peasant who tells them they must return to their starting point and follow a stream down instead of further ascending, i.e. they had already, and without knowing it, crossed the Alps. Disappointed, "For still we had hopes that pointed to the clouds," they start downward beset by a "melancholy slackening," which, however, is soon dislodged (VI.557–91, 616 ff.).

This naive event stands, however, within a larger, interdependent series of happenings: an unexpected revelation comes almost immediately (624–40), and the sequence is preceded by a parallel disappointment with the natural world followed by a compensatory vision (523 ff.). In addition to this pattern of blankness and revelation, of the soulless image and the sudden renewed immediacy of nature, we find a strange instance of the past flowing into the present. Wordsworth, after telling the story of his disappointment, is suddenly, in the very moment of composition, overpowered by a feeling of glory to which he gives expression in rapturous, almost self-obscuring lines (VI.592 ff.). Not until the moment of composition, some fourteen years after the event,[5] does the real reason behind his upward climb and subsequent melancholy slackening strike home; and it strikes so hard that he gives to the power in him, revealed by the extinction of the immediate external motive (his desire to cross the Alps) and by the abyss of intervening years, the explicit name Imagination:

> Imagination—here the Power so called
> Through sad incompetence of human speech,
> That awful Power rose from the mind's abyss
> Like an unfathered vapour that enwraps,
> At once, some lonely traveller. I was lost;
> Halted without an effort to break through;
> But to my conscious soul I now can say—
> "I recognise thy glory." (VI.592–99)

Thus Wordsworth's failure vis-à-vis nature (or its failure vis-à-vis him) is doubly redeemed. After descending, and passing through a gloomy strait (621 ff.), he encounters a magnificent view. And crossing, one might say, the gloomy gulf of time, his disappointment becomes retrospectively a prophetic instance of that blindness to the external world which is the tragic, pervasive, and necessary condition of the mature poet. His failure of 1790 taught him gently what now (1804) literally *blinds* him: the independence of imagination from nature.

I cannot miss my way, the poet exults in the opening verses of *The Prelude*. And he cannot, as long as he respects the guidance of nature, which leads him along a gradual via negativa to make his soul more than

---

[5] That the rising up of imagination occurred as Wordsworth was remembering his disappointment rather than immediately after it (i.e., in 1804, not in 1790) was first pointed out by W. G. Fraser in the *Times Literary Supplement* (April 4, 1929), p. 276.

"a mere pensioner / On outward forms" (VI.737 f.). It is not easy, however, to "follow Nature." The path, in fact, becomes so circuitous that a
poet follows least when he thinks he follows most. For he must cross a
strait where the external image is lost yet suddenly revived with more
than original immediacy. Thus a gentle breeze, in the first book, calls
forth a tempest of verse, but a splendid evening wanes into silence. A
magnificent hope, in the sixth book, dies for lack of sensuous food, but
fourteen years later the simple memory of failure calls up that hope
in a magnificent tempest of verse. When the external stimulus is too
clearly present the poet falls mute and corroborates Blake's strongest
objection: "Natural Objects always did and now do weaken, deaden, and
obliterate Imagination in Me." [6] The poet is forced to discover the
autonomy of his imagination, its independence from present joy, from
strong outward stimuli—but this discovery, which means a passing of the
initiative from nature to imagination, is brought on gradually, mercifully.

Wordsworth does not sustain the encounter with Imagination. His
direct cry is broken off, replaced by an impersonal construction—"here
the Power." It is not Imagination but his "conscious soul" he addresses
directly in the lines that follow. What, in any case, is the soul to do with
its extreme recognition? It has glimpsed the height of its freedom. At
the end of his apostrophe to Imagination, Wordsworth repeats the idea
that the soul is halted by its discovery, as a traveler by a sudden bank of
mist. But the simile this time suggests not only a divorce from but also
(proleptically) a return to nature on the part of the soul,

> Strong in herself and in beatitude
> That hides her, like the mighty flood of Nile
> Poured from his fount of Abyssinian clouds
> To fertilise the whole Egyptian plain.   (VI.613–16)

III

It follows that nature, for Wordsworth, is not an "object" but a
presence and a power; a motion and a spirit; not something to be wor-
shiped and consumed, but always a guide leading beyond itself. This
guidance starts in earliest childhood. The boy of *Prelude* I is fostered
alike by beauty and by fear. Through beauty, nature often makes the
boy feel at home, for, as in the Great Ode, his soul is alien to this world.
But through fear, nature reminds the boy from where he came, and
prepares him, having lost heaven, also to lose nature. The boy of *Prelude*

---

[6] Marginalia to Volume I of Wordsworth's *Poems* of 1815. I may venture the opinion
that Wordsworth, at the beginning of *The Prelude*, goes back to nature not to increase his chances of sensation but rather to emancipate his mind from immediate
external excitements, the "gross and violent stimulants" (1800 Preface to *Lyrical
Ballads*) of the city he leaves behind him.

I, who does not yet know he must suffer this loss as well, is warned by nature itself of the solitude to come.

I have suggested elsewhere how the fine skating scene of the first book (425–63), though painted for its own sake, to capture the animal spirits of children spurred by a clear and frosty night, moves from vivid images of immediate life to an absolute calm which foreshadows a deeper and more hidden life.[7] The Negative Way is a gradual one, and the child is weaned by a premonitory game of hide-and-seek in which nature changes its shape from familiar to unfamiliar, or even fails the child. There is a great fear, either in Wordsworth or in nature, of traumatic breaks: *Natura non facit saltus.*

If the child is led by nature to a more deeply meditated understanding of nature, the mature singer who composes *The Prelude* begins with that understanding or even beyond it—with the spontaneously creative spirit. Wordsworth plunges into *medias res,* where the *res* is Poetry, or Nature only insofar as it has guided him to a height whence he must find his own way. But Book VI, with which we are immediately concerned, records what is chronologically an intermediate period, in which the first term is neither Nature nor Poetry. It is Imagination in embryo: the mind muted yet also strengthened by the external world's opacities. Though imagination is with Wordsworth on the journey of 1790, nature seems particularly elusive. He goes out to a nature which seems to hide as in the crossing of the Alps.

The first part of this episode is told to illustrate a curious melancholy related to the "presence" of imagination and the "absence" of nature. Like the young Apollo in Keats' *Hyperion,* Wordsworth is strangely dissatisfied with the riches before him, and compelled to seek some other region:

> Where is power?
> Whose hand, whose essence, what divinity
> Makes this alarum in the elements,
> While I here idle listen on the shores
> In fearless yet in aching ignorance? [8]

To this soft or "luxurious" sadness, a more masculine kind is added, which results from a "stern mood" or "underthirst of vigor"; and it is in order to throw light on this further melancholy that Wordsworth tells the incident of his crossing the Alps.

The stern mood to which Wordsworth refers can only be his premonition of spiritual autonomy, of an independence from sense-experience foreshadowed by nature since earliest childhood. It is the "underground"

---

[7] *The Unmediated Vision* (New Haven, 1954), pp. 17–20.
[8] *Hyperion* III.103–07.

form of imagination, and *Prelude* II.315 ff. describes it as "an obscure sense / Of possible sublimity," for which the soul, remembering *how* it felt in exalted moments, but no longer *what* it felt, continually strives to find a new content. The element of obscurity, related to nature's self-concealment, is necessary to the soul's capacity for growth, for it vexes the latter toward self-dependence. Childhood pastures become viewless; the soul cannot easily find the source from which it used to drink the visionary power; and while dim memories of a passionate commerce with external things drive it more than ever to the world, this world makes itself more than ever inscrutable.[9] The travelers' separation from their guides, then that of the road from the stream (VI.568), and finally their trouble with the peasant's words that have to be "translated," express subtly the soul's desire for a *beyond*. Yet only when poet, brook, and road are once again "fellow-travellers" (VI.622), and Wordsworth holds to Nature, does that reveal—a Proteus in the grasp of the hero—its prophecy.

This prophecy was originally the second part of the adventure, the delayed vision which compensates for his disappointment (the "Characters of the great Apocalypse," VI.617–40). In its original sequence, therefore, the episode has only two parts: the first term or moment of natural immediacy is omitted, and we go straight to the second term, the inscrutability of an external image, which leads via the gloomy strait to its renewal. Yet, as if this pattern demanded a substitute third term, Wordsworth's tribute to "Imagination" severs the original temporal sequence, and forestalls nature's renewal of the bodily eye with ecstatic praise of the inner eye.

The apocalypse of the gloomy strait loses by this the character of a *terminal* experience. Nature is again surpassed, for the poet's imagination is called forth, at the time of writing, by the barely scrutable, not by the splendid emotion; by the disappointment, not the fulfillment. This (momentary) displacement of emphasis is the more effective in that the style of VI.617 ff., and the very characters of the apocalypse, suggest that the hiding places of power cannot be localized in nature.[10] Though the apostrophe to Imagination—the special insight that comes to Words-

---

[9] Cf. the Intimations Ode; also *Prelude* I.597 ff.

[10] Of the four sentences which comprise lines 617–40, the first three alternate the themes of eager and of restrained movement ("melancholy slackening . . . Downwards we hurried fast . . . at a slow pace"); and the fourth sentence, without explicit transition, commencing in mid-verse (line 624), rises very gradually and firmly into a development of sixteen lines. These depend on a single verb, an unemphatic "were," held back till the beginning of line 636; the verb thus acts as a pivot that introduces, without shock or simply as the other side of the coin, the falling and interpretative movement. This structure, combined with a skillful interchange throughout of asyndetic and conjunctive phrases, always avoids the sentiment of abrupt illumination for that of a majestic swell fed by innumerable sustaining events, and thereby strengthens our feeling that the vision, though climactic, is neither terminal nor discontinuous.

worth in 1804—is a real peripety, reversing a meaning already established, it is not unprepared. But it takes the poet many years to realize that nature's "end" is to lead to something "without end," to teach the travelers to transcend nature.

The three parts of this episode, therefore, can help us understand the mind's growth toward independence of immediate external stimuli. The measure of that independence is Imagination, and carries with it a precarious self-consciousness. We see that the mind must pass through a stage where it experiences Imagination as a power separate from Nature, that the poet must come to think and feel as if by his own choice, or from the structure of his mind.[11]

VI-a (557–91) shows the young poet still dependent on the immediacy of the external world. Imagination frustrates that dependence secretly, yet its blindness toward nature is accompanied by a blindness toward itself. It is only a "mute Influence of the soul, / An Element of nature's inner self" (1805, VIII.512–13).

VI-b (592–616) gives an example of thought or feeling that came from the poet's mind without immediate external excitement. There remains, of course, the memory of VI-a (the disappointment), but this is an internal feeling, not an external image. The poet recognizes at last that the power he has looked for in the outside world is really within and frustrating his search. A shock of recognition then feeds the very blindness toward the external world which helped to produce that shock.

In VI-c (617–40) the landscape is again an immediate external object of experience. The mind cannot separate in it what it desires to know and what it actually knows. It is a moment of revelation, in which the poet sees not as in a glass, darkly, but face to face. VI-c clarifies, therefore, certain details of VI-a and *seems* to actualize figurative details of VI-b.[12] The matter-of-fact interplay of quick and lingering movement, of up-and-down perplexities in the ascent (VI.567 ff.), reappears in larger letters; while the interchanges of light and darkness, of cloud and cloud-lessness, of rising like a vapor from the abyss and pouring like a flood from heaven have entered the landscape bodily. The gloomy strait also participates in this actualization. It is revealed as the secret middle term which leads from the barely scrutable presence of nature to its resurrected image. The travelers who move freely with or against the terrain, hurry-ing upward, pacing downward, perplexed at crossings, are now led narrowly by the pass as if it were their rediscovered guide.

---

[11] Cf. Preface (1802) to *Lyrical Ballads:* [The poet] has acquired a greater readiness and power in expressing . . . especially those thoughts and feelings which, by his own choice, or from the structure of his own mind, arise in him without immediate external excitement."

[12] VI-c was composed before VI-b, so while the transference of images goes structur-ally from VI-b to VI-c, *chronologically* the order is reversed.

The Prelude and The Recluse:
Wordsworth's Long Journey Home

by M. H. Abrams

In the "Prospectus" to his intended masterwork, *The Recluse,* Wordsworth announces that his "high argument" will be the capacity of the
mind of man, "When wedded to this goodly universe / In love and holy
passion," to transform the world into a paradise which will be "A simple
produce of the common day." [1] He then goes on to pray to the "prophetic
Spirit" that

> if with this
> I mix more lowly matter; with the thing
> Contemplated, describe the Mind and Man
> Contemplating; and who, and what he was—
> The transitory Being that beheld
> This Vision; when and where, and how he lived;—
> Be not this labour useless.

In this way Wordsworth designated and justified the personal narrative
which makes up the opening book of *The Recluse* he called *Home at
Grasmere,* as well as the entire poem that his wife later named *The
Prelude.* Wordsworth described the latter work as a "tributary" and also
"as a sort of portico to the Recluse, part of the same building." [2] The

"*The Prelude* and *The Recluse:* Wordsworth's Long Journey Home." From M. H.
Abrams, *Natural Supernaturalism: Tradition and Revolution in Romantic Literature*
(New York; W. W. Norton & Company, 1971). Copyright © 1971 by W. W. Norton
and Company, Inc., and Oxford University Press. Reprinted by permission of the
publishers. This essay incorporates a revised version of chapter 2, section 1, and chapter 5, section 2.

[1] Wordsworth excerpted the verse passage that he called "a kind of Prospectus of
the design and scope" of *The Recluse* from the conclusion to *Home at Grasmere* and
printed it in his Preface to *The Excursion* (1814). For the manuscript drafts, composed probably between 1800 and 1806, see M. H. Abrams, *Natural Supernaturalism*
(New York, 1971), Appendix.

[2] To DeQuincey, 6 March 1804, *Letters: The Early Years* (2d ed.; Oxford, 1967),
p. 454; to Beaumont, 3 June 1805, *ibid.*, p. 594.

time taken to compose *The Prelude* straddled the writing of the Prospectus, and the completed work was conceived as an integral part of the overall structure whose "design and scope" Wordsworth specified in that poetic manifesto. "The Poem on the growth of your own mind," as Coleridge recalled the plan in 1815, "was as the ground-plat and the Roots, out of which the Recluse was to have sprung up as the Tree"— two distinct works, but forming "one compleat Whole." [3] The role of *The Prelude*, as Wordsworth himself describes his grand design, is to recount the circumstances and mental growth of a "transitory Being," culminating in his achievement of a "Vision" and in the recognition that his mission is to impart the vision in the public and enduring form of an unprecedented kind of poem:

> Possessions have I that are solely mine,
> Something within which yet is shared by none . . .
> I would impart it, I would spread it wide,
> Immortal in the world which is to come.[4]

The Idea of The Prelude

In this era of constant and drastic experimentation with literary materials and forms, it is easy to overlook the radical novelty of *The Prelude* when it was completed in 1805. The poem amply justified Wordsworth's claim to have demonstrated original genius, which he defined as "the introduction of a new element into the intellectual universe" of which the "infallible sign is the widening the sphere of human sensibility." [5]

The Prelude is a fully developed poetic equivalent of two portentous innovations in prose fiction, of which the earliest examples had appeared in Germany only a decade or so before Wordsworth began writing his poem: the *Bildungsroman* (Wordsworth called *The Prelude* a poem on "the growth of my own mind") and the *Künstlerroman* (Wordsworth also spoke of it as "a poem on my own poetical education," and it far surpassed all German examples in the detail with which his "history," as he said, was specifically "of a *Poet's* mind").[6] The whole poem is written as a sustained address to Coleridge—"I speak bare truth / As if alone to thee in private talk" (X, 372–3); Coleridge, however, is an auditor *in absentia*, and the solitary author often supplements this form with an interior monologue, or else carries on an extended colloquy with the landscape in which the interlocutors are "my mind" and "the speaking

---

[3] To Wordsworth, 30 May 1815, *Collected Letters* (Oxford, 1956–9), IV, 573.
[4] *Home at Grasmere*, 11. 686–91, preceding the Prospectus.
[5] "Essay, Supplementary to the Preface of 1815."
[6] *Letters: The Early Years*, p. 518, Isabella Fenwick note to "There Was a Boy," and *The Prelude*, XIII, 408. (All references are to *The Prelude* of 1805, unless indicated by the date "1850.")

face of earth and heaven" (V, 11–12). The construction of *The Prelude* is radically achronological, starting not at the beginning, but at the end—during Wordsworth's walk to "the Vale that I had chosen" (I, 100), which telescopes the circumstances of two or more occasions but refers primarily to his walk to the Vale of Grasmere, that "hermitage" (I, 115) where he has taken up residence at that stage of his life with which the poem concludes.[7] During this walk an outer breeze, "the sweet breath of Heaven," evokes within the poet, "a corresponding mild creative breeze," a prophetic *spiritus* or inspiration which assures him of his poetic mission and, though it is fitful, eventually leads to his undertaking *The Prelude* itself; in the course of the poem, at times of imaginative dryness, the revivifying wind recurs in the role of a poetic leitmotif.[8]

Wordsworth does not tell his life as a simple narrative in past time but as the present remembrance of things past, in which forms and sensations "throw back our life" (I, 660–1) and evoke the former self which coexists with the altered present self in a multiple awareness that Wordsworth calls "two consciousnesses." There is a wide "vacancy" between the I now and the I then,

> Which yet have such self-presence in my mind
> That, sometimes, when I think of them, I seem
> Two consciousnesses, conscious of myself
> And of some other Being.   (II, 27–33)

The poet is aware of the near impossibility of disengaging "the naked recollection of that time" from the intrusions of "after-meditation" (III, 644–8). In a fine and subtle figure for the interdiffusion of the two consciousnesses (IV, 247–64), he describes himself as one bending from a drifting boat on a still water, perplexed to distinguish actual objects at the bottom of the lake from surface reflections of the environing scene, from the tricks and refractions of the water currents, and from his own intrusive but inescapable image (that is, his present awareness). Thus "incumbent o'er the surface of past time" the poet, seeking the elements of continuity between his two disparate selves, conducts a persistent exploration of the nature and significance of memory, of his power to sustain freshness of sensation and his "first creative sensibility" against the deadening effect of habit and analysis, and of manifestations of the enduring and the eternal within the realm of change and time. Only intermittently does the narrative order coincide with the order of actual oc-

---

[7] For convincing evidence that the chief prototype of the walk described in the "preamble" to *The Prelude* was Wordsworth's walk to Grasmere, see John Finch, "Wordsworth's Two-Handed Engine," *Bicentenary Wordsworth Studies*, ed. Jonathan Wordsworth (Ithaca, N.Y., 1970). But Wordsworth probably telescoped events from several walks in real life, to make the "preamble" to *The Prelude* a typological change of venue, signifying a new stage in his spiritual history.

[8] E.g., VII, 1–56; XI, 1–12.

currence. Instead Wordsworth proceeds by sometimes bewildering ellipses, fusions, and as he says, "motions retrograde" in time (IX, 8).

Scholars have long been aware that it is perilous to rely on the factual validity of *The Prelude,* and in consequence Wordsworth has been charged with intellectual uncertainty, artistic ineptitude, bad memory, or even bad faith. The poem has suffered because we know so much about the process of its composition between 1798 and 1805—its evolution from a constituent part to a "tail-piece" to a "portico" of *The Recluse,* and Wordsworth's late decision to add to the beginning and end of the poem the excluded middle: his experiences in London and in France. A work is to be judged, however, as a finished and free-standing product; and in *The Prelude* as it emerged after six years of working and reworking, the major alterations and dislocations of the events of Wordsworth's life are imposed deliberately, in order that the design inherent in that life, which has become apparent only to his mature awareness, may stand revealed as a principle which was invisibly operative from the beginning. A supervising idea, in other words, controls Wordsworth's account and shapes it into a structure in which the protagonist is put forward as one who has been elected to play a special role in a providential plot. As Wordsworth said in the opening passage, which represents him after he has reached maturity: in response to the quickening outer breeze

> to the open fields I told
> A prophecy: poetic numbers came
> Spontaneously, and cloth'd in priestly robe
> My spirit, thus singled out, as it might seem,
> For holy services. (I, 59–63)

Hence in this history of a poet's mind the poet is indeed the "transitory Being," William Wordsworth, but he is also the exemplary poet-prophet who has been singled out, in a time "of hopes o'erthrown . . . of dereliction and dismay" (II, 448–57), to bring mankind tidings of comfort and joy; as Wordsworth put it in one version of the Prospectus,

> that my verse may live and be
> Even as a light hung up in heaven to chear
> Mankind in times to come.

The spaciousness of his chosen form allows Wordsworth to introduce some of the clutter and contingency of ordinary experience. In accordance with his controlling idea, however, he selects for extended treatment only those of his actions and experiences which are significant for his evolution toward an inherent end, and organizes his life around an event which he regards as the spiritual crisis not of himself only, but of his generation: that shattering of the fierce loyalties and inordinate hopes

for mankind which the liberal English—and European—intellectuals had
invested in the French Revolution.

> Not in my single self alone I found,
> But in the minds of all ingenuous Youth,
> Change and subversion from this hour.
>
>   (X, 232–4)

The Prelude, correspondingly, is ordered in three stages. There is a process
of unified mental development which, although at times suspended, remains a continuum; this process is shattered by a crisis of apathy and
despair; but the mind then recovers an integrity which, despite admitted
losses, is represented as a level higher than the initial unity, in that the
mature mind possesses powers, together with an added range, depth, and
sensitivity of awareness, which are the products of the critical experiences
it has undergone. The discovery of this fact resolves a central problem
which has been implicit throughout *The Prelude*—the problem of how
to justify the human experience of pain and loss and suffering; he is now
able to recognize that his life is "in the end / All gratulant if rightly understood" (XIII, 384–5).

The narrative is punctuated with recurrent illuminations, or "spots of
time," and is climaxed by two major revelations. The first of these is
Wordsworth's discovery of precisely what he has been born to be and
to do. At Cambridge he had reached a stage of life, "an eminence," in
which he had felt that he was "a chosen Son" (III, 82 ff., 169), and on a
walk home from a dance during a summer dawn he had experienced an
illumination that he should be, "else sinning greatly, / A dedicated
Spirit" (IV, 343–4); but for what chosen, or to what dedicated, had not
been specified. Now, however, the recovery from the crisis of despair
after his commitment to the French Revolution comprises the insight
that his destiny is not one of engagement with what is blazoned "with
the pompous names / Of power and action" in "the stir / And tumult
of the world," but one of withdrawal from the world of action so that
he may meditate in solitude: his role in life requires not involvement,
but detachment.[9] And that role is to be one of the "Poets, even as
Prophets," each of whom is endowed with the power "to perceive / Something unseen before," and so to write a new kind of poetry in a new
poetic style. "Of these, said I, shall be my Song; of these . . . / Will I
record the praises": the ordinary world of lowly, suffering men and of
commonplace or trivial things transformed into "a new world . . . fit /
To be transmitted," of dignity, love, and heroic grandeur (XII, 220–379).
Wordsworth's crisis, then, involved what we now call a crisis of identity,
which was resolved in the discovery of "my office upon earth" (X, 921).

---

[9] *The Prelude,* XII, 44–76, 112–16. Cf. *Home at Grasmere,* ll. 664–752.

And since the specification of this office entails the definition, in the twelfth book, of the particular innovations in poetic subjects, style, and values toward which his life had been implicitly oriented, *The Prelude* is a poem which incorporates the discovery of its own *ars poetica*.

His second revelation he achieves on a mountain top. The occasion is the ascent of Mount Snowdon, which Wordsworth, in accordance with his controlling idea, excerpts from its chronological position in his life in 1791, before the crucial experience of France, and describes in the concluding book of *The Prelude*. As he breaks through the cover of clouds the light of the moon "upon the turf / Fell like a flash," and he sees the total scene as "the perfect image of a mighty Mind" in its free and continuously creative reciprocity with its milieu, "Willing to work and to be wrought upon" and so to "create / A like existence" (XIII, 36–119). What has been revealed to Wordsworth in this symbolic landscape is the grand locus of *The Recluse* which he announced in the Prospectus, "The Mind of Man— / My haunt, and the main region of my song," as well as the "high argument" of that poem, the union between the mind and the external world and the resulting "creation . . . which they with blended might / Accomplish." The event which Wordsworth selects for the climactic revelation in *The Prelude,* then, is precisely the moment of the achievement of "this Vision" by "the transitory Being" whose life he had, in the Prospectus, undertaken to describe as an integral part of *The Recluse.*

In the course of *The Prelude* Wordsworth repeatedly drops the clue that his work has been designed to round back to its point of departure. "Not with these began / Our Song, and not with these our Song must end," he had cried after the crisis of France, invoking the "breezes and soft airs" that had blown in the "glad preamble" to his poem (XI, 1 ff. and VII, 1 ff.). As he nears the end of the song, he says that his self-discovery constitutes a religious conclusion ("The rapture of the Hallelujah sent / From all that breathes and is") which is at the same time, as he had planned from the outset, an artistic beginning:

> And now, O Friend; this history is brought
> To its appointed close: the discipline
> And consummation of the Poet's mind.
>   . . . we have reach'd
> The time (which was our object from the first)
> When we may, not presumptuously, I hope,
> Suppose my powers so far confirmed, and such
> My knowledge, as to make me capable
> Of building up a work that should endure.
>   (XIII, 261–78)

That work, of course, is *The Recluse,* for which *The Prelude* was designed to serve as "portico . . . part of the same building." *The Prelude,* then, is an involuted poem which is about its own genesis—a prelude to itself. Its structural end is its own beginning; and its temporal beginning, as I have pointed out, is Wordsworth's entrance upon the stage of his life at which it ends. The conclusion goes on to specify the circular shape of the whole. Wordsworth there asks Coleridge to "Call back to mind / The mood in which this Poem was begun." At that time,

> I rose
> As if on wings, and saw beneath me stretch'd
> Vast prospect of the world which I had been
> And was; and hence this Song, which like a lark
> I have protracted. . . .   (XIII, 370–81)

This song, describing the prospect of his life which had been made visible to him at the opening of *The Prelude,* is *The Prelude* whose composition he is even now concluding. . . .

The Circuitous Journey

It is time to notice that Wordsworth's account of unity achieved, lost, and regained is held together, as various critics have remarked, by the recurrent image of a journey: like a number of works by his contemporaries, Wordsworth's "poem on my own poetical education" converts the wayfaring Christian of the Augustinian spiritual journey into the self-formative traveler of the Romantic educational journey. The poem in fact opens, as Elizabeth Sewell has said, "with the poet in a prospect of wide landscape and open sky," on a literal walk which serves as "the great over-all poetic figure or trope of a journey which he is about to undertake." [10] In the course of this episode the aimless wanderer becomes "as a Pilgrim resolute" who takes "the road that pointed toward the chosen Vale," and at the end of the first book the road translates itself into the metaphorical way of his life's pilgrimage:

> Forthwith shall be brought down
> Through later years the story of my life.
> The road lies plain before me. . . .
>   (1850; I, 91–3, 638–40)

The Prelude is replete with "the Wanderers of the Earth" (XII, 156), and after the period of childhood, its chief episodes are Wordsworth's own wanderings through the English countryside, the Alps, Italy, France, and Wales—literal journeys through actual places which modulate easily into symbolic landscapes traversed by a metaphorical wayfarer. This or-

[10] *The Orphic Voice: Poetry and Natural History* (New Haven, 1960), pp. 338–9.

ganizing figure works in two dimensions. In one of these, *The Prelude* represents the life which the poet narrates as a self-educative journey, "from stage to stage / Advancing," in which his early development had been "progress on the self-same path," the crisis following the French Revolution had been "a stride at once / Into another region," and the terminus was his achievement of maturity in "the discipline / And consummation of the Poet's mind." [11] In the second application, the poet repeatedly figures his own imaginative enterprise, the act of composing *The Prelude* itself, as a perilous quest through the uncharted regions of his own mind.

At times the vehicle for this latter poetic journey is a voyage at sea, connoting the wanderings of Odysseus in his search for home:

> What avail'd,
> When Spells forbade the Voyager to land,
> The fragrance which did ever and anon
> Give notice of the Shore? . . .
> My business was upon the barren sea,
> My errand was to sail to other coasts.
>
> (XI, 48–56; see I, 35–8)

Elsewhere Wordsworth's implied parallel is to Dante, who "Nell mezzo del cammin di nostra vita" had been granted a visionary journey, with a relay of guides, through hell and the earthly paradise to heaven:

> A Traveller I am,
> And all my Tale is of myself; even so,
> So be it, if the pure in heart delight
> To follow me; and Thou, O honor'd Friend!
> Who in my thoughts art ever at my side,
> Uphold, as heretofore, my fainting steps.
>
> (III, 196–201)

At the beginning of the ninth book, "as a traveller, who has gained the brow / Of some aerial Down" and "is tempted to review / The region left behind him," Wordsworth turns back to his earlier youth, before he moves reluctantly on into the discordant "argument" that begins with his residence in France—"Oh, how much unlike the past!" (1850: IX, 1–22). The eleventh book, narrating the process of Wordsworth's recovery, opens in a parallel to Milton's description of his epic journey back from hell to the realms of light (XI, 1–7; see *Paradise Lost*, III, 13–20). And through all these regions the imagined presence of Coleridge serves both as auditor and guide, heartening the exhausted poet in his pilgrimage and quest:

[11] *The Prelude*, XI, 43–4; X, 239–42; XIII, 270–1.

> Thou wilt not languish here, O Friend, for whom
> I travel in these dim uncertain ways
> Thou wilt assist me as a Pilgrim gone
> In quest of highest truth.   (XI, 390–3)

The last book of *The Prelude,* in symmetry with its first book, also opens with a literal walk which translates itself into a metaphor for the climactic stage both of the journey of life and of the imaginative journey which is the poem itself. This time the walk is not a movement along an open plain but the ascent of a mountain, the traditional place for definitive visions since Moses had climbed Mount Sinai. As in Hegel's contemporary *Phenomenology* the spirit, at the close of its educational journey, recognizes itself in its other, so Wordsworth's mind, confronting nature, discovers itself in its own perfected powers:

> A meditation rose in me that night
> Upon the lonely Mountain . . .
>   and it appear'd to me
> The perfect image of a mighty Mind.

In the earliest stage of its development Wordsworth's "Babe, / Nurs'd in his Mother's arms" had not only acquired "The gravitation and the filial bond . . . that connect him with the world," but had also, as "inmate of this *active* universe," established the beginnings of the reciprocative power by which

>   his mind . . .
> Creates, creator and receiver both,
> Working but in alliance with the works
> Which it beholds.—Such, verily, is the first
> Poetic spirit of our human life.
>   (II, 265–76)

On Mount Snowdon, in an evident parallel and complement to this early passage, his mind recognizes, in that image of itself "which Nature thus / Thrusts forth upon the senses," the same power, which has now developed into "the fulness of its strength." As mist and moonlight transform the natural scene, so higher minds by a similar "Power"

>   can send abroad
> Like transformation, for themselves create
> A like existence, and, whene'er it is
> Created for them, catch it by an instinct . . .
> Willing to work and to be wrought upon

by the works which they behold. An essential alteration, however, is that the mature poetic mind, whose infant perception had been a state of undifferentiated consciousness, has acquired self-consciousness, and is able to sustain the sense of its own identity as an individuation-in-unison with the objects it perceives. In Wordsworth's terse rendering,

> hence the highest bliss
> That can be known is theirs, the consciousness
> Of whom they are habitually infused
> Through every image, and through every thought,
> And all impressions. (XIII, 84–111)

I have remarked that *The Prelude* has a circular organization. This circularity of its form, we now see, reflects the circularity of its subject matter. In the opening passage of *The Prelude* the narrator is confirmed in his vocation as a poet-prophet and, in response to an impulse from the autumnal wood, chooses as his goal "a known Vale, whither my feet should turn," in the assurance "of some work of glory there forthwith to be begun." "Keen as a Truant or a Fugitive, / But as a Pilgrim resolute," and also (in a complementary pedestrian metaphor) "like a home-bound labourer," he then pursued his way until a three days' walk "brought me to my hermitage" (1850; I, 71–80, 90–107). At the end of *The Prelude* Wordsworth, having taken up his "permanent abode" (XIII, 338) in this hermitage, calls "back to mind" the occasion of its beginning. But *The Prelude* has a complex function, for it is designed not only as a poem in itself, but also as a "portico" to *The Recluse*. The spiritual journey thus circles back at its conclusion to the literal journey with which it had originated; but this beginning at once turns over into the opening book of Wordsworth's "work of glory," *The Recluse* proper, which describes his way of life in the chosen vale.[12] Only now does he identify the aspect of the vale which had all along made it the goal of his tortuous literal, spiritual, and poetic journey. That goal, as in all the ancient genre of the circuitous pilgrimage of life, is home—*Home at Grasmere.*

The initial passage of *Home at Grasmere* makes it clear that the place to which the poet has returned is not his literal home but one which, on his first overview of the "Vale below" when, solitary, he had chanced across it as "a roving School-boy," he had recognized to be his spiritual home. "Perfect was the Spot . . . stirring to the Spirit"; and he had immediately felt that "here / Must be his Home, this Valley be his World." Throughout his youth the vale had lingered in memory, "shedding upon joy / A brighter joy," and now the home of his imagining has become his actual home (the word reverberates through the opening passage):

---

[12] As de Selincourt points out (*Wordsworth's Poetical Works*, V, 365), the opening book of *The Recluse* "is in fact a continuation of his poetical autobiography from the place where *The Prelude* leaves off." This place, as we have seen, is also the place from which *The Prelude* has set out.

> And now 'tis mine, perchance for life, dear Vale,
> Beloved Grasmere (let the Wandering Streams
> Take up, the cloud-capt hills repeat, the Name),
> One of thy lowly Dwellings is my Home.
>
>   (1–59)

The place in which, "on Nature's invitation" (line 71), Wordsworth's literal and metaphoric wanderings have terminated is identified, after the venerable formula of the Christian quest, as a home which is also a recovered paradise. In his Pisgah-sight of it as a schoolboy he had looked upon it as a "paradise before him" (line 14); and it remains, after he takes up his abode in it, an "earthly counterpart" of heaven (line 642), which he describes in terms echoing Milton's description of the Garden of Eden, and in which Wordsworth and Dorothy, "A solitary pair" (line 255) are somewhat incongruously the Adam and Eve. The journey to this ultimate stage has taken him through "the realities of life so cold," but this had been a fortunate fall into experience, for "the cost" of what he has lost from the earlier stage of his life is greatly outweighed by "what I keep, have gain'd / Shall gain," so that

> in my day of Childhood I was less
> The mind of Nature, less, take all in all,
> Whatever may be lost, than I am now.

For him, man's ancient dream of felicity has been brought down from a transcendent heaven and located in this very world—

>   the distant thought
> Is fetch'd out of the heaven in which it was.
> The unappropriated bliss hath found
> An owner, and that owner I am he.
> The Lord of this enjoyment is on Earth
> And in my breast.[13]

Here he dwells, therefore, as a second and more fortunate Adam, because unlike his predecessor he possesses an Eden which has been gained:

> The boon is absolute; surpassing grace
> To me hath been vouchsafed; among the bowers
> Of blissful Eden this was neither given,
> Nor could be given, possession of the good
> Which had been sighed for, ancient thought fulfilled

[13] Lines 60 ff., MS variant, *Poetical Works*, V, 315–16.

> And dear Imaginations realized
> Up to their highest measure, yea and more.[14]

As in comparable passages in Hölderlin and Novalis (in Blake the parallel is more with Beulah than with the New Jerusalem), all the natural scene becomes alive, human, and feminine, and encloses the poet in an embrace of love:

> Embrace me then, ye Hills, and close me in. . . .
> But I would call thee beautiful, for mild
> And soft, and gay, and beautiful thou art,
> Dear Valley, having in thy face a smile
> Though peaceful, full of gladness.
>
> (lines 110–7)

And when the solitary pair had first entered this valley together in the winter season, its elements had addressed them as fellow beings:

> "What would ye," said the shower,
> "Wild Wanderers, whither through my dark domain?"
> The sunbeam said, "be happy." When this Vale
> We entered, bright and solemn was the sky
> That faced us with a passionate welcoming,
> And led us to our threshold

—a threshold which in an earlier version of the text had been that of "a home / Within a home, which was to be" (lines 168–73, and footnote). This terminus of all the poet's journeyings is not only home and paradise, but also a recovered unity and wholeness which he had experienced nowhere else except "as it found its way into my heart / In childhood"; for this "blended holiness of earth and sky" is

> A termination, and a last retreat,
> A Centre, come from wheresoe'er you will,
> A Whole without dependence or defect,
> Made for itself; and happy in itself,
> Perfect Contentment, Unity entire.
>
> (lines 135–51)

[14] Lines 103–9. As late as in a poem of 1811 Wordsworth parallels his "Departure from the Vale of Grasmere" to that of a tenant of "Elysian plains" or of "celestial Paradise," whom it might please to absent himself from felicity long enough to take a round trip to a lower realm.

> O pleasant transit, Grasmere! to resign
> Such happy fields, abodes so calm as thine. . . .
> Ne'er can the way be irksome or forlorn
> That winds into itself for sweet return.
>
> (*Poetical Works*, III, 64)

And only here does he find a human community. Man "truly is alone"
only in the "vast Metropolis," where he is "doomed / To hold a vacant
commerce . . . / With objects wanting life, repelling love," and where
"neighbourhood serves rather to divide / Than to unite." In this rural
place, however, all is on a human scale, a multeity-in-unity in which individuality is preserved in a society which is a family writ large, and which
finds itself thoroughly at home in its natural milieu.

> Society is here
> A true Community, a genuine frame
> Of many into one incorporate. . . .
> One household, under God, for high and low,
> One family, and one mansion, . . .
>   possessors undisturbed
> Of this Recess. . . . their glorious Dwelling-place.
>   (lines 592–624)

The poet's spiritual home, however, remains ineluctably a paradise of
this earth, for in the vale man differs "but little from the Man elsewhere"
and exhibits the common qualities of "selfishness, and envy, and revenge,
. . . / Flattery and double-dealing, strife and wrong" (lines 347–57). But,
he asks, is there not a strain of words that shall be "the acknowledged
voice of life," and so speak "of solid good / And real evil" in a higher
poetic harmony than that of the unalloyed pastoral fantasy—

> More grateful, more harmonious than the breath,
> The idle breath of softest pipe attuned
> To pastoral fancies?   (lines 401–9)

For this poetry of real life he dismisses the poetry of wish-fulfillment, "All
Arcadian dreams / All golden fancies of the golden Age" engendered by
man's "wish to part / With all remembrance of a jarring world" (lines
625–32). Confident of "an internal brightness," he assumes "his office" as a
mature artist and announces his manifesto: in this "peaceful Vale . . . /
A Voice shall speak, and what will be the Theme?" (lines 660–90, 751–3).

Home at Grasmere concludes with the answer to this question, in the
passage Wordsworth later excerpted to serve as the Prospectus to the
subject and argument of *The Recluse* and all its related poems. This statement in fact epitomizes, and proclaims as valid for other men, what the
poet himself has learned from the long and arduous journey of his life
that has just terminated in Grasmere Vale. The subject, he tells us, will
incorporate the poetic narrative of that life itself, in the account of "the
transitory Being" who had beheld the "Vision" which constituted his
poetic credential, and which it was his unique mission to impart. This
vision is of "the Mind of Man," through which he will undertake a poetic
journey that must ascend higher than Milton's heaven and sink deeper

than Milton's hell. Of this audacious poetic enterprise it will be the high argument that we can re-create the experienced world, and that this new world, despite the inescapable fact of evil and anguish—no less evident in the solitude of "fields and groves" than when they are "barricadoed . . . / Within the walls of cities"—will provide a sufficient paradise to which we have immediate access. Here we return to Wordsworth's figure for an imaginative apocalypse that will restore paradise, taken from the vision of the marriage of the Lamb in the biblical Apocalypse and adapted to his naturalistic premises of mind and its relations to nature. Only let a man succeed in restoring his lost integrity, by consummating a marital union between his mind and a nature which, to the sensual in their sleep of death, has become a severed and alien reality, and he shall find "Paradise, and groves Elysian, . . . A simple produce of the common day."

Wordsworth and the Paradox
of the Imagination

by Cleanth Brooks

Wordsworth's great "Intimations" ode has been for so long intimately connected with Wordsworth's own autobiography, and indeed, Wordsworth's poems in general have been so consistently interpreted as documents pertaining to that autobiography, that to consider one of his larger poems as an object in itself may actually seem impertinent. Yet to do so for once at least is not to condemn the usual mode of procedure and it may, in fact, have positive advantages.

Wordsworth's spiritual history is admittedly important: it is just possible that it is ultimately the important thing about Wordsworth. And yet the poems are structures in their own right; and, finally, I suppose, Wordsworth's spiritual biography has come to have the importance which it has for us because he is a poet.

At any rate, it may be interesting to see what happens when one considers the "Ode" as a poem, as an independent poetic structure, even to the point of forfeiting the light which his letters, his notes, and his other poems throw on difficult points. (That forfeiture, one may hasten to advise the cautious reader, need not, of course, be permanent.) But to enforce it for the moment will certainly avoid confusion between what the poem "says" and what Wordsworth in general may have meant; and it may actually surprise some readers to see how much the poem, strictly considered in its own right, manages to say, as well as precisely what it says.

If we consider the "Ode" in these terms, several observations emerge. For one thing, the poem will be seen to make more use of paradox than is commonly supposed. Of some of these paradoxes, Wordsworth himself must obviously have been aware; but he was probably not aware, the reader will conjecture, of the extent to which he was employing paradox.

The poem, furthermore, displays a rather consistent symbolism. This may be thought hardly astonishing. What may be more surprising is the fact that the symbols reveal so many ambiguities. In a few cases, this ambiguity, of which Wordsworth, again, was apparently only partially aware, breaks down into outright confusion. Yet much of the ambiguity is rich and meaningful in an Empsonian sense, and it is in terms of this ambiguity that many of the finest effects of the poem are achieved.

There are to be found in the "Ode" several varieties of irony; and some of the themes which Wordsworth treats in the poem are to be successfully related only through irony. Yet the principal defect of the "Ode" results from the fact that Wordsworth will not always accept the full consequences of some of his ironical passages.

Lastly, as may be surmised from what has already been remarked, the "Ode" for all its fine passages, is not entirely successful as a poem. Yet, we shall be able to make our best defense of it in proportion as we recognize and value its use of ambiguous symbol and paradoxical statement. Indeed, it might be maintained that, failing to do this, we shall miss much of its power as poetry and even some of its accuracy of statement.

It is tempting to interpret these propositions as proof of the fact that Wordsworth wrote the "Ode" with the "dark" side of his mind—that the poem welled up from his unconscious and that his conscious tinkering with it which was calculated to blunt and coarsen some of the finest effects was, in this case, held to a minimum. But it hardly becomes a critic who has just proposed to treat the poem strictly as a poem, apart from its reflections of Wordsworth's biography, to rush back into biographical speculation. It is far more important to see whether the generalizations proposed about the nature of the poem are really borne out by the poem itself. This is all the more true when one reflects that to propose to find in the poem ambiguities, ironies, and paradoxes will seem to many a reader an attempt to fit the poem to a Procrustean bed—in fine, the bed in which John Donne slept comfortably enough but in which a Romantic poet can hardly be supposed to find any ease.

In reading the poem, I shall emphasize the imagery primarily, and the success or relative failure with which Wordsworth meets in trying to make his images carry and develop his thought. It is only fair to myself to say that I am also interested in many other things, the metrical pattern, for example, though I shall necessarily have to omit detailed consideration of this and many other matters.

In the "Ode" the poet begins by saying that he has lost something. What is it precisely that he has lost? What does the poem itself say? It says that things uncelestial, the earth and every common sight, once seemed apparelled in celestial light. The word "apparelled" seems to me important. The light was like a garment. It could be taken off. It was

not natural to the earth; it *has* been taken off. And if the celestial light
is a garment, the earth must have been clad with the garment by someone (the garment motif, by the way, is to appear later with regard to the
child: "trailing clouds of glory do we come").

The earth, which has had to be apparelled in the garment of light, is
counterbalanced by the celestial bodies like the sun, moon, and stars of
the next stanza. These are lightbearers capable of trailing clouds of glory
themselves, and they clothe the earth in light of various sorts. One is
tempted here to say that the poles of the basic comparison are already
revealed in these first two stanzas: the common earth on which the glory
has to be conferred, and the sun or moon, which confers glory. We can
even anticipate the crux of the poem in these terms: has the child been
clothed with light? Or does he himself clothe the world about him in
light? But more of this later.

This celestial apparel, the garment of light, had, the speaker says, the
glory and the freshness of a dream. A dream has an extraordinary kind
of vividness often associated with strong emotional coloring. It frequently represents familiar objects, even homely ones, but with the
familiarity gone and the objects endowed with strangeness. But the dream
is elusive, it cannot be dissected and analyzed. (Even if Wordsworth could
have been confronted with Dr. Freud, he would, we may surmise, have
hardly missed seeing that Freud's brilliant accounts of dreams resemble
science less than they do poems—"Odes on the Intimations of all too
human humanity from unconscious recollections of early childhood.")
Moreover, the phrase, taken as a whole, suggests that the glory has the
unsubstantial quality of a dream. Perhaps this is to overload an otherwise
innocent phrase. But I should like to point out as some warrant for this
suggestion of unsubstantiality that "dream" is rhymed emphatically with
"To me did *seem*," and that it is immediately followed by "It is not now
as it hath been of yore." The dream quality, it seems to me, is linked
definitely with the transience of the experience. Later in the poem, the
dream is to be connected with "visionary gleam," is to be qualified by
the adjective "fugitive," and finally is to be associated with "Those
shadowy recollections."

The ambiguous character of the child's vision as remembered by the
man is implicit, therefore, in the first stanza of the poem. What the
speaker has lost, it is suggested, is something which is fleeting, shadowy,
and strange, but something which possesses a quality of insight and
wholeness which no amount of other perception—least of all patient
analysis—will duplicate. It is *visionary;* that is, like a vision, a revelation.
But visionary perhaps also suggests something impractical, not completely
real. Perhaps most interesting of all, the speaker, a little later in the
"Ode," has it fade into the light of common day, which is inimical to

both its freshness and its glory. The vision which has been lost is at once more intense and less intense than common daylight.

The second stanza, I think, is very important in defining further the relation of the visionary gleam to the man and to the earth. Ostensibly, this second stanza simply goes on to define further the nature of the thing lost: it is not mere beauty; nature is still beautiful, but a special quality has been lost. Yet the imagery seems to me to be doing something else beneath this surface statement, and something which is very important. In contrast to the earth, we have the rainbow, the moon, the stars, and the sun—all examples of celestial light; and to these we may add the rose by the sort of extension, not too difficult to be sure, by which Cowley treats it as light in his "Hymn to Light." Wordsworth says that the rainbow and the rose are beautiful. We expect him to go on to say the same of the moon. But here, with one of the nicest touches in the poem, he reverses the pattern to say, "The moon doth with delight / Look round her when the heavens are bare." The moon is treated as if she were the speaker himself in his childhood, seeing the visionary gleam as she looks round her with joy. The poet cannot see the gleam, but he implies that the moon can see it, and suggests how she can: she sheds the gleam herself; she lights up and thus creates her world. This seems to me a hint which Wordsworth is to develop later more explicitly, that it is the child, looking round him with joy, who is at once both the source and the recipient of the vision. In this stanza even the sunshine (though as the source of common day it is to be used later in the poem as the antithesis of the visionary gleam) participates in the glory—"The sunshine is a glorious birth." The word *birth*, by the way, suggests that it is a dawn scene: it is the childhood of the sun's course, not the maturity. Like the moon, the sun joyfully creates its world. The poet is giving us here, it seems to me, some very important preparation for Stanza V, in which he is to say "Our birth is but a sleep and a forgetting: / The Soul that rises with us, our life's Star, / Hath had elsewhere its setting. . . ." Surely, it is perfectly clear here that the child, coming upon the world, trailing his clouds of glory, is like the sun or moon which brings its radiance with it, moonlight or starlight or dawn light.

I shall not try to prove here that Wordsworth consciously built up the imagery of Stanza II as preparation for Stanza V. In one sense I think the question of whether or not Wordsworth did this consciously is irrelevant. What I am certain of is this: that the lines

> The Moon doth with delight
> Look round her. . . .

strike any sensitive reader as fine to a degree which their value as decoration will not account for. Certainly it is a testimony of many readers

that the famous passage "Our birth is but a sleep, etc." has registered
with a special impact, with more impact than the mere "beauty" of the
images will account for. The relation of both passages to the theme,
and their mutual interrelations seem to me one way of accounting for
their special force.

This relation of both passages to the theme is so important, however,
that I should like for the moment to pass over consideration of Stanzas
III and IV in order to pursue further the central symbolism of light as
treated in Stanza V. The basic metaphor from line sixty-seven onward has
to do with the child's moving away from heaven, his home—the shades
of the prison house closing about him—the youth's progress further and
further from the day-spring in the east. We should, however, if the
figure were worked out with thorough consistency, expect him to arrive
at darkness or near darkness, the shades of the prison house having
closed round the boy all but completely—the youth having traveled into
some darkened and dismal west. Yet the tantalizing ambiguity in the
symbol which we have noticed earlier, continues. The climax of the
process is not darkness but full daylight: "At length the Man perceives
it die away, / And fade into the light of common day." We have a contrast, then, between prosaic daylight and starlight or dawn light—a contrast between kinds of light, not between light and darkness. There is a
further difficulty in the symbolism: the sunlight, which in Stanza II was
a glorious birth, has here become the symbol for the prosaic and the
common and the mortal.

I point out the ambiguities, not to convict the poet of confusion, but
to praise him for his subtlety and accuracy. I suggest that the implied
comparison of the child to the sun or the moon is still active here, and
that Wordsworth is leaning on his earlier figure more heavily than most
of his critics have pointed out, or than, perhaps, he himself realized. If
the sun, at his glorious birth, lights up a world with the glory and freshness of a dream, with a light which persists even after he has begun
to ascend the sky, yet the sun gradually becomes the destroyer of his
earlier world and becomes his own prisoner. Indeed it is very easy to read
the whole stanza as based on a submerged metaphor of the sun's progress:
the soul is like our life's star, the sun, which has had elsewhere its setting.
It rises upon its world, not in utter nakedness. The trailing clouds of
glory suggest the sunrise. The youth is like the sun, which, as it travels
farther from the east, leaves the glory more and more behind it, and
approaches prosaic daylight. But it is the sun itself which projects the
prosaic daylight, just as the man projects the common day which sur-
rounds him, and upon which he now looks without joy.

I do not insist that we have to read the stanza as a consistent parallelism
between the growing boy and the rising sun. Certainly other metaphors
intrude: that of the darkening prison house, for example. But whether

or not we bring the dominant symbolism to the surface, there is no question, I think, that it is at work within the stanza. And it *is* a symbolism: we are not permitted to pick up the metaphors when we please and drop them when we please. Light plays throughout the poem, and the "Ode," one must remember, closes with another scene in which sunlight again figures prominently:

> The Clouds that gather round the setting sun
> Do take a sober colouring from an eye
> That hath kept watch o'er man's mortality. . . .

Here, by the way, the hint that it is the child who confers the "gleam" upon the world becomes explicit. The clouds take their sober coloring from the eye. Even if we make "eye" refer to the sun as the eye of day, we have but brought the basic metaphors into closer relationship. If the sun, the eye of heaven, after it has watched over mortality, is sobered, so is the eye of the man who has kept the same watch. The parallel between the sun and the developing child which we noticed in Stanza V is completed.

To some readers, however, the occurrence of the word "shades" may still render such an interpretation bizarre. But such a reader will have to prepare himself to face another even more startling ambiguity in the central symbol. Blindness and darkness in this poem are not the easy and expected antitheses to vision and light. The climax of man's falling away from his source is, as we have seen, not the settling down of complete darkness, but of common day. In Stanza IX when the poet pays his debt of gratitude to the childhood vision he actually associates it with blindness and darkness:

> But for those obstinate questionings
> Of sense and outward things,
> Fallings from us, vanishings;
> Blank misgivings. . . .
>
> But for those first affections,
> Those shadowy recollections,
>   Which, be they what they may,
> Are yet the fountain light of all our day,
> Are yet a master light of all our seeing. . . .

The supernal light, the master-light of all our seeing, is here made to flow from the shadowy recollections. Even if we argue that "shadowy" means merely "fitful," "fugitive," we shall still find it difficult to discount some connection of the word with shades and darkness. And if we consider the changing points of view in the "Ode," we shall see that it is inevitable that light should shift into dark and dark into light. For the man who has become immersed in the hard, white light of common day, the recollections of childhood are shadowy; just as from the standpoint of the poet, such a man, preoccupied with his analysis and dissection, must appear merely blind.

As a matter of fact, I think we shall have to agree that there is method in Wordsworth's paradoxes: he is trying to state with some sensitiveness the relation between the two modes of perception, that of the analytic reason and that of the synthesizing imagination. They do have their relationships; they are both ways of seeing. The ambiguities which light and darkness take on in this poem are, therefore, not confusions, as it seems to me, but necessary paradoxes.

A further treatment of the relationship in which Wordsworth is certainly making a conscious use of paradox seems to clinch the interpretation given. I refer to the passage in which the child is addressed as

> Thou best Philosopher, who yet dost keep
> Thy heritage, thou Eye among the blind,
> That, deaf and silent, read'st the eternal deep. . . .

> Why with such earnest pains dost thou provoke
> The years to bring the inevitable yoke,
> Thus blindly with thy blessedness at strife?

The child who sees, does not know that he sees, and is not even aware that others are blind. Indeed, he is trying his best (or soon will try his best) to become blind like the others. Yet, in this most extravagant passage in the poem, Wordsworth keeps the balance. In the child we are dealing with the isolated fact of vision.[1] The eye, taken as an organ of sense, is naturally deaf and silent. The child cannot tell what he reads in the eternal deep, nor can he hear the poet's warning that he is actually trying to cast away his vision. If the passage seems the high point of extravagance, it is also the high point of ironic qualification. How blind is he who, possessed of rare sight, *blindly* strives to forfeit it and become blind!

In pursuing the implications of the light-darkness symbolism, however, I do not mean to lose sight of the "Ode" as a rhetorical structure. To this matter—the alternation of mood, the balance of stanza against stanza, the metrical devices by which the poet attempts to point up these contrasts—to this matter, I shall be able to give very little attention. But I do not mean to desert altogether the line of development of the poem. It is high time to turn back to Stanzas III and IV.

With Stanza III the emphasis is shifted from sight to sound. It is a

---

[1] Cf. I. A. Richards' discussion of this passage in *Coleridge on Imagination* (London, 1934), pp. 133 ff. [Quotations in this essay from *Coleridge on Imagination* are reprinted by permission of W. W. Norton & Company, Inc., New York.]

very cunning touch. The poet has lamented the passing of a glory from the earth. But he can, he suggests, at least *hear* the mirth of the blessed creatures for whom the earth still wears that glory. Stanza III is dominated by sound: the birds' songs, the trumpets of the cataracts, echoes, the winds—presumably their sound—one can't *see* them. Even the gamboling of the lambs is associated with a strong auditory image—"As to the tabor's sound." Hearing these sounds, the poet tries to enter into the gaiety of the season. He asks the shepherd boy to shout, and he goes on to say in Stanza IV,

> Ye blessed Creatures, I have heard the call
> Ye to each other make. . . .

The effect is that of a blind man trying to enter the joyful dawn world. He can hear the blessed creatures as they rejoice in the world, but he himself is shut out from it. If one argues against this as oversubtle—and perhaps it is—and points out that after the poet says,

> . . . I have heard the call
> Ye to each other make

he goes on immediately to say

> I *see*
> The heavens laugh with you in your jubilee,

we are not left entirely without a rejoinder. One can point out that at this point another strong auditory image intervenes again to make sound the dominant sense, not sight. One sees a smile, but laughter is vocal. The heavens are laughing with the children. The poet does in a sense enter into the scene; certainly he is trying very hard to enter into it. But what I notice is that the poet seems to be straining to work up a gaiety that isn't there. If his heart is at the children's festival, it is their festival, after all, not his. I hasten to add that this sense of a somewhat frenetically whipped-up enthusiasm is dramatically quite appropriate. (The metrical situation of the stanza, by the way, would seem to support the view that the strained effect is intentional.) The poet under the influence of the morning scene, feeling the winds that blow "from the fields of sleep," tries to relive the dream. He fails.

But to return to the contrast between sight and sound, the poet should be saying at the climax of his ecstasy,

> I *see*, I *see*, with joy I *see!*

not,

> I hear, I hear, with joy I hear!

Consequently, we are not surprised that the sudden collapse of his afflatus occurs in the very next line, and occurs with the first particular object which is concretely visualized in this stanza:

—But there's a Tree, of many, one,
A single Field which I have looked upon. . . .

The influences of the May morning will no longer work.

I have already discussed the manner in which the first two stanzas of the "Ode" charge the imagery of the famous fifth stanza. I should like to take a moment to glance at another aspect of this stanza. The poet, in "explaining" the loss of vision, says,

Our birth is but a sleep and a forgetting. . . .

The connection with

The glory and the freshness of a dream

of Stanza I is obvious, but I think few have noticed that the expected relation between the two is neatly reversed. Our life's star is rising: it is dawn. We expect the poet to say that the child, in being born, is waking up, deserting sleep and the realm of dream. But instead, our birth, he says, is a sleep and a forgetting. Reality and unreality, learning and forgetting, ironically change places.

Parallel ambiguities are involved in the use of "earth." In general, earth is made to serve as a foil for the celestial light. For example, when the poet writes,

. . . when meadow, grove, and stream,
The earth and every common sight,

it is almost as if he had said "even the earth," and this is the implication of "While earth *herself* is adorning," in Stanza IV. Yet, logically and grammatically, we can look back and connect "earth" with "meadow, grove, and stream"—all of which are aspects of earth—just as properly as we can look forward to connect "earth" with "every common sight." The poet himself is willing at times in the poem to treat the earth as the aggregate of all the special aspects of nature, at least of terrestrial nature. This surely is the sense of such a line as

. . . there hath passed away a glory from the earth

where the emphasis suggests some such statement as: the whole world has lost its glory.

But these somewhat contradictory aspects of the word "earth" overlay a far more fundamental paradox: in general, we think of this poem as a celebration of the influence of nature on the developing mind, and surely, to a large degree, this is true. The poem is filled with references to valleys,

mountains, streams, cataracts, meadows, the sea. Yet, though these aspects
are so thoroughly interwoven with the spontaneous joy of the child
which the poet has himself lost, it is the earth which is responsible for
the loss. Stanza VI is concerned with this paradox:

> Earth fills her lap with pleasures of her own. . . .

What are these pleasures? They would seem to be suspiciously like the
pleasures which engage the children on this May morning and in which
the speaker of the poem regrets that he cannot fully indulge. It is true
that the next stanza of the "Ode" does emphasize the fact that the world
of human affairs, as the stanza makes clear, is seized upon by the child
with joy, and that this is a process which is eminently "natural":

> Fretted by sallies of his mother's kisses,
> With light upon him from his father's eyes!

Earth, "even with something of a Mother's mind," "fills her lap with
pleasures."

> Yearnings she hath in her own natural kind.

What are these yearnings but yearnings to involve the child with herself? We can translate "in her own natural kind" as "pertaining to her,"
"proper to the earth"; yet there is more than a hint that "natural" means
"pertaining to nature," and are not the yearnings proper to the earth,
natural in this sense, anyway?

In trying to make the child forget the unearthly or supernatural glory,
the Earth is acting out of kindness. The poet cannot find it in him to
blame her. She wants the child to be at home. Here we come close upon a
Wordsworthian pun, though doubtless an unpremeditated pun. In calling the Earth "the homely Nurse" there seems a flicker of this suggestion:
that Earth wants the child to be at home. Yet "homely" must surely
mean also "unattractive, plain." [2] She is the drudging common earth after
all, homely, perhaps a little stupid, but sympathetic, and kind. Yet it is
precisely this Earth which was once glorious to the poet, "Apparelled in
celestial light."

This stanza, though not one of the celebrated stanzas of the poem, is
one of the most finely ironical. Its structural significance too is of first
importance, and has perhaps in the past been given too little weight. Two
of its implications I should like to emphasize. First, the stanza definitely
insists that the human soul is not merely natural. We do not of course,
as Wordsworth himself suggested, have to take literally the doctrine about

---

[2] It has been objected that "homely" in British English does not have this sense.
Perhaps it does not today, but see Milton's *Comus*:

> It is for homely features to keep home,
> They had their name thence. . . .

pre-existence; but the stanza makes it quite clear, I think, that man's soul brings an alien element into nature, a supernatural element. The child is of royal birth—"that imperial palace whence he came"—the Earth, for all her motherly affection, is only his foster-mother after all. The submerged metaphor at work here is really that of the foundling prince reared by the peasants, though the phrase, "her Inmate Man," suggests an even more sinister relation: "Inmate" can only mean inmate of the prison-house of the preceding stanza.

The second implication is this: since the Earth is really homely, the stanza underlies what has been hinted at earlier: namely, that it is the child himself who confers the radiance on the morning world upon which he looks with delight. The irony is that if the child looks long enough at that world, becomes deeply enough involved in its beauties, the celestial radiance itself disappears.

In some respects, it is a pity that Wordsworth was not content to rely upon this imagery to make his point and that he felt it necessary to include the weak Stanza VII. Presumably, he thought the reader required a more explicit account. Moreover, Wordsworth is obviously trying to establish his own attitude toward the child's insight. In the earlier stanzas, he has attempted to define the quality of the visionary gleam, and to account for its inevitable loss. Now he attempts to establish more definitely his attitude toward the whole experience. One finds him here, as a consequence, no longer trying to recapture the childhood joy or lamenting its loss, but withdrawing to a more objective and neutral position. The function of establishing this attitude is assigned to Stanza VII. The poet's treatment of the child here is tender, but with a hint of amused patronage in the tenderness. There is even a rather timid attempt at humor. But even if we grant Wordsworth's intention, the stanza must still be accounted very weak, and some of the lines are very flat indeed. Moreover, the amused tenderness is pretty thoroughly over-balanced by the great stanza that follows. I am not sure that the poem would not be improved if Stanza VII were omitted.

If Stanza VII patronizes the child, Stanza VIII apparently exalts him. What is the poet's attitude here? Our decision as to what it is—that is, our decision as to what the poem is actually saying here—is crucial for our interpretation of the poem as a whole. For this reason I believe that it is worth going back over some of the ground already traversed.

Coleridge, one remembers, found the paradoxes which Wordsworth uses in Stanza VIII too startling. Several years ago, in his *Coleridge on Imagination,* I. A. Richards answered Coleridge's strictures. He replies to one of Coleridge's objections as follows:

> The syntax is "faulty" only in that the reader may be required to reflect. He may have to notice that *eye* is metaphorical already for *philosopher*—that the two conjointly then have a meaning that neither

would have apart. "An idea in the mind is to a Natural Law as the power of seeing is to light," said Coleridge himself. As an eye, the philosopher is free from the need to do anything but respond to the laws of his being. *Deaf* and *silent* extend the metaphor by perfectly consentaneous movements. . . . The child will not hear (cannot understand) our words; and he will tell us nothing. That which Wordsworth would derive from him he cannot give; his silence (as we take it through step after step of interpretation, up to the point at which it negates the whole *overt* implication of the rest of Wordsworth's treatment) can become the most important point in the poem. We might look to Lao Tzu to support this: "Who knows speaks not; who speaks knows not." But it is enough to quote, from Coleridge himself, "the words with which Plotinus supposes NATURE to answer a similar difficulty. 'Should anyone interrogate her, how she works, if graciously she vouchsafe to listen and speak, she will reply, it behoves thee not to disquiet me with interrogatories, but to understand in silence even as I am silent, and work without words.' "

Before going further with Richards, however, the reader may wonder how far Wordsworth would be prepared to accept this defense of the lines, particularly in view of Richards' statement that the child's silence "*can* become the most important point in the poem." *Did* it become the most important part for Wordsworth? And regardless of how we answer that question, *does* it become such for us? How is it that the child is an eye among the blind?

Because he "yet [doth] keep / [His] heritage"; because he still dreams and remembers, for all that birth is a sleep and a forgetting; because he is still near to God, who is our home. This, I take it, is what Richards calls the "*overt* implication of . . . Wordsworth's treatment." But it is not so simple as this in Wordsworth's poem. We have seen the hints of another interpretation: the suggestion that the child is like the moon which "with delight / Look[s] round her," and the association of the joyous vision of the child with the child's own joyous activity, and further, with the joyous activity of the birds and the lambs. Is the poem theistic or pantheistic? Coleridge was certainly alive to the difficulties here. He went on to question:

> . . . In what sense can the magnificent attributes, above quoted, be appropriated to a *child,* which would not make them equally suitable to a *bee,* or a *dog,* or a *field of corn;* or even to a ship, or to the wind and waves that propel it?

Richards' answer is forthright:

> . . . why should Wordsworth deny that, in a much less degree, these attributes are equally suitable to a bee, or a dog, or a field of corn? What else had he been saying with his
>
> > And let the young lambs bound
> > As to the tabor's sound!

And what else is Coleridge himself to say in Appendix B of his *Statesman's Manual?* "Never can I look and meditate on the vegetable creation without a feeling similar to that with which we gaze at a beautiful infant. . . ."

Whatever Coleridge was to say later, there can be little doubt as to what Wordsworth's poem says. The lambs and birds are undoubtedly included, along with the children, in the apostrophe, "Ye blessed Creatures." It will be difficult, furthermore, to argue that the poet means to exclude the moon, the stars, and the sun. (If Wordsworth would have excluded the bee and the dog, the exclusion, we may be sure, would have been made on other grounds—not philosophical but poetic.) The matter of importance for the development of the poem is, of course, that the child is father to the man, to the man Wordsworth, for example, as the birds, the lamb, and the moon are not. But it is also a point of first importance for the poem that the child, whatever he is to develop into later, possesses the harmony and apparent joy of all these blessed creatures. It may not be amiss here to remind ourselves of Coleridge's definition of joy with which Wordsworth himself must have been familiar: ". . . a consciousness of entire and therefore well being, when the emotional and intellectual faculties are in equipoise."

Consider, in this general connection, one further item from the poem itself, the last lines from the famous recovery stanza, Stanza IX:

> Nor all that is at enmity with joy,
> Can utterly abolish or destroy!
> > Hence in a season of calm weather
> > Though inland far we be,
> Our Souls have sight of that immortal sea
> > Which brought us hither,
> > Can in a moment travel thither,
> And see the Children sport upon the shore,
> And hear the mighty waters rolling evermore.

Wordsworth has said that the child as the best philosopher "read'st the eternal deep," and here for the first time in the poem we have the children brought into explicit juxtaposition with the deep. And how, according to the poem, are these best philosophers reading it? By sporting on the shore. They are playing with their little spades and sand-buckets along the beach on which the waves break. This is the only explicit exhibit of their "reading" which the poem gives. It seems to corroborate Richards' interpretation perfectly.

In writing this, I am not trying to provoke a smile at Wordsworth's expense. Far from it. The lines are great poetry. They are great poetry because, although the sea is the sea of eternity, and the mighty waters are rolling evermore, the children are not terrified—are at home—are

filled with innocent joy. The children exemplify the attitude toward
eternity which the other philosopher, the mature philosopher, wins to
with difficulty, if he wins to it at all. For the children are those

> On whom these truths do rest,
> Which we are toiling all our lives to find.

The passage carries with it an ironic shock—the associations of innocence
and joy contrasted with the associations of grandeur and terror—but it
is the kind of shock which, one is tempted to say, is almost normal in the
greatest poetry.

I asked a few moments ago how the child was an "Eye among the
blind." The poem seems to imply two different, and perhaps hostile,
answers: because the child is from God and still is close to the source
of supernal light; *and,* because the child is still close to, and like, the
harmonious aspects of nature, just as are the lamb or the bee or the dog.
According to the first view, the child is an eye among the blind because
his soul is filled with the divine; according to the second, because he is
utterly natural. Can these two views be reconciled? And are they reconciled in the poem?

Obviously, the question of whether "divine" and "natural" can be
reconciled in the child depends on the senses in which we apply them to
the child. What the poem is saying, I take it, is that the child, because
he is close to the divine, is utterly natural—natural in the sense that he
has the harmony of being, the innocence, and the joy which we associate
with the harmonious forms of nature. Undoubtedly Wordsworth found
a symbol of divinity in such "beauteous forms" of nature; but the poem
rests on something wider than the general context of Wordsworth's
poetry: throughout the entire Christian tradition, the lamb, the lilies
of the field, etc., have been used as such symbols.

But we may protest further and say that such a reading of "nature"
represents a selection, and a loaded selection at that, one which has
been made by Wordsworth himself—that there are other accounts of
nature which will yield "naturalism" which is hostile to the claims to
the divine. It is profitable to raise this question, because an attempt to
answer it may provide the most fundamental explanation of all for the
ambiguities and paradoxes which fill the "Ode."

Richards says that from "Imagination as a 'fact of mind'" there are
"two doctrines which Coleridge (and Wordsworth) at times drew from
it as to a life in or behind Nature." The two doctrines he states as follows:

> 1. The mind of the poet at moments, penetrating "the film of familiarity
> and selfish solicitude," gains an insight into reality, reads Nature as a
> symbol of something behind or within Nature not ordinarily perceived.

[In the "Ode," the child, untarnished by "the film of familiarity and selfish solicitude," sees nature clad in a *celestial* light.]

2. The mind of the poet creates a Nature into which his own feelings, his aspirations and apprehensions, are projected. [In the "Ode," the child projects his own joy over nature as the moon projects its light over the bare heavens.]

In the first doctrine man, through Nature, is linked with something other than himself which he perceives through her. In the second, he makes of her, as with a mirror, a transformed image of his own being.

But Richards interrupts the process of determining which of these doctrines Coleridge held and which, Wordsworth, to raise two questions which he suggests have a prior status: the questions are, namely, "(1) Are these doctrines necessarily in opposition to one another? (2) What is the relation of any such doctrine to the fact of mind from which it derives?" And Richards goes on to argue:

The Imagination projects the life of the mind not upon Nature . . . [in the sense of the whole] field of the influences from without to which we are subject, but upon a Nature that is already a projection of our sensibility. The deadest Nature that we can conceive is already a Nature of our making. It is a Nature shaped by certain of our needs, and when we "lend to it a life drawn from the human spirit" it is reshaped in accordance with our other needs. [We may interrupt Richards to use Wordsworth's own phrasing from "Tintern Abbey": ". . . all this mighty world / Of eye, and ear,—both what they half create, / And what perceive. . . ."] But our needs do not originate in us. They come from our relations to Nature . . . [as the whole field of influences from without]. We do not create the food that we eat, or the air that we breathe, or the other people we talk to; we do create, from our relations to them, every image we have "of" them. *Image* here is a betraying and unsatisfactory word; it suggests that these images, with which all that we can know is composed, are in some way insubstantial or unreal, mere copies of actualities other than themselves—figments. But *figment* and *real* and *substantial* are themselves words with no meaning that is not drawn from our experience. To say of anything that it is a figment seems to presuppose things more real than itself; but there is nothing within our knowledge more real than these images. To say that anything is an image suggests that there is something else to which it corresponds; but here all correspondence is between images. In short, the notion of reality derives from comparison between images, and to apply it as between images and things that are not images is an illegitimate extension which makes nonsense of it.

This deceiving practice is an example of that process of abstraction which makes it almost inevitable that the two doctrines . . .—the projective and the realist doctrines of the life in Nature—should be conceived as contradictory. "If projected, not real; if real, not projected," we shall say, unless we are careful to recall that the meanings of *real* and *projected* derive from the imaginative fact of mind, and that when they are thus

put in opposition they are products of abstraction and are useful only for
other purposes than the comprehension of the fact of mind.

This is all very well, I can hear someone say; but even if we grant that
the realist and projective doctrines are not necessarily in opposition, what
warrant have we for believing that *Wordsworth* believed they were not
in opposition? In trying to answer this objection, I should agree that
merely to point out that both realist and projective doctrines seem to
occur in the "Ode" is not to give an answer. We can argue for the reconciliation of these doctrines only if we can find where these doctrines im-
pinge upon each other. Where do they meet? That is to say, where is
the real center of the poem? What is the poem essentially about?

The poem is about the human heart—its growth, its nature, its development. The poem finds its center in what Richards has called the
"fact of imagination." Theology, ethics, education are touched upon.
But the emphasis is not upon these: Wordsworth's rather awkward note
in which he repudiates any notion of trying to inculcate a belief in pre-
existence would support this view. The greatness of the "Ode" lies in
the fact that Wordsworth is about the poet's business here, and is not
trying to inculcate anything. Instead, he is trying to dramatize the
changing interrelations which determine the major imagery. And it is
with this theme that the poem closes. Thanks are given, not to God—at
least in this poem, not to God—but to

> . . . the human heart by which we live,
> Thanks to its tenderness, its joys, and fears. . . .

It is because of the nature of the human heart that the meanest flower
can give, if not the joy of the celestial light, something which the poet
says is not sorrow and which he implies is deeper than joy: "Thoughts
that do often lie too deep for tears."

If the poem is about the synthesizing imagination, that faculty by
which, as a later poet puts it,

> Man makes a superhuman
> Mirror-resembling dream

the reason for the major ambiguities is revealed. These basic ambiguities,
by the way, assert themselves as the poem ends. Just before he renders
thanks to the human heart, you will remember, the poet says that the
clouds do not give *to,* but take *from,* the eye their sober coloring. But in
the last two lines of the stanza, the flower does not take *from,* but gives
to, the heart. We can have it either way. Indeed, the poem implies that
we must have it *both* ways. And we are dealing with more than optics.
What the clouds take from the eye is more than a sober coloring—the
soberness is from the mind and heart. By the same token, the flower,
though it gives a color—gives more, it gives thought and emotion.

It has not been my purpose to present this statement of the theme as a discovery; it is anything but that. Rather, I have tried to show how the imagery of the poem is functionally related to a theme—not vaguely and loosely related to it—and how it therefore renders that theme powerfully, and even exactly, defining and refining it. But I can make no such claim for such precision in Wordsworth's treatment of the "resolution," the recovery. In a general sense we know what Wordsworth is doing here: the childhood vision is only one aspect of the "primal sympathy"; this vision has been lost—is, as the earlier stanzas show, inevitably lost—but the primal sympathy remains. It is the faculty by which we live. The continuity between child and man is actually unbroken.

But I must confess that I feel the solution is asserted rather than dramatized. Undoubtedly, we can reconstruct from Wordsworth's other writings the relationship between the primal sympathy and the joy, the "High instincts" and the "soothing thoughts," but the relationship is hardly digested into poetry in the "Ode." And some of the difficulties with which we meet in the last stanzas appear to be not enriching ambiguities but distracting confusions: e.g., the years bring the philosophical mind, but the child over which the years are to pass is already the best philosopher. There is "something" that remains alive in our embers, but it is difficult for the reader to define it in relation to what has been lost. If we make a desperate effort to extend the implied metaphor—if we say that the celestial light is the flame which is beautiful but which must inevitably burn itself out—the primal sympathy is the still-glowing coal—we are forced to realize that such extension is overingenious. The metaphor was not meant to bear so much weight. With regard to this matter of imagery, it would be interesting to compare with the "Ode" several poems by Vaughan which embody a theme very closely related to that of the "Ode." And lest this remark seem to hint at an inveterate prejudice in favor of the metaphysicals, I propose another comparison: a comparison with several of Yeats's poems which deal with still another related theme: unity of being and the unifying power of the imagination. Such comparisons, I believe, would illuminate Wordsworth's difficulties and account for some of the "Ode's" defects. Yet, in closing this account of the "Ode," I want to repudiate a possible misapprehension. I do not mean to say that the general drift of the poem does not come through. It does. I do not mean that there is not much greatness in the poem. There is. But there is some vagueness—which is not the same thing as the rich multiplicity of the greatest poetry; and there are some loose ends, and there is at least one rather woeful anticlimax.

But if the type of analysis to which we have subjected the "Ode" is calculated to indicate such deficiencies by demanding a great deal of the imagery, it is only fair to remind the reader that it focuses attention on the brilliance and power of the imagery, a power which is sustained almost throughout the poem, and with which Wordsworth has hardly been sufficiently credited in the past. Even the insistence on paradox does not create the defects in the "Ode"—the defects have been pointed out before—but it may help account for them. Indeed, one can argue that we can perhaps best understand the virtues and the weaknesses of the "Ode" if we see that what Wordsworth wanted to say demanded his use of paradox, that it could only be said powerfully through paradox, and if we remember in what suspicion Wordsworth held this kind of poetic strategy.

Wordsworth: The Baptized Imagination

by John Jones

What is new and Christian in *The Excursion* is not always ineffectual. Wordsworth can still write persuasively of things that he has seen, though his gaze is now heavenward:

> homeward the shepherds moved
> Through the dull mist, I following—when a step,
> A single step that freed me from the skirts
> Of the blind vapour, opened to my view
> Glory beyond all glory ever seen
> By waking sense or by the dreaming soul!
> The appearance, instantaneously disclosed,
> Was of a mighty city—boldly say
> A wilderness of building, sinking far
> And self-withdrawn into a boundless depth,
> Far sinking into splendour—without end!
> Fabric it seemed of diamond and of gold,
> With alabaster domes, and silver spires,
> And blazing terrace upon terrace. . . .   [II, 828 ff.]

And while his eyes are raised to the Kingdom of Heaven, he still stands on earth; so that there is fugue-like movement of finite and infinite through the passage. The immediate occasion of the experience is clearly stated:

> By earthly nature had the effect been wrought
> Upon the dark materials of the storm
> Now pacified. . . .

But no less clear, as he returns to it, is the sight of

> that marvellous array
> Of temple, palace, citadel, and huge
> Fantastic pomp of structure without name. . . .

Finally, the contrast of familiar valley and city that has suddenly usurped it, becomes explicit:

> This little Vale, a dwelling-place of Man,
> Lay low beneath my feet; 'twas visible—
> I saw not, but I felt that it was there.
> That which I *saw* was the revealed abode
> Of Spirits in beatitude. . . .
> . . . there I stood and gazed:
> The apparition faded not away,
> And I descended.

Wordsworth sees Paradise as a jewelled and holy city, as the New Jerusalem of Revelation. That the city should play this part is at once remarkable, since it has hitherto been very unimportant to him. The city of social and satirical poetry appears scarcely at all, because he was not this kind of poet. The city has no place within the greater landscape: if it has any poetic function, it is the negative one of circumscribing the unmanageable. This is not to say that all Wordsworth's poetry of the city is bad: sometimes, as in *The Prelude's* description of the "anarchy and din" of St. Bartholomew's Fair, the countryman's wide-eyed stare, his fearful amazement, his almost unwilling fascination, are vividly conveyed. And once or twice, as when he saw London from Westminster Bridge "all bright and glittering" in the dress of early morning, or, in a fine poem which he left unpublished,

> white with winter's purest white, as fair,
> As fresh and spotless as he ever sheds
> On field or mountain,[1]

the city is suddenly transmuted, and one can just understand how he came to see that other that has no need of sun or moon to shine upon it.

Even so, the *Excursion* city is a new thing—Paradise in an exact Christian and literary sense. It would be a tidy thesis that followed Wordsworth's imaginative course from the Garden of Eden in his greater landscape to the New Jerusalem in his late poetry. But it would not be true. The landscape is paradisal only in that difficult sense in which Wordsworth's early poetry is optimistic. Neither is it Christian nor is it the Never Never Land of Classical and Rousseauite myth: it is northern

---

[1] ["St. Paul's," in *Poetical Works*, ed. de Selincourt and Darbishire, vol. 4, 374–75 —ED.]

and severe, with a terrible simplicity that the pastoral Wordsworth of
Arnold's tradition could not have compassed. And Wordsworth did not
see his landscape as he now sees the holy city. Then, the point of his
vision was the literalness that enabled him, as he insisted in a hundred
different ways, to see things as they are. Now there is a duality which he
openly admits. The valley "was visible," yet he did not see it. What he
saw—and he italicizes the word so that there shall be no mistake—was
"the revealed abode" of the blessed. "Revealed" emphasizes the divine
gift of second-sight. We must believe that Wordsworth was in the spirit
when he beheld this vision.

Nor does Wordsworth's spiritual eye report anything grey or ghostly:
the picture is as brilliant and as substantial as that described in Revelation. This directness of visual appeal owes much to the philosophical
innocence that allowed Wordsworth to write about the Kingdom of
Heaven unalarmed by the huge difficulties at least as old as Plato's
Parmenides, that attend belief in a transcendent order of reality. In this
Excursion passage he is entirely concerned, like Blake, to report what
he saw, in the faith that visions justify themselves; and, like Blake, he
sees his problem as one of adequate description. Sustained prophetic
frenzy is very rare in Wordsworth, but he is clearly attracted to the
lunatic state, as to childhood, for its privileged access to the supernatural.
A late poem about a woman driven mad by the pain of bereavement
ends thus:

> Nor of those maniacs is she one that kiss
> The air or laugh upon a precipice;
> No, passing through strange sufferings towards the tomb,
> She smiles as if a martyr's crown were won:
> Oft, when light breaks through clouds or waving trees,
> With outspread arms and fallen upon her knees
> The Mother hails in her descending Son
> An Angel, and in earthly ecstasies
> Her own angelic glory seems begun.[2]

The Christianity of this poetry is very unlike that which inspired the
almost incredible final couplet of his *Address to a Skylark*:

> I, with my fate contented, will plod on,
> And hope for higher raptures, when life's day is done.

Anything but mean and pinched, its nature is already being unfolded
in the architecture and jewelry of the holy city, and in the ceremonious
action of lunacy—demoniac with those that "laugh upon a precipice"
and adoring with the woman "fallen upon her knees": for art and sym-

---

[2] *The Widow on Windermere Side.*

bolic action and eternity precious and unbreathing are the subject of his late poetry.

The Immortality Ode once more proves a turning-point. Arnold, and many since Arnold, have been offended by what they take for an unwordsworthian element in the ode's imagery and diction. The child comes earthward from an "imperial palace." The lambs that "bound As to the tabor's sound" discover the rhythm of their game in the Old Testament. The ode is suggestive of ritual form in "jubilee," "festival," "wedding," "funeral"; in "my head hath its coronal," in "the gladness of the May," in "other palms are won." Critics are right to complain, but wrong to take no further interest in these discordancies.

The same thing happens in *The Prelude,* and is partly responsible for the discreteness of the later version.

> Witness, ye Solitudes! where I received
> My earliest visitations   [XIII, 123–24]

in the 1805 text becomes in 1850

> compassed round by mountain solitudes,
> Within whose solemn temple I received
> My earliest visitations. . . .   [1850 ed., XIV, 139–41]

Wordsworth is not simply indulging his taste for circumlocution. The God-graven temple of earth is one of the most persistent images in his late poetry, and one aspect of his changed attitude to the entire natural order. The idea of God as mere Creator is still repugnant to him: he follows his own advice, which was, we have seen, to "say as little as possible about *making*." [3] But God the loving and careful Artist—Wordsworth's theory of art, unlike Coleridge's, was not a theory of making—and God the Sustainer are both familiar.

Again, in the 1805 *Prelude,* he speaks of men of great soul who, in their dealings "with all the objects of the universe,"

> for themselves create
> A like existence; and, whene'er it is
> Created for them, catch it by an instinct.
>   [1805 ed., XIII, 94–96]

In 1850, "all the objects" becomes "the whole compass," indicative of Wordsworth's loss of concentration upon particularity and the reciprocal principle; and the rest is much altered:

> for themselves create
> A like existence; and whene'er it dawns
> Created for them, catch it, or are caught

[3] [In *Letters,* 1811–20, ed. de Selincourt, p. 619—ED.]

> By its inevitable mastery,
> Like angels stopped upon the wing by sound
> Of harmony from Heaven's remotest spheres.
> [1850 ed., XIV, 94-99]

Clearly Wordsworth has come to dislike "instinct," with its natural and optimistic associations. In its place he introduces the equivocal "catch it, or are caught," and adds to this the angel simile. The simile is worth attention: it is more than a Miltonic flourish, just as the retreat from instinct is not mere cowardice or dishonesty. Wordsworth's movement from nature is also a movement towards art. There is an ever-increasing emphasis upon craftsmanship in his talk about poetry, and in his practice there is more of literary. Because of this, criticism that fails to use the criterion of Derivative with great tact may well go astray. Thus in the present case, the obvious Miltonism of the last line must not hide the sudden arrest of "angels stopped upon the wing," which is very effective and not quite Miltonic. And as for the general, angels work hard and successfully in Wordsworth's late poetry, speaking of heaven and earth as he requires them.

Angels live in heaven, but are sometimes seen by men. Thus they are persuaded by the beauty of spring on earth to "quit their mansions unsusceptible of change" [4] and walk abroad. Or a merciful errand may bring them here: Wordsworth tells how

> their own untroubled home
> They leave, and speed on nightly embassy
> To visit earthly chambers.[5]

They may have a purpose less specific than this comforting of sufferers. When attention seems wholly directed towards earth they sometimes remind us unexpectedly of the other order:

> In sunny glade,
> Or under leaves of thickest shade,
> Was such a stillness e'er diffused
> Since earth grew calm while angels mused? [6]

This extreme delicacy with firmness of suggestion is the angelic task. Their transcendentalism is often, as here, a matter of being convincingly apart; or, like the child, of coming from the courts of the holy city. And they have their natural counterparts, in Wordsworth's late poetry, in the heavenly bodies: in the moon, looking down upon the earth's "unsettled

---

[4] *Vernal Ode.*
[5] *The Cuckoo Clock.*
[6] *The Triad.*

atmosphere," [7] in order to "shield from harm the humblest of the sleeping"; and the sun, "source inexhaustible of life and joy," worshipped once as "a blazing intellectual deity." [8] *The Excursion* opens with the prayer that the poem may shine "star-like," secure from "those mutations that extend their sway Throughout the nether sphere"; [9] and it closes[10] with the analogy, too carefully developed, of the sun and the Deity. The invisible sun, shedding light on evening clouds, is called "this local transitory type Of thy paternal splendours." And when Wordsworth hears the cuckoo, his favourite among sky creatures,

> Wandering in solitude, and evermore
> Foretelling and proclaiming,[11]

he is now put in mind of

> the great Prophet, styled *the Voice of One*
> *Crying amid the wilderness.*

Everything in nature speaks of its Original to one who listens

> in the power, the faith,
> Of a baptized imagination.

Angels and shining things of earth serve Wordsworth's purpose in another way. Consider this glance at the world through a magnifying glass:

> Glasses he had, that little things display,
> The beetle panoplied in gems and gold,
> A mailèd angel on a battle-day;
> The mysteries that cups of flowers enfold. . . .[12]

Unnatural in the way of art in its jewelled proportion, the universe becomes a bright pageant that relates to God with a fineness too elusive for the wide-meshed vocabulary of symbol and analogy. Mastery of scale, in the shift from beetle to angelic wars, is another aspect of Wordsworth's

---

[7] *To the Moon.*
[8] *To the Clouds.*
[9] The very sharp contrast of Star-Poem and "nether sphere" only appears in later versions of the Preface. In his first draft Wordsworth merely expresses the hope

> that my song may live, and be
> Even as a light hung up in heaven to cheer
> The world in times to come.
> [In *Poetical Works,* vol. 5, 6 —Ed.]

[10] Bk. IX, 590–633.
[11] *The Cuckoo at Laverna.*
[12] *Within our happy Castle . . .*

understanding of God the Artist; and later, in the great *Vernal Ode,*
he exploits it to marvellous effect. He is resting his "tired lute," after a
song of time and immortality, when there steals upon his ear

> the soft murmur of the vagrant Bee.
> —A slender sound! Yet hoary Time
> Doth to the *Soul* exalt it with the chime
> Of all his years;—a company
> Of ages coming, ages gone;
> (Nations from before them sweeping,
> Regions in destruction steeping,)
> But every awful sound in unison
> With that faint utterance, which tells
> Of treasure sucked from buds and bells,
> For the pure keeping of those waxen cells.

Then Wordsworth describes her pausing in flight, so that he can observe
her parts:

> o'er this tempting flower
> Hovering, until the petals stay
> Her flight, and take its voice away!—
> Observe each wing!—a tiny van!
> The structure of her laden thigh,
> How fragile! yet of ancestry
> Mysteriously remote and high;
> High as the imperial front of man;
> The roseate bloom on woman's cheek;
> The soaring eagle's curvèd beak;
> The white plumes of the floating swan;
> Old as the tiger's paw. . . .

Scale is important for this reason, that by beating the bounds of
creation, from the nature of time to the bee's humming and from her
wing and thigh to tiger's paw, Wordsworth is able to suggest how God
must see his own work. There is artistic love and justice in the handling
of each element, none preferred before the rest since there is no small and
no great within the work of art, but mutual support towards the end of
coherence and beauty. Everything is intelligible in terms of everything
else, as, by divine transposition, the temporal order in the voice of the
bee; and the whole leans on the Artist's imaginative will. The idea of
service directed to God's glory replaces the self-sustaining structure of
the greater landscape: in terse little poems, not unlike those of Yeats's old
age, Wordsworth sees the shadow of a daisy fulfil its nature by protecting

a dew-drop from the sun,[13] or moon and planet together in the sky and wonders which is queen and which attendant.[14]

In natural things there is a new bright meaning: beak and plume and paw are the elements of a living heraldry, closely related to Wordsworth's jewelry and architecture, and adding to these the more urgent quality of ceremonious action. Only a poet grown old in wisdom would dare to use the conventions of "hoary time," "imperial front," "roseate bloom," because they exactly serve his purpose. The utterly conventional can thus approach the command of style proper to divinity.

Another aspect of heraldic nature is its anthropomorphism, mythical and heroic. Wordsworth at one time protested against the use of Classical mythology, as a kind of decadence. In a sonnet to a brook he said:

> If wish were mine some type of thee to view,
> Thee, and not thee thyself, I would not do
> Like Grecian Artists, give thee human cheeks,
> Channels for tears; no Naiad shouldst thou be. . . .[15]

The root of his objection is the offence that this sort of thing gives to his philosophy of inner and outer, the independence of each and the "ennobling interchange" between them. Nor in truth did he recant, for his late poetry is not in this sense anthropomorphic. Natural objects are not men in disguise; but there is a certain key, reached again through a kind of divine transposition, in which human inference may be drawn from all the music of the world. He speaks of trees that "tear The lingering remnant of their yellow hair," [16] of the eagle "shedding where he flew Loose fragments of wild wailing," [17] of waterfalls "white-robed" [18] priestlike, perhaps, as Keats's "moving waters." The only Roman among the English Romantics, Wordsworth still went to Greece for his mythology, and he made of it something strong and personal. Because things are seen in God's eye, the anthropomorphism of nature is curiously without human prejudice or condescension.

The same bee of the *Vernal Ode* is called

> a warrior bold,
> Radiant all over with unburnished gold,
> And armed with living spear for mortal fight;
> A cunning forager
> That spreads no waste, a social builder; one

[13] *To a Child, Written in her Album.*
[14] *The Crescent-moon.*
[15] *Brook! whose society . . .*
[16] *One who was suffering tumult . . .*
[17] *A dark plume fetch me . . .*
[18] *The Excursion*, Bk. III. 48.

In whom all busy offices unite
With all fine functions that afford delight.

In his *Georgics,* Vergil compares bees to men, and later, in *The Æneid,*
men to bees: a coming full circle that has been related to his poetry's
development.[19] Wordsworth is doing neither—or both. Warrior, forager,
social builder are impartial titles, above and between the bee-world and
the man-world, which have both an equal claim to them. And again the
angelic brightness of description marks a divine authenticity, the impress
of the Just Artist's hands on all his creatures. Art in this way becomes
the heart of Wordsworth's late poetry, and figures like the humming-bee
its agents. Through the bee's embracing of all functions, warlike, peaceful,
utilitarian, ornamental, art achieves the controlled boundlessness proper
to itself. If the bee-world can be described in terms intelligible to men,
but without reducing bees to men in miniature, we will know better
how God sees us, and what it is like to be concerned in heaven for
happenings on earth. Art helps in this because of its power to lay
paradox to rest: it is at once the hardest work and the purest play;
it matters finally and finally it does not matter, since love which is
richness of art is not quite love which is richness of life—yet it is still
love, and godlike in the artist's simultaneous detachment and participation; so that heat and light are undiminished, and he can escape, though
only in imagination, the precise human self-involvement that makes
divine compassion unattainable.

The flowers of Wordsworth's poetry are no longer studied with literal
passion, to discover what they are. Already, in the Immortality Ode, the
"pansy at my feet" is completely formal, introduced with the barest of
gestures to confirm Wordsworth's story of lost childhood, and interesting
only for its relevance to the human predicament. Flowers, like the
Vernal Ode bee, supply a transcendental correlative for the root situations
of men. "The flowers themselves," with

> all their glistening,
> Call to the heart for inward listening—
> And though for bridal wreaths and tokens true
> Welcomed wisely; though a growth
> Which the careless shepherd sleeps on,
> As fitly spring from turf the mourner weeps on—
> And without wrong are cropped the marble tomb to strew.[20]

Again there is convention and ceremony, and the comprehension at re-
move peculiar to art.

In a very late poem, *Love Lies Bleeding,* the same elements are present,

[19] W. F. J. Knight, *Roman Vergil,* pp. 167, 170.
[20] *The Triad.*

and their organization is most subtle. Wordsworth's theme is the red
flower that is always drooping, seems always to be dying, yet never dies,
its "life passing not away":

> A flower how rich in sadness! Even thus stoops,
> (Sentient by Grecian sculpture's marvellous power),
> Thus leans, with hanging brow and body bent
> Earthward in uncomplaining languishment,
> The dying Gladiator. So, sad Flower!
> ('Tis Fancy guides me willing to be led,
> Though by a slender thread,)
> So drooped Adonis, bathed in sanguine dew
> Of his death-wound, when he from innocent air
> The gentlest breath of resignation drew;
> While Venus in a passion of despair
> Rent, weeping over him, her golden hair
> Spangled with drops of that celestial shower.
> She suffered, as Immortals sometimes do. . . .

The flower is compared with the sculptured figure that seems to be alive,
and then with the mythical—the fighter and the lover who were both
killed in sport. This is a large achievement in very small compass; ranging from flesh to stone and from stone to story, learning from each the
same lesson which is also different because of their varying conditions.
The passage has a great and almost anonymous distinction, like the blue
of sky, and seems to resolve the inexplicable in its subject through some
mystery of style. Wordsworth the unfanciful has reached an extreme of
fancy which before and since has been the province of old imaginations.

This preoccupation with mere art is seen to be nothing limited. The
starlit dome, in Yeats's *Byzantium,*

> disdains
> All that man is,
> All mere complexities,
> The fury and the mire of human veins.

Wordsworth also moves towards art, but not in order to oppose it to
nature as Yeats does. His art is not in this way disdainful: there is no
parallel to Yeats's rhetorical ascent towards his "artifice of eternity."
Wordsworth placed the same human limits on art as on nature, but the
difference between the two orders, as he experienced it, helped him in his
poetry. *Love Lies Bleeding* has an added richness in its expression of
suffering through art. All the figures suffer, in the modes of statuesque,
literary and pictorial; until in the end suffering and immortality are
brought together.

It was the fact of suffering that first set Wordsworth thinking about

the necessity of "another and a better world": struck down by his brother's
death, he suggested an answer which may easily prove small and rigid; a
philosophy of pain, of life to be undergone but not assented to. That he
escaped such an issue is due to his taking firm hold of the fact that God
too must suffer. We have already studied *Hart-Leap Well* as an essay
in the problem of pain, in which Wordsworth is undecided whether he
is writing a landscape poem about an animal that dies where it was born,
or asserting God's love for "unoffending creatures" like the hart. There is
a third possibility, not hinted at in the poem, but clearly in Wordsworth's
mind when he wrote some blank-verse lines a very short time before *Hart-
Leap Well* itself. He says that a trance came over him when he stood at
the well, thinking about the

> hunted beast, who there
> Had yielded up his breath, the awful trance,
> The vision of humanity, and of God
> The Mourner, God the Sufferer, when the heart
> Of his poor Creatures suffers wrongfully. . . .[21]

Hart-Leap Well was written too soon for Wordsworth to turn this experience to account. Later, in *Love Lies Bleeding* and in other poems, he
is able to think of sadness as a kind of wealth, and suffering not without
its divine likeness. And Wordsworth's Christianity also becomes rich,
through acceptance of the consequences of the Incarnation. Eternal movement from heaven earthward, there manifested, justifies poetic effort; for
although the poet must nourish his imagination at the "secondary founts"
of time and space, he is still being "tutored for eternity."

In this there is a leaning on God, in His guarantee of the world for
poets as for all men. Wordsworth accepts Bradley's dramatic conclusion
that appearance *is* reality, but the conclusion rests in the life of the
Trinity, as a matter of faith. In his early poetry the star is an important
feature of the greater landscape: it helps the Pedlar, in his childhood, to
reach thought-in-sense, and is one of the types of eternity. Now it serves
a general transcendental purpose, and is of particular interest for its
power "to testify of Love and Grace divine." The stars appear

> to mortal eye,
> Blended in absolute serenity,
> And free from semblance of decline;

and the certain mortality of stars does not gainsay this appearance:

> What if those bright fires
> Shine subject to decay,
> Sons haply of extinguished sires,

[21] [*Home at Grasmere*, MS variant, in *Poetical Works*, vol. 5, 319—Ed.]

> Themselves to lose their light, or pass away
> Like clouds before the wind,
> Be thanks poured out to Him whose hand bestows,
> Nightly, on human kind
> That vision of endurance and repose.

Often, as here in the *Vernal Ode,* reliance on the hand that sustains through mortal change and gratitude to the hand that bestows, are found together. In *The Primrose of the Rock,* Wordsworth thinks of the flower as a "link in Nature's chain," and traces this chain, link by link, to God. His late lyrical verse, Christian and conventional rather in the manner of eighteenth-century hymns, has been underestimated by those anxious to see this much and to see no more. Originality has many kinds: Wordsworth, like Burke, his counsellor in politics, can handle received ideas with authority deriving from a serene largeness of scale and vital control of emphasis. This primrose he sees, in its stem

> faithful to the root,
> That worketh out of view;
> And to the rock the root adheres
> In every fibre true.
>
> Close clings to earth the living rock,
> Though threatening still to fall;
> The earth is constant to her sphere;
> And God upholds them all:
> So blooms this lonely Plant, nor dreads
> Her annual funeral.

The immortality of succession becomes very dear to Wordsworth, as an earthly witness of eternal creative purpose. It also helps him in his personal struggle for humility and abatement of natural egotism: he is always trying to see himself a creature, to impress his finitude. In 1845 he instructed his printer to place a short passage of blank verse at the beginning of the volume, because, he said, "I mean it to serve as a sort of Preface." [22] This is not a good poem, but it catches this particular quality of his old age. He is once more watching the night sky, and the stars, some brilliant others dim, all owing their light to God. And he addresses himself thus:

> Then, to the measure of the light vouchsafed,
> Shine, Poet! in thy place, and be content.

His putting himself in his place has important consequences. Humility issues into thanks to God for all good things, and especially for the

---

[22] ["If thou indeed . . . ," in *Poetical Works,* vol. 1, pp. 1, 317—ED.]

beauty of nature. Again perfectly conventional, his attitude is still worth consideration. What he calls "the religion of gratitude" can be seen at work in his poetry: gratitude is at the centre of his religious life because, as he declares, "gratitude is the handmaid to hope, and hope the harbinger of faith." [23] It is as if he returned in different spirit to his first belief in the necessary connexion of poetry and pleasure. Pleasure that is coloured by gratitude to the giver is a sacrificial thing: the very taking joy becomes a handing back to God. As the motto of his Ecclesiastical Sonnets Wordsworth uses an adaptation of George Herbert's couplet:

> A verse may finde him, who a sermon flies
> And turn delight into a sacrifice:[24]

which makes the point entirely clear; and like other borrowings in thought and language, it shows how subtle is the question of originality.

Wordsworth's youth must not be set in judgment over his old age: nor, of course, must it be denied, as Wordsworth did when he pretended that he wrote the Preface to the *Lyrical Ballads* because "prevailed upon by Mr. Coleridge." [25] When he was a young man he felt impelled to attack the accepted canons of poetic orthodoxy. When he was old, he became orthodox himself. Both states deserve serious regard; yet there is general willingness to forgive his youth ignorant and dogmatic theorising and much bad poetry, while age is scarcely listened to. Wordsworth found, as an honest man must, that orthodoxy is no easier than its opposite; and he could not achieve it without a partial recantation. In particular, there is his changed attitude to the conventional in diction and imagery, which at his best he makes the controlled means of serving new ends. But this change is itself enough to deny his poetry a hearing: the eye lights on "hoary time" and "roseate bloom" in the *Vernal Ode*, and a great poem goes unread.

Convention is thus on the circumference and at the centre of Wordsworth's late poetry: convention that is a plain matter of style leads to convention less plain and already approached through God's artistic manner, through the heraldry of nature and through action determined by accustomed forms—still a matter of style, or concern with the How of things. The last of these, style in ceremony, takes him furthest in his Christian poetry: indeed it proves to be almost the whole truth, since the religion of gratitude makes the imagination everywhere ceremonious, intent to cast experience into a form acceptable to God.

Small wonder, then, that Wordsworth has a lot to say about the ritual of belief. He likes to compare the incense that "curls in clouds Around angelic Forms" depicted on cathedral roof with the "flower-incense" of the

[23] *Letters,* 1821–30 (ed. de Selincourt), p. 204.
[24] *The Church-porch.*
[25] *Letters,* 1831–40 (ed. de Selincourt), p. 910.

fields and "unwearied canticles" of birds and streams.[26] In a more exact sense he is fascinated by the externals of worship. *Processions* is a study of Pagan and Christian within these terms. He recounts how

> mid the sacred grove
> Fed in the Libyan waste by gushing wells,
> The priests and damsels of Ammonian Jove
> Provoked responses with shrill canticles;
> While, in a ship begirt with silver bells,
> They round his altar bore the hornèd God,
> Old Cham, the solar Deity, who dwells
> Aloft, yet in a tilting vessel rode,
> When universal sea the mountains overflowed.

He then turns to "Roman Pomps":

> The feast of Neptune—and the Cereal Games,
> With images, and crowns, and empty cars;
> The dancing Salii—on the shields of Mars
> Smiting with fury; and a deeper dread
> Scattered on all sides by the hideous jars
> Of Corybantian cymbals, while the head
> Of Cybele was seen, sublimely turreted.

And finally to "Christian pageantries": to

> The Cross, in calm procession, borne aloft
> Moved to the chant of sober litanies,

and his sight, one Sunday morning, of Swiss worshippers

> winding, between Alpine trees
> Spiry and dark, around their House of prayer.

This again is a small poem, but powerful in its dealing with ritual forms. Of all stylistic patterns, Wordsworth sees that of ritual as the most vital and comprehensive: within it he can blend sight and sound and movement in transcendental dedication. It is the favourite retreat of the baptized imagination; and while it serves perfectly the wish to touch all spiritual conditions, it can do so without the narrowness of judgment that seems unavoidable in any direct comparison of creeds. Thus in *Processions* the frenzy and compulsion of pagan rites are justly stated, but without prejudice to the poet's Christianity.

The finest achievement in this kind is the ode *On the Power of Sound*; and not in this kind only, for all the materials of his late poetry are here blended with supreme felicity. As physical eyesight failed, Wordsworth

---

[26] *Devotional Incitements.*

read few books, and he must have seen less as he walked abroad; but he still composed aloud, murmuring by the hour verses to himself. This too, I think, brought him to art in his old age, and a new love for the words themselves: unashamed delight in rhetorical utterance and much experimenting with the regular and the Pindaric ode, its fittest vehicles. Praise of sound, in the present poem, is also homage to poetry, as the thing that he was born to do.

Wordsworth approaches his subject, which is the divinity of sound, by way of the familiar road from nature to art. The voices of all natural things, streams and living creatures; echoes of voice

> From rocky steep and rock-bestudded meadows
> Flung back, and, in the sky's blue caves, reborn:

the voice that furthers action:

> the peasant's whistling breath that lightens
> His duteous toil of furrowing the green earth;

the voice that sustains patriot and martyr; the voice that renders the lunatic

> aghast, as at the world
> Of reason partially let in—

all lead him to the conclusion stated at the exact middle of the poem:

> Point not these mysteries to an Art
> Lodged above the starry pole . . . ?

In its second half the ode enquires more closely how sound can be art, or "tutored passion." Working with his favourite elements of story and ritual, Wordsworth achieves an astonishing result:

> The Gift to king Amphion
> That walled a city with its melody
> Was for belief no dream:—thy skill, Arion!
> Could humanize the creatures of the sea,
> Where men were monsters. A last grace he craves,
> Leave for one chant;—the dulcet sound
> Steals from the deck o'er willing waves,
> And listening dolphins gather round.
> Self-cast, as with a desperate course,
> 'Mid that strange audience, he bestrides
> A proud One docile as a managed horse;
> And singing, while the accordant hand
> Sweeps his harp, the Master rides;
> So shall he touch at length a friendly strand,

And he, with his preserver, shine starbright
In memory, through silent night.

The next stanza opens in heightened and frantic splendour:

The pipe of Pan, to shepherds
Couched in the shadow of Maenalian pines,
Was passing sweet; the eyeballs of the leopards,
That in high triumph drew the Lord of vines,
How did they sparkle to the cymbal's clang!
While Fauns and Satyrs beat the ground
In cadence,—and Silenus swang
This way and that, with wild-flowers crowned.

Myth, the kingship of story, a city walled with music; salvation in knowing what song to sing, and bright eternity reached through artistic action
—the tale is of some great skill truly learnt, spiritual and gracious like
the poetry itself, before it shifts to the terrible brilliance of the leopards'
eyeballs and the beating on the ground.

Suddenly Wordsworth returns to the natural order, addressing those
"who are longing to be rid Of fable," and bidding them

hear
The little sprinkling of cold earth that fell
Echoed from the coffin-lid.

He then asks why Nature cannot achieve the artistic modulation of her
own voices, adding, as a premonition of the truth, this fine Pythagorean
comment:

By one pervading spirit
Of tones and numbers all things are controlled,
As sages taught, where faith was found to merit
Initiation in that mystery old.
The heavens, whose aspect makes our minds as still
As they themselves appear to be,
Innumerable voices fill
With everlasting harmony;
The towering headlands, crowned with mist,
Their feet among the billows, know
That Ocean is a mighty harmonist. . . .

The Greek answer has already been anticipated by

What more changeful than the sea?
But over his great tides
Fidelity presides,

from another of the late odes.[27] It prepares Wordsworth for his own conclusion. There is a kind of artistry, a meaningful ordering, in nature; in
the ebb and flow of air and wash of sea. He had said so long ago, in the
poetry of solitude and relationship, building thereon a magnificent and
single structure. Glory is not now vanished, nor the affirmative, enfold-
ing optimism of creative purpose: rather, delight becomes a sacrifice, and
all this sounding movement confessional of the religion of gratitude:

> All worlds, all natures, mood and measure keep
> For praise and ceaseless gratulation, poured
> Into the ear of God, their Lord!

And so to the final stanza, telling how sound was before the beginning,
and will survive the end:

> A Voice to Light gave Being;
> To Time, and Man his earth-born chronicler;
> A Voice shall finish doubt and dim foreseeing,
> And sweep away life's visionary stir;
> The trumpet (we, intoxicate with pride,
> Arm at its blast for deadly wars)
> To archangelic lips applied,
> The grave shall open, quench the stars.

Not sound exactly, but a Voice, which is also, in the poem's final line,
"the WORD that shall not pass away." He is using a Semitic and European
highroad in this language of the Word, a convention that becomes com-
mandingly personal in his apocalyptic vision of Thought Self-Voiced, of
divine Action-in-Utterance perfecting the Christian mystery of life. What
can be understood by the Word that was made flesh? For this essay the
answer must rest in the energy and coherence of Wordsworth's transcendental symbolism.

I would not claim too much. There is no *Tempest* lying unregarded
in this late work, or even such poetry as would reverse the universal
judgment that the best is early. Even so, it has been grossly underestimated,
too easily slipped into place to serve large theories of Romantic defeat.
The final privacy of greatness in style has escaped notice. Wordsworth was
not silenced by the music of Christianity, nor stifled by Victorian morals.
He was profoundly changed. He writes now of stories and strange ritual
acts, of "doubt and dim foreseeing," of the witness of faith and the
spiritual eye: his waterfall-trumpeter is now the archangel.

[27] *The Triad.*

Chronology of Important Dates

1770   Born 7 April at Cockermouth, Cumberland.

1778   His mother, Ann Wordsworth, dies.

1779   Enters Hawkshead Grammar School, near Esthwaite Lake in the heart of the Lake Country. Boards at the cottage of Ann Tyson.

1783   His father, John Wordsworth, dies.

1787–91   At St. John's College, Cambridge University.

1790   Walking tour with a college friend, Robert Jones, in France, Switzerland, and Germany, one year after the fall of the Bastille.

1791   Tours North Wales with Robert Jones and climbs Mount Snowdon.

1791–92   Lives in France; becomes a fervent advocate of the French Revolution; has a love affair with Annette Vallon, who on December 15, 1792, bears his daughter, Anne-Caroline.

1793   Publishes *An Evening Walk* and *Descriptive Sketches*.

1795   A friend, Raisley Calvert, dies and leaves Wordsworth a legacy sufficient to allow him to live by his poetry.

1795–98   With his sister Dorothy settles at Racedown, Dorset, then at Alfoxden. Close association with Coleridge, living nearby at Nether Stowey, 1797–98.

1798   September: Publishes *Lyrical Ballads, with a Few Other Poems* with Coleridge; the "other poems" included "Tintern Abbey." The second edition, with Wordsworth's great "Preface," was published in 1800.

1798–99   Spends a cold and lonely winter with Dorothy at Goslar, Germany.

1799   Settles with Dorothy at Dove Cottage, Grasmere. Writes the first version of *The Prelude*, in two parts.

1802   Marries Mary Hutchinson.

1805   February 6: His brother, John Wordsworth, drowned in the wreck of his ship, the *Abergavenny*. May: *The Prelude*, in thirteen books, completed but left unpublished.

1807   Publishes *Poems in Two Volumes,* often said to mark the end of "the great decade" of his poetry.

1810–12   Estranged from Coleridge; their reconciliation fell short of the old intimacy.

1813–42   Distributor of stamps (i.e., tax collector) for Westmorland. May 1813: Moves to Rydal Mount, near Ambleside.

1814   Publishes *The Excursion.*

1835   Dorothy suffers a permanent mental collapse.

1843   Succeeds Robert Southey as poet laureate.

1850   April 23: Dies at Rydal Mount. July: *The Prelude,* in fourteen books, published posthumously.

Notes on the Editor and Contributors

M. H. ABRAMS, the editor of this volume, is Professor of English at Cornell. His writings on the romantic period include *The Mirror and the Lamp: Romantic Theory and the Critical Tradition* (1953) and *Natural Supernaturalism: Tradition and Revolution in Romantic Literature* (1971).

HAROLD BLOOM, Professor of English at Yale, has written, among other books, *Shelley's Mythmaking* (1959), *Blake's Apocalypse* (1963), and *The Visionary Company: A Reading of English Romantic Poetry* (1961).

A. C. BRADLEY, Professor of Poetry at Oxford and one of the most distinguished scholar-critics of his day, wrote *Shakespearean Tragedy* (1904) and *Oxford Lectures on Poetry* (1909).

CLEANTH BROOKS, one of the best known of the American "New Critics," is Professor of English at Yale. Among his books are *Modern Poetry and the Tradition* (1939), *The Well Wrought Urn* (1947), and *William Faulkner* (1963).

JOHN F. DANBY, Professor of English at the University College of North Wales, has published *The Simple Wordsworth: Studies in the Poems, 1797–1807* (1960) and *William Wordsworth: "The Prelude" and Other Poems* (1963).

PAUL DE MAN, after having taught at Harvard, Cornell, Johns Hopkins, and Zurich, is Professor of Comparative and French Literature at Yale. He has written a number of essays on romantic and postromantic European literature, as well as *Blindness and Insight: Essays in the Rhetoric of Contemporary Criticism* (1971).

DAVID RUSSELL FERRY, Professor of English at Wellesley College, is a poet and critic, and author of *The Limits of Mortality: An Essay on Wordsworth's Major Poems* (1959).

GEOFFREY H. HARTMAN is Professor of English and Comparative Literature at Yale. His books include *The Unmediated Vision* (1954), *Wordsworth's Poetry, 1787–1814* (1964), and *Beyond Formalism: Literary Essays, 1958–1970* (1970).

NEIL HERTZ, who teaches English literature at Cornell, has written various essays in criticism and is at work on a study of the Miltonic tradition through Wordsworth.

JOHN JONES, a Fellow of Merton College, Oxford, is author of a study of Wordsworth's poetry, *The Egotistical Sublime* (1954), of *On Aristotle and Greek Tragedy* (1962), and of *John Keats's Dream of Truth* (1969).

ROBERT D. MAYO is Professor of English at Northwestern University, a scholar in English fiction and periodical literature, and author of *The English Novel in the Magazines, 1740–1815* (1962).

STEPHEN MAXFIELD PARRISH, Professor of English at Cornell, is coauthor (with Hyder Rollins) of *Keats and the Bostonians* (1951) and author of *The Art of the Lyrical Ballads* (1972). He is also general editor of the Cornell Wordsworth Series of editions, from the manuscripts, of all Wordsworth's long poems.

DAVID PERKINS, Associate Professor of English at Harvard, has written *The Quest for Permanence: The Symbolism of Wordsworth Shelley and Keats* (1959) and *Wordsworth and the Poetry of Sincerity* (1964) and has edited the anthology *English Romantic Writers* (1967).

LIONEL TRILLING is one of the most distinguished of contemporary critics and essayists, University Professor at Columbia, whose critical writings include *Matthew Arnold* (1939), *The Liberal Imagination* (1950), *The Opposing Self* (1955), and *Beyond Culture: Essays on Learning and Literature* (1965).

ALFRED NORTH WHITEHEAD was the eminent mathematician, philosopher, and essayist who, with Bertrand Russell, wrote *Principia Mathematica* (1910–13), the foundation work of modern symbolic logic. His most widely read books, combining his philosophical ideas with excursions into intellectual history, are *Science and the Modern World* (1926) and *Adventures of Ideas* (1933).

JONATHAN WORDSWORTH, a descendant of the poet's brother Christopher, is a Fellow of Exeter College, Oxford, and a Trustee of the Wordsworth Library at Dove Cottage. He is the author of *The Music of Humanity: A Critical Study of Wordsworth's "Ruined Cottage"* (1969) and of various essays on Wordsworth.

Selected Bibliography

I. EDITIONS

The standard edition of the poems (exclusive of *The Prelude*) is *The Poetical Works*, edited by Ernest de Selincourt and Helen Darbishire (5 vols., Oxford, 1940–49). The same scholars have edited *The Prelude*, with the texts of 1805 and 1850 on facing pages (revised edition, Oxford, 1959); a new edition of these two versions of *The Prelude*, edited by J. C. Maxwell, is available in a Penguin paperback (1971). A convenient one-volume collection of all Wordsworth's poems, including *The Prelude* of 1850, was edited by Thomas Hutchinson for Oxford Standard Authors (revised by E. de Selincourt, London, 1950).

The Letters of William and Dorothy Wordsworth was edited by de Selincourt in six volumes, Oxford, 1935–39; a revised version, edited by C. L. Shaver, is in process, 1967– . A useful collection of the *Literary Criticism of William Wordsworth* was edited by Paul M. Zall (Lincoln, Neb., 1966).

II. BIOGRAPHY

Harper, George McLean. *William Wordsworth: His Life, Works, and Influence.* 2 vols., London, 1916; rev. 1929.

Margoliouth, H. M. *Wordsworth and Coleridge, 1795–1835.* London, 1953.

Moorman, Mary. *William Wordsworth.* 2 vols., Oxford, 1957, 1965.

III. CRITICAL STUDIES

James V. Logan, *Wordsworthian Criticism: A Guide and Bibliography* (Columbus, Ohio, 1961), combines a summary history of the critical treatments of Wordsworth with a bibliographical listing of critical books and essays, 1850–1944. For criticism since 1944, see Elton F. Henley and David H. Stamm, *Wordsworthian Criticism, 1945–1964* (New York, 1965), and the annual bibliography of "The Romantic Movement" in *English Literary History* (to 1949), *Philological Quarterly* (1950–1964), and *English Language Notes* (1965–).

Early critical writings on Wordsworth which have had enduring influence: S. T. Coleridge, *Biographia Literaria* (1817), especially Chapter XXII; William Hazlitt, in *Lectures on the English Poets* (1818) and in *The Spirit of the Age*

(1825); Matthew Arnold, "Wordsworth," *Essays in Criticism: Second Series* (London, 1888); Walter Raleigh, *Wordsworth* (London, 1903); A. C. Bradley, in *Oxford Lectures on Poetry* (London, 1909).

A. BOOK-LENGTH STUDIES OF THE POETRY

Bateson, F. W. *Wordsworth: A Reinterpretation.* London, 1954.

Danby, John F. *The Simple Wordsworth: Studies in the Poems, 1797–1807.* New York, 1960.

Darbishire, Helen. *The Poet Wordsworth.* Oxford, 1950.

Ferry, David. *The Limits of Mortality: An Essay on Wordsworth's Major Poems.* Middletown, Conn., 1959.

Hartman, Geoffrey H. *The Unmediated Vision.* New Haven, Conn., 1954.

———. *Wordsworth's Poetry, 1787–1814.* New Haven, Conn., 1964.

Jones, John. *The Egotistical Sublime: A History of Wordsworth's Imagination.* London, 1954.

Marsh, Florence. *Wordsworth's Imagery.* New Haven, Conn., 1952.

Miles, Josephine. *Wordsworth and the Vocabulary of Emotion.* Berkeley, 1942.

Murray, Roger N. *Wordsworth's Style: Figures and Themes in the "Lyrical Ballads" of 1800.* Lincoln, Neb., 1967.

Perkins, David. *The Quest for Permanence: The Symbolism of Wordsworth Shelley and Keats.* Cambridge, Mass., 1959.

———. *Wordsworth and the Poetry of Sincerity.* Cambridge, Mass., 1964.

Sperry, W. L. *Wordsworth's Anti-Climax.* Cambridge, Mass., 1933.

Woodring, Carl. *Wordsworth.* Boston, 1964.

Wordsworth, Jonathan. *The Music of Humanity: A Critical Study of Wordsworth's "Ruined Cottage."* London, 1969.

B. "THE PRELUDE"

Abrams, M. H. *Natural Supernaturalism: Tradition and Revolution in Romantic Literature.* New York, 1971. See especially chapters 1, 2, 5–7.

Gallie, W. B. "Is *The Prelude* a Philosophical Poem?" *Philosophy*, 22 (1947).

Havens, R. D. *The Mind of a Poet.* 2 vols. Baltimore, 1941. A detailed commentary on *The Prelude,* traditional in its views.

Lindenberger, Herbert. *On Wordsworth's "Prelude."* Princeton, 1963.

Wordsworth, Jonathan. "The Growth of a Poet's Mind." *Cornell Library Journal* (Spring 1970). Discusses the manuscript version of the two-part *Prelude* of 1799.

C. WORDSWORTH'S IDEAS AND THEIR SOURCES

Beach, Joseph Warren. *The Concept of Nature in Nineteenth-Century English Poetry.* New York, 1956.

Beatty, Arthur. *William Wordsworth: His Doctrine and Art in Their Historical Relations.* Madison, 1922; rev. 1927. Discloses, but overemphasizes, the influence of David Hartley's associationist psychology.

Durrant, Geoffrey. *Wordsworth and the Great System: A Study of Wordsworth's Poetic Universe.* Cambridge, England, 1970.

Stallknecht, Newton P. *Strange Seas of Thought: Studies in William Wordsworth's Philosophy of Man and Nature.* Bloomington, Ind., 1945; rev. 1958.

Willey, Basil. " 'Nature' in Wordsworth." In Willey, *The Eighteenth-Century Background.* London, 1950.

D. CRITICAL ESSAYS

Following is a highly selective list of essays not included in this anthology that indicates the diversity of subjects and views in recent criticism of Wordsworth's poems.

Abrams, M. H. "English Romanticism: The Spirit of the Age." In *Romanticism Reconsidered,* edited by Northrop Frye. New York, 1963. Reprinted in *Romanticism and Consciousness,* edited by Harold Bloom. New York, 1970.

————. "Wordsworth and Coleridge on Diction and Figures," *English Institute Essays* (1952).

Benziger, James. "Tintern Abbey Revisited." *PMLA,* 65 (1950).

Brooks, Cleanth. "Wordsworth and Human Suffering: Notes on Two Early Poems." In *From Sensibility to Romanticism,* edited by F. W. Hilles and Harold Bloom. New York, 1965.

Bush, Douglas. "Wordsworth: A Minority Report." In *Wordsworth Centenary Studies,* edited by G. T. Dunklin. Princeton, 1951. An attempt to show Wordsworth's limitations as a poet for the present age.

Davie, Donald. "Dionysus in *Lyrical Ballads.*" In *Wordsworth's Mind and Art,* edited by A. W. Thomson. London, 1969.

————. "Syntax in the Blank Verse of Wordsworth's *Prelude.*" *Articulate Energy* (1955).

de Man, Paul. "Symbolic Landscape in Wordsworth and Yeats." In *In Defense of Reading,* edited by R. A. Brower and Richard Poirier. Cambridge, Mass., 1962.

Empson, William. "Sense in *The Prelude.*" In Empson, *The Structure of Complex Words.* London, 1952.

Frost, Robert. "A Tribute to Wordsworth" (1950). *Cornell Library Journal* (Spring 1970).

Grob, Alan. "Wordsworth's 'Nutting.' " *Journal of English and Germanic Philology,* 51 (1962). Argues against the interpretation by Perkins (see Perkins's essay in this volume) and by Ferry, in *The Poetry of Mortality* (Middletown, Conn., 1959).

Hartman, Geoffrey. "Wordsworth, Inscriptions, and Romantic Nature Poetry." In *From Sensibility to Romanticism,* edited by F. W. Hilles and Harold Bloom. New York, 1965.

Huxley, Aldous. "Wordsworth in the Tropics." In Huxley, *Collected Essays*. New York, 1959.

Knight, G. Wilson. "The Wordsworthian Profundity." In Knight, *The Starlit Dome: Studies in the Poetry of Vision*. London, 1941.

Langbaum, Robert. "The Evolution of Soul in Wordsworth's Poetry." In Langbaum, *The Modern Spirit*. New York, 1970.

Leavis, F. R. "Wordsworth." In Leavis, *Revaluation: Tradition and Development in English Poetry*. London, 1936.

Pottle, Frederick A. "The Eye and the Object in the Poetry of Wordsworth." In *Wordsworth Centenary Studies*, edited by G. T. Dunklin. Princeton, 1951. Reprinted in *Romanticism and Consciousness*, edited by Harold Bloom. New York, 1970.

Trilling, Lionel. "The Immortality Ode." In Trilling, *The Liberal Imagination*. New York, 1942. Reprinted in *English Romantic Poets*, edited by M. H. Abrams. New York, 1960.

Williams, Charles. "Wordsworth." In Williams, *The English Poetic Mind*. Oxford, 1932. Reprinted in *English Romantic Poets*, edited by M. H. Abrams. New York, 1960.

Woolley, Mary Lynn. "Wordsworth's Symbolic Vale as It Functions in *The Prelude*." *Studies in Romanticism*, 7 (1968).

Wordsworth, Jonathan. "The Climbing of Snowdon." In *Bicentenary Wordsworth Studies in Memory of John Alban Finch*. Ithaca, N.Y., 1970. In opposition to the "apocalyptic" reading of this passage in *The Prelude* by David Ferry and Geoffrey Hartman.

———. "William Wordsworth 1770–1969." *Proceedings of the British Academy*, 60 (1969).

Index of Titles

This index lists the poems and prose-writings by Wordsworth that are discussed in the critical essays. Page-numbers in **boldface** indicate fairly extensive discussion; other references are printed in *italics*.